Modernizing SAP with AWS

A Comprehensive Journey to Cloud
Migration, Architecture,
and Innovation Strategies

Tushar Srivastava

Apress®

Modernizing SAP with AWS: A Comprehensive Journey to Cloud Migration, Architecture, and Innovation Strategies

Tushar Srivastava
Cumming, GA, USA

ISBN-13 (pbk): 979-8-8688-1578-2   ISBN-13 (electronic): 979-8-8688-1579-9
https://doi.org/10.1007/979-8-8688-1579-9

Managing Director, Apress Media LLC: Welmoed Spahr
Acquisitions Editor: Celestin Suresh John
Development Editor: James Markham
Editorial Assistant: Gryffin Winkler

Cover designed by eStudioCalamar

Cover image designed by Ruchi Ukhade

Distributed to the book trade worldwide by Springer Science+Business Media New York, 1 New York Plaza, New York, NY 10004. Phone 1-800-SPRINGER, fax (201) 348-4505, e-mail orders-ny@springer-sbm.com, or visit www.springeronline.com. Apress Media, LLC is a Delaware LLC and the sole member (owner) is Springer Science + Business Media Finance Inc (SSBM Finance Inc). SSBM Finance Inc is a **Delaware** corporation.

For information on translations, please e-mail booktranslations@springernature.com; for reprint, paperback, or audio rights, please e-mail bookpermissions@springernature.com.

Apress titles may be purchased in bulk for academic, corporate, or promotional use. eBook versions and licenses are also available for most titles. For more information, reference our Print and eBook Bulk Sales web page at http://www.apress.com/bulk-sales.

Any source code or other supplementary material referenced by the author in this book is available to readers on GitHub. For more detailed information, please visit https://www.apress.com/gp/services/source-code.

If disposing of this product, please recycle the paper

Dedicated to my children, Aarika and Ayaan,
whose sense of wonderment and curiosity motivates me to
appreciate the simple joys that surround all of us, and, if not for them,
this book would have been completed six months earlier!

Table of Contents

About the Author

Tushar Srivastava has been working in sales and account management roles in technology since 2001. Currently, he is a principal account manager, and in his most recent role, he was a principal specialist for SAP on AWS at Amazon Web Services (AWS). He is a thought leader in this domain, guiding customers in modernizing SAP systems with AWS technology, specifically SAP infrastructure modernization, and extending SAP capabilities with cloud technologies like machine learning and artificial intelligence.

Tushar holds a Bachelor of Technology (Mechanical Engineering) degree from the National Institute of Technology, Kurukshetra, India, and an MBA from the Indian Institute of Technology, Bombay. He currently resides in the Atlanta metro area in the United States and plays the guitar in his spare time.

About the Technical Reviewer

Bidwan Baruah brings 19 years of IT experience as a cloud architect and technology advisor. He has led various implementation, upgrade, and migration projects of SAP solutions for customers around the globe. He has also been an SAP customer and, as an SAP architect, led the successful execution of a large-scale SAP digital transformation project for a leading organization. Currently serving as a senior solutions architect at Amazon Web Services (AWS), Bidwan specializes in guiding enterprises through the complexities of cloud migration and digital transformation, particularly in integrating SAP environments with AWS services. In this role, he has assisted a number of Fortune 100 and other leading enterprises in North America with migrating and modernizing their SAP workloads on AWS, making him a sought-after advisor for leveraging cloud technologies to drive business innovation. Bidwan is deeply committed to educating and empowering professionals, regularly sharing his expertise through speaking engagements and technical publications. He is also the principal author of the book *Evolve from Infrastructure to Innovation with SAP on AWS*.

Acknowledgments

Having never written a book before, when I was first approached to write this book, I was not sure if I would be able to take on such a project all by myself. Little by little, paragraph by paragraph, this book took shape and a life of its own. And that is when I realized I did not work on this book alone. Writing this book has been an exciting journey, and I would like to thank Preksha, my life partner, for being the steady supportive hand all throughout and my parents, Mr. Omkant and Mrs. Sarita, for planting the seed of a love for books at a very early age.

I have been fortunate to have many mentors all through my professional life, and this book has been a product of all the words of wisdom and guidance received from them, especially Carl Bachor, who has been a friend and guide during my time at AWS. I would also like to thank all my colleagues at AWS with whom I spent countless hours discussing technical concepts, especially Deep Kwatra, who was my sounding board all through the duration of the writing process. I would also like to thank all the amazing customers past and present that I had the privilege of serving, and it is based on those experiences that I was able to paint a vivid picture of a fictional customer at the center of this book, Nimbus Airlines. Specifically, I would like to thank Mukesh Kakani, Nathan Souer, and Ashok Satapathy (CHS Inc.), as well as Jana Branham and Paul Shook (Ergon Inc.), for kindly agreeing to contribute case studies for this book.

My team at Apress deserves a special thanks for pushing me hard and helping me explore my limits as a writer. Thank you, Deepa, Celestin, and Jim.

Lastly, I would like to thank my lifelong friends Ajay and Amit, who hardly had much involvement in the book, but have been a great influence in shaping who I am today and, consequently in some way, this book that you are reading now …

Introduction

Dear reader, if you are reading this book, chances are you have had some interaction with SAP systems. Over the past few years, customers have been putting a priority on modernizing SAP, specifically leveraging cloud technology. This book covers the fundamental concepts of modernizing SAP on AWS. While the most common approach has been rehosting SAP on AWS, more recently, customers have been looking at options like SAP RISE as well as the whole complement of AWS services that can be leveraged to enhance the capabilities of SAP, including monitoring services, analytics, SAP DevOps, as well as newer concepts including machine learning (ML), artificial intelligence (AI), and its newer avatar, generative AI.

This is not a textbook; rather, it covers the SAP modernization on AWS through the journey of a fictional enterprise, "Nimbus Airlines." Nimbus goes through a detailed process of modernizing SAP and evaluating AWS services, and in the process, you, the reader, will learn about the fundamental concepts, just like Nimbus did. In that respect, even if you have no background of SAP, you can still enjoy reading through the customer's journey.

I must emphasize that while the technical details in the book are accurate, the story is fictional and real-world scenarios are very different from how they are described in this book. I would consider this book successful if you get more clarity about modernizing SAP with AWS while being able to relate with the characters in this book.

Who This Book Is For

This book is written for senior executives, enterprise architects, as well as system analysts who have a responsibility toward building and managing SAP systems for their enterprise. Service providers of SAP implementation and managed services will also gain insights from this book.

The main personas will benefit from the book in the following way:

- **Senior Executives**: As an executive, you will get a flavor of key options and decisions that are relevant for executives in the context of leveraging AWS cloud for modernizing SAP. As more and more organizations adopt cloud, after reading the book, executives would be well positioned to apply these learnings within their own enterprise or even as a thought leader for advisory firms.

- **Enterprise Architects**: They will learn about all the technical concepts of AWS cloud that are relevant to modernizing SAP. They would be able to implement the learnings either in their own enterprise or in a consulting role for other customers.

- **System Analysts**: Analysts including SAP Basis administrators and technical analysts will learn about key architectural patterns relevant for architecting SAP systems on AWS, including compute, storage, networking, high availability (HA), disaster recovery (DR), and innovation. They will learn best practices, which can be implemented in day-to-day work, as well as grow in their career in the field of cloud computing.

What This Book Covers

Chapter 1, Cloud Fundamentals and Overview of AWS, covers the evolution of cloud computing and the basic building blocks of AWS and helps understand its key features, specifically in the context of running SAP systems.

Chapter 2, AWS and SAP Technical Partnership, covers the technical partnership between SAP and AWS, technical considerations for SAP infrastructure, and key features of engineering collaboration between SAP and AWS.

Chapter 3, Day 1 Customer Conversations: Why SAP on AWS, provides an overview of some of the key hardware and infrastructure-related challenges faced by customers and how running SAP on AWS can help address those.

Chapter 4, Design of the AWS Cloud, covers the design of the AWS cloud infrastructure, including concepts of regions, Availability Zones (AZs), data centers, connectivity, and other related concepts. The chapter outlines how this design is relevant for SAP deployments.

Chapter 5, Designing the AWS Infrastructure for SAP, covers how to architect the optimized AWS infrastructure (compute, network, storage, and other services) for running SAP workloads on AWS.

Chapter 6, Designing the Operating Model, covers details on the day-to-day SAP operations, including high availability, disaster recovery, security, automation of ongoing tasks, and monitoring.

Chapter 7, Innovation Beyond Infrastructure with SAP on AWS, covers three pillars of innovations on SAP with AWS cloud, including data analytics, applications and APIs (Application Programming Interfaces), and artificial intelligence and machine learning.

Chapter 8, Migration Execution and Ramping Up to Cloud, provides an overview of migration strategies and AWS tools that can be used for ramping up SAP systems on AWS.

Chapter 9, Customer Case Studies, covers real-life customer case studies that provide insights into how other customers have modernized SAP with AWS technology.

CHAPTER 1

Cloud Fundamentals and Overview of AWS

This chapter first covers the evolution of cloud computing and key milestones along the way. Next, it covers at a high level the benefits that cloud computing offers to modern enterprises. The chapter then covers the birth of Amazon Web Services as a cloud service provider (CSP) and the basic building blocks of AWS. These topics are relevant for the SAP practitioner as they help to set the context of how cloud computing and AWS specifically play a role in modernizing SAP systems. At the end of the chapter, you'll understand how the AWS cloud is architected and understand its features specifically in the context of running SAP systems.

> It was 9 AM on a regular morning when Thomas was settling down with a cup of his favorite black coffee and waiting for his laptop to boot up. As he was looking through his notes for his "to-do" list, he noticed a congratulatory email pop up, wishing him on his two-year "Amaversary," or Amazon anniversary. Time had flown by so fast, and it felt like just yesterday when Thomas accepted the role of "**SAP Specialist**" within the "Amazon Web Services" division of Amazon. The division itself started in 2006, and his team, the "**SAP on AWS**" group, was a recent addition. A smile broke out on Thomas's face as he was reading the emails and the congratulatory chat messages from colleagues that started pouring in with all sorts of "emojis" appended.

> His thoughts wandered off to two years ago when he had walked out of his "loop interview" - a day-long set of interviews with different people testing him on his skills and Amazon's "**leadership principles**" (a set of guidelines for how Amazonians think about behaviors within the business). Though he felt he did well, he was not sure what to expect; after all Amazon did have a high recruiting bar. A few days later the offer came through, which

© Tushar Srivastava 2025
T. Srivastava, *Modernizing SAP with AWS*, https://doi.org/10.1007/979-8-8688-1579-9_1

Thomas gladly accepted. With a bit of nervousness and a lot of excitement, Thomas started his "Day 1" at AWS. Having spent much of his professional career in the SAP ecosystem, his excitement stemmed from the fact that he would get to use his SAP skills, and the nervousness was rooted in the fact that he had only a high-level knowledge of the fundamentals of "cloud computing." Reassurances came from colleagues who said that he would get ample learning opportunities.

*That learning opportunity came up as Thomas completed his initial onboarding, which, apart from general information, also was a window into Amazon's culture and history. His manager had sent him the link to the "**AWS Certified Cloud Practitioner**" certification and the associated learning material. Over the next few days, Thomas spent time learning the fundamentals of AWS and in the process was awed by both the scale of the cloud infrastructure and the variety of microservices that provided point solutions serving various needs of an organization.*

Even before digging into the learning material, Thomas spent time reading various blogs and books about the evolution of cloud computing and reflecting on his own experiences as a mainframe programmer during his early career.

A Brief History of Cloud Computing

In the dawn of computing, businesses and institutions operated large mainframe computers, necessitating substantial capital and physical space. As technology evolved, the paradigm shifted toward personal computers (PCs) and on-premises servers. However, the twenty-first century ushered in a new era with the concept of "cloud computing" – the delivery of computing services, including servers, storage, databases (DBs), networking, and more, over the internet. The concept of "cloud computing" evokes imagery of vast, nebulous data networks operating beyond the realm of traditional computing. Yet, this now-ubiquitous term was born from a confluence of ideas, innovations, and necessities spanning several decades. The foundation of cloud computing can be traced back to the times when computers were mammoth structures, occupying entire rooms, and when the idea of accessing computing power from a distant location seemed like science fiction.

The evolution of cloud computing is not merely a technological story – it is intertwined with economic shifts, changing business paradigms, and societal transformations. The promise of on-demand access, scalability, and flexible cost structures has made cloud computing the backbone of modern-day businesses, from startups to multinational corporations. Moreover, its historical development offers insight into the ingenuity and vision of pioneers who perceived a future where computing power would be as accessible as any utility service, like electricity or water.

The Dawn of the Digital Age

In the annals of computational history, the mainframe era stands as a testament to early innovation and the precursors of modern cloud concepts. Before desktop PCs became a household staple, mainframes, with their monumental size and striking presence, were the epicenters of computing. **Mainframes**, the veritable giants of their day, emerged in the 1950s and 1960s. Companies like IBM, UNIVAC, and Honeywell began producing these machines that were renowned for their sheer processing power and ability to handle vast amounts of data. However, their size reflected the infancy of computational technology – entire rooms were dedicated to hosting a single mainframe, with intricate cooling systems and dedicated power supplies.

The Thin Client Paradigm: The Precursors to Distributed Computing

Connected to these mainframes were the so-called "dumb terminals" or thin clients. Lacking in processing power and storage of their own, these devices served primarily as input and output conduits, relying entirely on the mainframe for computational tasks. This setup allowed multiple users to access the mainframe's resources simultaneously from different terminals, essentially creating a primitive form of shared and centralized computing.

Resource Time Sharing: An Early Nod to Cloud Concepts

One of the significant innovations of this era was time sharing. Instead of dedicating the mainframe's resources to a single task at a time, time sharing allowed the machine to switch between tasks rapidly, giving users the illusion of simultaneous processing. This idea was revolutionary – it maximized resource efficiency and laid the groundwork for today's multi-tenant cloud environments.

The Shift Toward Decentralization

However, as technology advanced, the computational landscape began to shift. The advent of the microprocessor in the 1970s heralded the era of personal computers, moving away from the centralized mainframe model. Yet, the principles of shared resources and distributed access, inherent in mainframes and thin clients, did not fade but evolved, setting the stage for modern cloud architecture.

Virtualization: The Heart of the Cloud

At its core, cloud computing thrives on the efficient and flexible utilization of resources. This is made possible primarily through **virtualization** – a technology that, while not exclusive to cloud computing, plays a pivotal role in its success. Virtualization's magic lies in its ability to abstract, partition, and isolate the underlying hardware resources, enabling multiple virtual environments on a single physical machine.

The roots of virtualization can be traced back to the mainframes of the 1960s. The goal was straightforward: optimize the costly and vast resources of mainframes by allowing them to run multiple applications and processes simultaneously without interference. IBM was notably at the forefront, introducing its CP-40 and CP/CMS systems, pioneering the concept of **virtual machines (VMs)**. Virtualization operates on the principle of abstraction. Inserting a layer – the hypervisor – between the hardware and the operating system (OS) allows the creation of multiple virtual instances or VMs. These VMs believe they have access to actual physical resources, but in reality, they interact with a virtual representation of those resources:

- **Type 1 hypervisor** (**bare metal**) is installed directly on the physical hardware. This kind of hypervisor has direct access to resources and is responsible for distributing them among VMs. Examples include VMware vSphere/ESXi, Microsoft Hyper-V, and Oracle VM Server for x86.

- **Type 2 hypervisor** (**hosted**) operates atop a conventional operating system (the host OS). This hypervisor relies on the underlying OS for resource management. Examples include VMware Workstation, Oracle VirtualBox, and Parallels Desktop.

The Benefits of Virtualization in Cloud Computing

Virtualization offers many benefits in the context of cloud computing. Some important ones are as below:

- **Resource Optimization**: By running multiple VMs on a single server, providers can maximize resource utilization, leading to cost savings and energy efficiency.

- **Isolation and Security**: VMs operate in isolated environments. If one VM crashes or is compromised, others remain unaffected.

- **Flexibility and Agility**: Virtualization allows for rapid provisioning and scaling of resources. VMs can be easily cloned, migrated, or backed up, providing a dynamic and responsive infrastructure.

- **Legacy Application Support**: Older applications designed for specific environments can be run in VMs that mimic those environments, extending the application's lifecycle and ensuring business continuity. With the context above, we will next look at the birth of modern cloud computing.

Birth of Modern Cloud Computing

As the twenty-first century dawned, the IT landscape witnessed the convergence of various technological advancements, laying the foundation for the modern cloud era. The rise of the internet and the maturation of virtualization techniques, combined with increasing computational power and falling storage costs, created the perfect storm for the emergence of the modern cloud infrastructure.

The Precursors to Modern Cloud Solutions

While the idea of on-demand computing resources wasn't new, the early 2000s marked a turning point in making this vision commercially viable and accessible.

Before that, customers had either one of the two options below:

- **Grid Computing**: Before the widespread adoption of cloud, grid computing was seen as a method to harness computational power across various domains and disciplines. It involved connecting geographically dispersed computers, typically used in research and complex computational problems, to function as a singular mega-resource.

- **Utility Computing**: Championed by companies like Sun Microsystems, the idea here was that computational resources would eventually be consumed in a manner similar to traditional utilities like water or electricity – only pay for what you use.

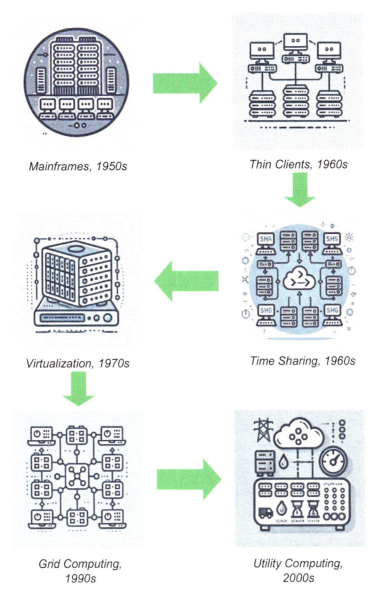

Mainframes, 1950s

Thin Clients, 1960s

Virtualization, 1970s

Time Sharing, 1960s

Grid Computing, 1990s

Utility Computing, 2000s

Figure 1-1. *Evolution of Modern Computing*

Some Key Milestones in Modern Cloud Evolution

Cloud computing did not start with a big bang, but with incremental gains spread over many years and across many organizations. Here are some key milestones in the early evolution of modern cloud computing:

- **Salesforce (1999)**: With its launch, Salesforce brought the concept of delivering enterprise applications via a website. This software as a service (SaaS) model heralded the age where software wasn't something you purchased and installed but accessed over the internet.

- **Amazon Web Services (2006)**: Amazon, sensing an opportunity to monetize its surplus in-house infrastructure capabilities, introduced AWS. Amazon Simple Storage Service (Amazon S3) and Elastic Compute Cloud (EC2) provided scalable storage and computing capacity in the cloud, allowing users to run applications on Amazon's infrastructure. This marked the solidification of the infrastructure as a service (IaaS) model.

- **Google Apps (2006)**: Google introduced a suite of business productivity tools, such as Gmail, Google Drive, and Google Docs, delivered entirely online, further solidifying the SaaS market.

- **Cloud Security Concerns and the CSA (2009)**: The **Cloud Security Alliance (CSA)** was formed to promote best practices to ensure security assurance within cloud computing.

- **Microsoft Azure (2010)**: Microsoft entered the cloud market with Azure, providing a wide range of cloud services including those for computing, analytics, storage, and networking.

- **OpenStack Launch (2010)**: An open source cloud computing platform designed to facilitate the easy deployment of cloud services. It received backing from major industry players, including NASA and Rackspace.

- **Docker's Introduction (2013)**: Docker introduced containerization to the mainstream, allowing for more efficient and flexible application deployment compared with traditional virtualization.

- **Serverless Computing (2014)**: AWS launched Lambda, introducing the idea of serverless computing where developers could run code in response to events without managing the server infrastructure, heralding the **function as a service (FaaS)** era.

- **Kubernetes Momentum (2017 Onward)**: While introduced by Google in 2014, Kubernetes (an open source container orchestration platform) started gaining immense momentum around 2017, becoming a de facto standard for container orchestration.

- **Edge Computing Emergence (Late 2010s)**: Recognizing the need for processing data closer to its source, especially for Internet of Things (IoT) devices, companies started pushing for edge computing solutions, where computations are performed on edge devices rather than centralized data centers.

- **Hybrid and Multi-cloud Strategies (Late 2010s Onward)**: Businesses began to deploy hybrid cloud strategies, using a mix of private and public cloud resources, and multi-cloud strategies, leveraging services from multiple public cloud providers to avoid vendor lock-in and improve resilience.

- **Increased Emphasis on Cloud Governance and Management (2020s)**: As organizations adopted multi-cloud environments, tools and practices for managing costs, performance, and security across diverse cloud platforms became paramount.

Each of these milestones represents significant shifts in the way businesses and developers approach IT infrastructure, development, and deployment, showcasing the rapid pace of innovation and adoption in the realm of cloud computing.

Paradigm Shift in Business and IT Operations

The rise of cloud computing has not merely been a technological evolution – it has ushered in a transformative shift in business models, operational dynamics, and IT management. This metamorphosis is reflective of the monumental changes that cloud technology has brought to the table, redefining the way organizations function and strategize in the modern digital era.

Even in the short time span that cloud computing has been around, it is starting to have a positive impact on business outcomes. Some key benefits include the following.

Cost-Effective IT Management

One of the immediate benefits of cloud computing has been the direct and indirect impact on cost. Most organizations look at the following benefits when building a case for cloud adoption:

- **Reduced Capital Expenditure (CapEx)**: Traditional IT infrastructure required heavy up-front investments in physical hardware, software licenses, and data centers. Cloud computing introduced a model where businesses could access the resources they needed on a pay-as-you-go basis, dramatically reducing initial capital expenses.

- **Operational Expenditure (OpEx) Model**: Moving from a CapEx to an OpEx model, businesses now had more predictable IT costs, only paying for the resources they consumed. This flexibility allowed for more agile financial planning and resource allocation.

Enhanced Agility and Scalability

Apart from cost, the immediate benefits of cloud lie in the scalability and agility offered as detailed below:

- **Rapid Provisioning**: Previously, deploying new infrastructure or scaling existing resources could take weeks or even months. With cloud services, businesses can now provision resources in mere minutes, responding swiftly to market demands. Also, the cloud provides automation and infrastructure as code capabilities to make the provisioning even more rapid.

- **On-the-Fly Scalability**: Cloud environments allow for automatic scaling, both vertically and horizontally, depending on the workload. This elasticity ensures optimal performance without wastage of resources.

Focus on Core Business Operations

The cloud offers the ability for teams to focus more on core business as below:

- **Shift from IT Management**: With the management complexities handled by cloud service providers, businesses could shift their focus from IT operations to core business functionalities, driving value and innovation.

- **Access to Cutting-Edge Technologies**: Cloud platforms often come equipped with the latest tools, applications, and services. Companies, especially startups and SMEs, benefit by leveraging these advanced technologies without in-house R&D.

Accelerated Digital Transformation

Moving on to additional benefits, cloud computing helps in accelerating transformation as below:

- **Collaboration and Remote Work**: Cloud solutions, especially SaaS products like collaboration tools and office suites, have enabled seamless remote work and global collaboration, a trend further amplified in the wake of the COVID-19 pandemic.

- **Data-Driven Decision-Making**: Cloud platforms facilitate the collection, storage, and analysis of vast datasets. This democratization of data analytics allows businesses to harness insights and make informed decisions.

New Business Models and Revenue Streams

Enterprises have started to drive additional benefits from the cloud besides cost and efficiency. Cloud is now leveraged to grow revenue as seen below:

- **SaaS, PaaS, and IaaS Models**: The cloud gave birth to new service-oriented models, allowing vendors to offer software, platforms, or infrastructure as services, revolutionizing software distribution and IT resource provisioning.

- **API Economy**: Cloud-native architectures and microservices have spurred the growth of the API economy. Companies now design, build, and monetize APIs, creating new revenue streams and partnership ecosystems.

The ascendancy of cloud computing represents more than just a shift in technology. It signifies a foundational change in how businesses conceptualize and implement their strategies, operations, and growth trajectories. As the cloud continues to evolve, its influence on business models and IT practices will only grow more profound, solidifying its role as a cornerstone of modern enterprise.

With these fundamentals in view, Thomas was confident and more than ready to start reviewing the material for his Cloud Practitioner certification, which started with the fundamentals of Amazon's foray into cloud computing.

Emergence of Amazon Web Services (AWS)

The story of **AWS** begins not with a vision of global cloud domination but rather with Amazon's internal need for scalable and efficient infrastructure. Today, AWS stands as a juggernaut in the cloud industry, but its genesis was rooted in Amazon's journey as an ecommerce platform. There were a few fundamental challenges that Amazon was dealing with that led to focus in this area:

- **Amazon's Scalability Challenge**: In the early 2000s, Amazon, primarily known as an online bookstore, was rapidly expanding its offerings. As the company grew, so did its IT infrastructure. However, even as Amazon was growing and hiring more technical staff, they were unable to speed up the process of application development. As Andy Jassy noted in many public fora, the key issue identified was that teams were spending months just to provision resources (database/compute/storage) even before writing a single line of application code. Each team spent time building these resources for their projects, and no one paid much attention to scale or reuse these resources across teams. Scaling and managing infrastructure for a global ecommerce platform was a complex task, and rapid deployment of services and features was becoming increasingly crucial to stay ahead of competitors.

- **The Vision of a Shared, Standardized Infrastructure**: Amazon's leadership realized that a more standardized, centralized approach to infrastructure was needed. The vision was to build a suite of infrastructure services – including computing power, storage, and databases – that internal teams could tap into as needed. The concept was simple yet revolutionary - break down infrastructure into fundamental, reusable components that any team within Amazon could use to build and run their systems. This shift was not just technological but cultural; it required teams to think about resources as services rather than physical hardware. Amazon began its foray into this new paradigm by creating a service for internal use called the "Merchant.com" platform. This allowed third-party retailers to leverage Amazon's ecommerce platform, but more importantly, it laid the foundation for offering services externally. This experiment also helped the internal teams to execute in a more disciplined way allowing better collaboration between teams.

- **Birth of the "Infrastructure Services" Idea**: As the story goes, during a leadership retreat at Jeff Bezos's house in 2003, the executive leaders spent time identifying Amazon's core competencies. As the discussion continued, the team realized that Amazon had also become quite good at running computer infrastructure services and scalable/reliable data centers. Sensing an opportunity beyond internal needs, Amazon started to toy with the idea of offering these infrastructure services to external developers and businesses. In 2002, Amazon launched the Amazon Web Services platform, but it wasn't the AWS we know today. This initial version offered a limited set of tools, including a service for retrieving website data and another for building simple web-based applications.

- **AWS's Public Debut**: 2006 was a landmark year for AWS. Amazon introduced **Amazon Simple Storage Service** (**S3**) and later **Amazon Elastic Compute Cloud** (**EC2**). These services were transformative.

  - **Amazon S3:** Allowed users to store vast amounts of data on the cloud, making it accessible from anywhere

  - **Amazon EC2:** Provided scalable computing capacity in the cloud, letting users run applications without investing in physical hardware

These services democratized infrastructure, enabling startups to large enterprises to access world-class infrastructure without hefty up-front costs. The success of Amazon S3 and EC2 created a snowball effect. AWS began rolling out a plethora of services, catering to various computing needs – from databases to machine learning. The pay-as-you-go model, combined with the breadth of offerings, made AWS an attractive proposition for businesses worldwide.

> *As Thomas understood more and more of the history of cloud computing, he was looking to understand how cloud computing would be relevant in the context of SAP, which had been his primary domain expertise over the years. Right out of college, Thomas started off his professional career in a mid-sized consulting firm that specialized in SAP solutions and services. Thomas was part of an "academy" where fresh graduates like him underwent an eight-week program to train on the technical fundamentals of SAP and then got assigned to projects as "**SAP Basis**" administrators. Though this was years ago, it seemed like yesterday for Thomas who learned quite a bit during the eight weeks and especially as a shadow administrator for three months under a tenured employee working on specific real-world customer systems. Over the years, Thomas quickly gained experience working across different projects supporting various customers both in day-to-day production support and implementations.*

> *Having spent a few years and becoming a seasoned SAP Basis administrator, Thomas felt the urge to learn additional skills that could help him become even more relevant to his customers. The next logical step for him was to get trained in a "functional" domain like **Order-to-Cash** or **Procure-to-Pay**, and that was what Thomas did. He worked with his manager who was supportive of him going back to the "academy" for functional expertise and coming back as a more rounded consultant. And that was what Thomas exactly did. He spent ten weeks learning about the Order-to-Cash cycle including sales order processing, availability check, delivery, billing, accounts receivable, and, most importantly, financial reporting. He now understood very well how the technical foundation of the SAP system that he was supporting helped the "functional expert" run business process transactions in the system, which had a very real-world impact in terms of goods reaching customers and invoices being paid. Thomas now had a better appreciation for how his day-to-day work helped support his customers run their business. Thomas soon became a much sought-after "techno-functional" consultant who would be called upon to troubleshoot problems, talk to clients, and help explain solutions and also gather requirements for new implementations.*

Soon word spread (and it did fast in small organizations), and Thomas was called in on "pre-sales" cycles to run "demos" of SAP solutions. Essentially as part of the sales cycle for acquiring new customers, the sales team leaned on Thomas as the subject matter expert who could demonstrate the solution and earn trust with the customer to help advance the sales cycle. Thomas's pleasant demeanor combined with sharp expertise made him a favorite of the sales teams so much so that there was a request from leadership to move him permanently to the sales team as a full-time "pre-sales" solution expert. The new role came with travel and an opportunity to engage with a diverse set of prospective clients, which Thomas relished. Very soon, Thomas was spending a lot of time on the road, visiting prospective customers, doing presentations by the day and solution demos in the afternoon. His ability to talk about both technical foundation and functional business processes helped him stand apart from other pre-sales engineers. Life was good!

And as Thomas contemplated during his initial onboarding at AWS, he kept going back to thinking, How will AWS help SAP customers run better? *And to answer that question, Thomas first needed to complete the next stage of his learning journey, which was understanding the basics of AWS cloud.*

What Is Cloud Computing?

In its simplest form, **cloud computing** is the on-demand delivery of IT resources like compute power, storage, applications, and databases, among others, over the internet or remote connection while paying only for what you consume. Think of it like the water connection to a family home. In today's modern houses, a water connection comes from a large reservoir over a main pipeline and then gets distributed over the house to the kitchen, bathrooms, and backyard and is accessed via a faucet.

Likewise, a **cloud service provider** creates "*reservoirs*" of these IT resources, and organizations and individuals can access them via a main pipeline (like "Direct Connect"). Much before the modern water distribution system became ubiquitous, people dug water wells within the house/community, while some people simply walked to a natural water source and filled up containers and carried them back to their homes. This is similar to legacy IT environments where an organization may build its own IT infrastructure (like a water well) or buy infrastructure piecemeal from a hardware vendor (carrying water).

Cloud Computing Service Models

Cloud computing is an evolving domain, and so are the **cloud computing models**. A key phrase common in the cloud computing world is "*as a service.*" A quick internet search (using the custom date range feature) shows that this phrase started appearing around the late 1990s and early 2000s. This phrase is key to understanding the nature of modern cloud computing where organizations and individuals are not paying for products, hardware, or even licenses. Instead, they are paying for a "service." In the very early days of the public cloud, the common IT resources available were storage and compute. Over the years it has evolved into more complex resources all the way up to complete end-to-end solutions. Largely there are the following models:

- **Infrastructure as a Service (IaaS)**: An IaaS model is when a cloud service provider delivers basic computing infrastructure like compute, storage, and networking. While this was the starting point of cloud computing, it remains the most common IT resources consumed. The cloud service providers have evolved these services so that now customers have a wide variety of choices of infrastructure to pick from. Some of this infrastructure is now purpose-built for specific needs, and the range of services help serve needs from individuals to startups and to large organizations. The typical consumers for IaaS were (and are) the infrastructure analysts and IT infra architects.

- **Platform as a Service** (**PaaS**): The early adopters of cloud computing were mostly startups who were trying to build a product or a service of their own. While the IaaS model helped provision the infrastructure, there were still some ways of being able to start building the application. That is when the cloud service providers started providing additional services like development tools, business intelligence (BI) services, middleware, and database management services among others. The developers could focus on building the applications on top of this "platform" or environment without having to worry about infrastructure building and managing the infrastructure associated with development of the application. The application development teams are the biggest consumers of PaaS services.

- **Software as a Service** (**SaaS**): As developers started building applications on the cloud, it also became an attractive mechanism to deliver those applications (or software) to their customers. Traditionally, software was delivered via a license model where it was shipped via a "compact disk." The end users typically click the executable file to install the software and use it on the device where it was installed. The ability to conduct commerce over the internet and securely process payments opened a channel for development teams to deliver the "software" as a subscription service leading to the SaaS boom. The end users or business users are the actual users of SaaS, whether you use an email service like "Gmail" or log into "Salesforce. com" for work.

There are some newer service models like function as a service/container as a service, which are further derivatives of the core models.

Now that we have reviewed the fundamentals and evolution of cloud computing, we will dive deep into the building blocks of AWS cloud itself.

The Building Blocks of AWS Cloud

In the context of SAP, AWS provides a secure, scalable, and high-performance infrastructure to run mission-critical SAP workloads. With services like Amazon EC2 for compute and Amazon S3 and Elastic Block Store (EBS) for storage, AWS enables flexible deployment and efficient management of SAP systems such as SAP RISE, S/4HANA, and SAP Business Technology Platform (BTP) among others. Additionally, AWS offers tools for automation, monitoring, backup, disaster recovery, and analytics, helping organizations reduce costs, improve agility, and accelerate innovation in their SAP environments.

While there are many components to AWS, the core fundamentals on which the cloud infrastructure is built are detailed below.

Storage (Amazon S3)

One of the key fundamental aspects of running an IT application is the ability to store data. And that is what Amazon S3 exactly offered when it was launched, providing object storage through a web interface. In spring 2006, AWS announced *Amazon S3 (Simple Storage Service)*, noting that developers can store any number of blocks of data in Amazon S3, providing an availability factor of 99.99% while costing about 15 cents a month to store 1 GB of data.

Over the years Amazon S3 has evolved to be a scalable object storage service designed to store and retrieve any amount of data from anywhere on the web. Some of the key features of Amazon S3 are

- **Durability and Availability**: Amazon S3 provides 99.999999999% (11 9s) durability over a given year, ensuring data is safe and reliable. Different levels of availability can be chosen based on storage classes

- **Storage Classes**: Various storage classes, like S3 Standard, S3 Intelligent-Tiering, S3 Standard-IA (Infrequent Access), and S3 One Zone-IA, cater to different use cases and cost points.

- **Security**: Provides robust capabilities for access control, encryption in transit, and encryption at rest.

- **Versioning**: Allows users to preserve, retrieve, and restore every version of every object stored in an Amazon S3 bucket, making it useful for backup and recovery.

- **Data Lifecycle Management**: Set policies to transition data to more cost-effective storage classes or archive/delete them.

- **Transfer Acceleration**: Enables faster file transfers to and from Amazon S3 by using Amazon CloudFront's globally distributed edge locations.

- **Event Notifications**: Automatically triggers workflows, alerts, or other actions based on changes to objects.

There are various usage scenarios for Amazon S3 including

- **Backup and Storage**: Use Amazon S3 as a highly durable and available backup storage.

- **Big Data and Analytics**: Store vast amounts of data for big data analytics.

- **Content Distribution**: Store content, like images or videos, and distribute them using integrations like Amazon CloudFront.

- **Static Website Hosting**: Host static websites directly from an Amazon S3 bucket without needing a server.

- **Data Lakes**: Combine data across various sources and allow different analytical tools to process it.

Compute (Amazon EC2)

As with storage, the computing power forms the fundamental building block of IT infrastructure that enables IT applications to process transactions and follow instructions. After Amazon S3 was announced in the spring of 2006, **Amazon EC2 (Elastic Compute Cloud)** was announced in the summer of 2006, again via a blog post by Jeff Barr, and was open for limited beta testing. As of 2025, EC2 now offers a wide range of compute instances that are optimized for specific needs and uses. Fundamentally, EC2 runs on top of physical host machines. However, spinning up an EC2 instance does not allocate the entire host to the user. Instead, the user is sharing the host with multiple other instances. This concept is known as *multi-tenancy* and is enabled by a software known as "*hypervisor*," which is responsible for isolating the virtual machines from one another even as they share the same host. Some key features of EC2 are

- **Elasticity**: Quickly scale up or down based on demand, making it easier to handle changes in traffic and optimize costs.

- **Variety of Instances**: EC2 offers a wide range of instance types optimized for various use cases, including computation, memory, storage, and GPU-based tasks.

- **Customizable**: Choose the memory, CPU (central processing unit), instance storage, and boot partition size that's right for your choice of application.

- **Integrated**: EC2 integrates with most AWS services like Amazon RDS, Amazon S3, and others, offering a complete environment for running applications.

- **Secure**: Amazon EC2 works in conjunction with Amazon Virtual Private Cloud (VPC) to provide security and robust networking functionality. This includes private IP addressing, security group assignment, and encrypted data storage.

- **Temporary Storage**: EC2 instances can leverage instance storage, which provides temporary block-level storage for the instance.

- **Elastic Load Balancing (ELB)**: Distributes incoming application traffic across multiple targets, such as EC2 instances, containers, and IP addresses, in one or more Availability Zones.

- **Auto-scaling**: Ensures that you have the right amount of compute capacity. Automatically increases the number of instances during demand spikes and decreases capacity during lulls.

At a high level, some of the key usage scenarios are

- **Web Servers**: Use EC2 to host scalable and fault-tolerant websites or web applications.

- **Big Data Analysis**: Utilize EC2's high-performance compute instances for distributed data processing.

- **Batch Processing**: Handle large amounts of data and tasks efficiently.

- **Backup and Recovery**: Facilitate backup services for business continuity.

- **Development and Test Environments**: Quickly provision and deprovision environments for development and testing.

Pricing

Amazon EC2 follows a pay-as-you-go model, where you pay for the compute capacity you use. There are multiple ways to purchase and use EC2 instances:

- **On-Demand Instances**: Pay for the compute capacity by the hour or second, with no long-term commitments or up-front payments.

- **Reserved Instances**: Reserve an instance for a set period (one or three years) in exchange for a significant discount compared with on-demand pricing.

- **Spot Instances**: Bid on unused EC2 instances, which can lead to cost savings if your applications have flexible start and end times.

- **Dedicated Hosts**: Physical servers dedicated to your use, helpful for regulatory requirements that do not allow multi-tenant virtualization.

Networking and Connectivity to AWS

As noted below, one of the key aspects of cloud computing is the delivery of services over the internet or remote connection. And that is why networking and connectivity became an important pillar in the foundational design of AWS. Let's look at it in detail:

- **Amazon VPC**: The **Amazon Virtual Private Cloud** is a logically isolated section of the AWS cloud where you can launch AWS resources in a virtual network. As more and more users are logging onto AWS and launching resources, the VPC lets you provision a logically isolated section of the AWS cloud where you can launch AWS resources in a virtual network that you define. The VPC also lets you group the resources into "*subnets*," which are a range of IP addresses in your VPC. These subnets can be either "*public subnets*" that can be accessed publicly , for instance, a website, or "*private subnets*" that can be accessed only through a private network, such as a database with customer data and historical orders placed. The subnets within a VPC can communicate with each other, for example, an application residing in a public subnet (say a website) needs to communicate with a database residing in the private subnet.

- **Connectivity to AWS**: Once the VPC is established, you need to establish connectivity to the VPC. Access to the VPC can be either by an "*internet gateway*" that allows public traffic from the internet to access your VPC or a "*virtual private gateway*" that allows protected (encrypted) internet traffic to enter the VPC. Additionally, a virtual private gateway empowers you to create a secure virtual private network (VPN) link between your VPC and a secluded network, like an on-premises data center or an internal corporate network. With a virtual private gateway, inbound traffic to the VPC is restricted to approved networks. AWS Direct Connect is a service designed to facilitate the establishment of a dedicated connection between your VPC and your organization's data center or corporate office.

The difference between the virtual private gateway and AWS Direct Connect is that in AWS Direct Connect, the network traffic does not traverse over the internet.

- **Access Controls and Traffic Management**: As the connectivity is established to the AWS cloud, the next logical step is to ensure there are right access controls of who can enter the VPC and manage the incoming and outgoing traffic. "*Amazon Route 53*" is a service that connects user requests to the AWS infrastructure (or even infrastructure outside of AWS). Amazon Route 53 can also be used to define routing rules (geo based, failover, latency based) or other complex routing rules that may consider multiple variables. Route 53 also monitors network health and can make routing decisions based on those inputs. Any time a user tries to interact with an application hosted in AWS, the request comes as a **packet** (a unit of data) over the internet or private network. This packet is checked for rules before it can reach a subnet. The VPC component that checks for these permissions is a "*network access control list*" or *network ACL* (sometimes also pronounced as "*knackle*"). Simply speaking, the NACL is a firewall that controls inbound and outbound traffic at the subnet level. Just like passport control officers at international airports, the network ACL checks for rules as the packet makes a request to enter or exit the subnet. Once the data packet has been checked at the subnet level, it is then checked at the EC2 instance level using an "*AWS security group*." Each instance in a subnet can be assigned a security group (a virtual firewall) to control incoming and outgoing traffic. While NACLs work at the subnet level and security groups at the EC2 instance level, another key difference is that NACLs perform *stateless* packet filtering, while security groups perform *stateful* packet filtering. Simply speaking, stateless means checking packets every time they cross both inbound and outbound, not remembering the previous decision and checking the rules again whether to allow or deny the packet. Stateful packet filtering means the previous request is remembered and allowed to proceed accordingly. Also, another key difference to note is NACLs have both "ALLOW" and "DENY" rules, while security groups only have "ALLOW" rules. So, if no rules are set, then no inbound traffic is allowed. Lastly, the default NACLs allow both inbound and outbound traffic until rules are specifically set up, while default security groups deny all inbound traffic until rules are set up; however, all outbound traffic is allowed by default.

Other Services

While Amazon EC2, Amazon S3, and networking form the core of AWS services, over the years AWS has evolved to provide additional services to meet specific needs. Even compute and storage have their own specific nuances. The services cover infrastructure, purpose-built services, and management services. A holistic view of AWS services looks something like this:

- **Analytics**: Tools to analyze data, process vast amounts of unstructured data, and gain insights.

- **Application Integration**: A suite of services that enable communication between decoupled components within microservices, distributed systems, and serverless applications.

- **Blockchain**: Offers managed blockchain services to create scalable blockchain networks.

- **Business Applications**: End-to-end solutions serving one particular need.

- **Cloud Financial Management**: Collection of practices, tools, and strategies aimed at helping AWS customers better understand and manage their cloud costs and usage.

- **Compute**: Provides scalable computing capacity in the AWS cloud, allowing the deployment of applications without investing in hardware.

- **Containers**: Suite of services and tools for building, deploying, and managing containerized applications. Containers package an application with all of its dependencies into a standardized unit, which facilitates consistent deployment across different environments.

- **Database**: Provides managed relational and NoSQL database services for transactional, analytical, and caching use cases.

- **Developer Tools**: Tools and services to aid developers in managing and automating the AWS application development and deployment process.

- **End User Computing**: Tools to provide a secure, managed environment for users accessing virtual desktops and applications.

- **Frontend Web and Mobile**: Set of tools and services designed specifically to aid developers in building, deploying, and scaling frontend web and mobile applications. These services simplify the process of launching full-stack applications, managing user authentication, content delivery, and more.

- **Internet of Things**: Services that allow devices to connect to the cloud and interact with other devices and cloud applications.

- **Machine Learning**: Provides tools and platforms to develop, train, and deploy machine learning models.

- **Management and Governance**: Services to manage, monitor, and automate AWS resources.

- **Media Services**: Suite of specialized services designed to facilitate the creation, processing, and management of video and audio content. These services cover a wide range of media-related workflows, from content creation and storage to processing, delivery, and analysis.

- **Migration and Transfer**: Tools to move applications, data, and workloads to AWS.

- **Networking and Content Delivery**: Contains services that enable isolated cloud networking, domain name registration, and fast content delivery.

- **Quantum Technologies**: Tools and services to explore and experiment with quantum computing.

- **Robotics**: Provides a development environment to simulate, test, and deploy intelligent robotics applications.

- **Satellite**: Services to connect, process, and transfer data with satellites.

- **Security, Identity, and Compliance**: Ensures data protection and secure user access to AWS resources.

- **Storage**: Offers a range of storage services that allow you to store, access, and back up data in the cloud.

The Scale of AWS's Global Infrastructure

Cloud service providers like AWS provide services across the globe to millions of users. Also, the services provided by AWS operate in a highly reliable, scalable, and available manner. To decode this a bit, AWS users are based in almost every remote corner of the planet. Also, these services have to *be highly reliable*, which means that the systems do not go down unpredictably and expectations for uptime keep going up. For example, if a customer is operating an ecommerce website, they would not want the systems to go down at all; hence, cloud service providers have built-in *fault tolerance*. The services also must operate in a highly available manner, which means they cannot slow down or have degraded performance at any point. Going back to the ecommerce example, the website cannot slow down just because there are too many users logged into the system. Similarly, the services need to be *highly scalable*. One of the key tenets of cloud services is that you can increase the capacity on demand and not wait for provisioning to be done over weeks or days.

Such diverse and complex needs cannot be fulfilled by setting up one, two, or even ten data centers. Rather, as AWS pioneered the concept of cloud computing, it proactively invested in building a network of data centers across the globe that are connected but at the same time fulfil defined criteria for geographic proximity, isolated power and cooling connection, and even things like accounting for flood plains and earthquake zones. AWS's global infrastructure is the underlying foundation of AWS services, designed to provide high availability, reliability, and scalability for its cloud offerings. This infrastructure allows AWS to operate on a global scale, serving millions of customers around the world. To understand AWS's scale of global infrastructure, it is good to understand it literally from the ground up.

- **AWS Region**: A region is a specific geographical area where AWS has multiple Availability Zones. Each region is isolated from other regions, ensuring that events in one region don't directly impact another region. The AWS regions are built closest to the high demand of business traffic, including locations like Paris, Tokyo, Sao Paulo, Dublin North Virginia, and Ohio (both in the United States), among others. An AWS region is a physical location in the world where we have multiple Availability Zones.

- **Availability Zones**: An Availability Zone (AZ) comprises one or more distinct data centers, each equipped with redundant power, networking, and connectivity, housed in separate facilities. These AZs provide the infrastructure needed to support production applications and databases with enhanced availability, fault tolerance, and scalability compared with a single data center setup. Each AZ operates as an autonomous failure zone, ensuring physical separation within a metropolitan area and placement in lower-risk flood plains (specific flood zone categorization varies by AWS region). Positioned tens of miles apart, AZs maintain proximity to minimize latency while also mitigating risk; in the event of a disaster in one part of the region, the separation reduces the likelihood of multiple AZs being affected. Alongside separate uninterruptible power supply (UPS) systems and onsite backup generation facilities, data centers situated across various Availability Zones are strategically linked to independent substations. This setup aims to minimize the potential impact of power grid events, ensuring that any such occurrence only affects a single Availability Zone, thus enhancing overall system resilience.

- **Local Zones**: These are a type of extension of regions placed in metropolitan areas, providing even lower latency to end users in those areas. They are useful for applications that require single-digit millisecond latency, like real-time gaming, media and entertainment, and machine learning inference at the edge.

- **Edge Locations**: Edge locations are sites deployed in major cities and metropolitan areas globally, distinct from regions and AZs. They are used by Amazon CloudFront (AWS's content delivery network) to cache content closer to end users, reducing latency. AWS has many more edge locations than regions, ensuring content is delivered quickly to end users wherever they are located.

The AWS network backbone ensures high-speed communication between the regions, AZs, and points of presence (local zones and edge locations) providing lower latency, higher transfer speeds, and enhanced security for data transfer between the sites.

An important point to note is that each region is isolated from every other region in the sense that no data goes in or out of the user environment in that region without the user explicitly granting permission for that data to be moved. Regional data sovereignty is part of the critical design of AWS regions with data being subject to the local laws and statutes of the country where the region lives.

With the way the AWS global infrastructure is designed, a user has the following key factors to consider when picking a region:

- **Compliance**: Depending on your organization location and local compliance laws, you may have to run all your data within, say, boundaries of the United Kingdom.

- **Proximity to Users**: Selecting a region closest to a majority of your users helps to get the necessary data to them faster. For example, if your users are in India, you should pick a region in India to provide them the lowest latency.

- **Service Availability Within a Region**: Since AWS keeps releasing new services, all of them may not be available in all regions. Hence, if the users would need a specific service, then you need to pick a region that offers that service.

- **Price**: The cost of running services varies within regions due to factors like tax laws, local labor pricing, etc. So this is another factor when picking the right region.

As of April 2025, AWS operates 34 regions with 108 Availability Zones with 400+ edge locations (for up-to-date locations and numbers, refer the AWS public website).

Security and Compliance in AWS Cloud

Finally, one of the most critical aspects of running applications in remote locations is security and compliance that not only meets an organization's security needs but also the regulatory and compliance needs of the framework that the organization operates in. AWS talks about the "*shared responsibility model*" of the cloud, which essentially means that AWS is responsible for the "*security of the cloud*" (hardware, software, networking, and facilities), while the customer is responsible for "*security in the cloud*" (applications and data). An analogy is securing the house. The builder is responsible for the quality-built doors, walls, etc., while the house owner is responsible for closing the locks. Similarly, all the services that AWS offers have to be secured. This is provided by AWS as

- **Physical Protection**: AWS's global network of data centers adhere to strict physical security measures. These include professional security staff, video surveillance, intrusion detection, and other advanced technologies to ensure the safety of physical infrastructure.

- **Infrastructure Protection**: Provided via *AWS Shield*, a managed Distributed Denial of Service (DDoS) protection service, *AWS WAF* (Web Application Firewall) that protects web applications from common web exploits, and *Amazon Inspector* that is an automated security assessment tool to find vulnerabilities and deviations from best practices.

- **Network Protection**: Provided via Amazon VPC, which offers a private, isolated section of the AWS cloud where you can launch resources; security groups, which act as a virtual firewall for EC2 instances, controlling inbound and outbound traffic; **network access control lists (NACLs)** that provide a rule-based tool for controlling network traffic in and out of subnets; and VPC peering, which is a secure and direct network route via private IP addresses. AWS Direct Connect provides a dedicated network connection from on-premises to AWS, and Amazon Route 53 is an encrypted **Domain Name System (DNS)** service.

- **Data Protection**: Via Amazon S3, offering server-side encryption with Amazon S3–managed keys (SSE-S3) or AWS **Key Management Service (KMS)**-managed keys; Amazon RDS, which supports encryption at rest and in transit; **AWS KMS**, which allows you to create and control cryptographic keys; and **AWS Secrets Manager and AWS Systems Manager Parameter Store**, which help in safeguarding access credentials and other secrets.

- **Identity and Access Management (IAM)**: The following are the components of IAM:

  - **IAM**: Allows administrators to grant granular permissions to different AWS services and resources. Helps in defining who can take what action on a specific resource

  - **IAM Roles**: Temporary permissions that can be granted to resources, like EC2 instances

  - **IAM Multi-factor Authentication (MFA)**: Adds an extra layer of protection on user access

- **Detective Controls**: The following are the components of detective controls:

  - **AWS CloudTrail**: Logs all API calls, allowing auditing and review

  - **Amazon GuardDuty**: Provides intelligent threat detection based on machine learning

  - **Amazon Macie**: Uses machine learning to identify and protect personally identifiable information (PII)

  - **VPC Flow Logs**: Capture information about IP traffic going in and out of network interfaces

- **Incident Response**: The following are the components of incident response:

  - **Amazon CloudWatch**: Monitors your environment, setting alerts for unusual activity

  - **AWS Config**: Provides a detailed view of the configuration of AWS resources, recording changes

- **Security Services and Tools**: AWS provides an array of tools for deep security visibility and automation, such as AWS Security Hub, a unified view of security alerts, and AWS Trusted Advisor, which provides real-time guidance to provision resources following best practices.

As Thomas reviewed all this material, the enormity of the AWS cloud dawned upon him. Cloud computing, which had been an abstract concept, was slowly emerging as a more structured and contextually relevant concept that would have a huge impact on his professional life.

Though he was nervous on the date of his "Cloud Practitioner" certification examination, all the material he read and the videos he saw helped him ace the exam. He proudly shared his achievement on "LinkedIn," and of course, congratulatory messages dropped in on his feed from friends, colleagues, and, of course, strangers who just happened to be on his LinkedIn network!

But that was two years ago …and all of a sudden Thomas's phone rang. He glanced quickly at the screen and saw a familiar name pop up …

CHAPTER 2

AWS and SAP Technical Partnership

This chapter covers the technical partnership between AWS and SAP and how that helps SAP customers. The chapter first covers the evolution of the partnership, then at a high level the technical considerations for SAP infrastructure, and lastly some key features of the engineering collaboration between the two companies.

Thomas let the phone ring a bit before pensively picking up the phone. "Hello, buddy ... What's my favorite 'cloud guy' up to ..." said a chirpy voice on the other end. That voice was Andrew Grant, who was always excited as if he just hit the jackpot in Vegas.

"I am doing good, Andy. What about you?" was all Thomas could muster weakly. While he really liked Andrew, he just could not keep up with his energy, and it felt nauseating at times. Thomas loathed himself for that but wisely kept his thoughts to himself. After all Andrew Grant, Industry Account Executive *at SAP, was not just a work partner but had become a good friend over the years.*

"Hey, Thomas, I think we should get together for drinks this week since we need to catch up on our joint account planning, and also I think there is an opportunity that we could work together on." Thomas's eyes lit up at the mention of the word "opportunity." It meant that there was a customer somewhere out there who was looking to modernize their SAP systems, and cloud technologies were a key to that transformation. However, he knew that he had to make sure that he did his part in the joint account planning exercise, which he had not started yet. He knew he had to drag himself to get that done; else, he would not get much from Andy.

Working with Andy and others from SAP had been integral to Thomas's success, in fact the success of their entire team. The "SAP on AWS" group focused on modernizing customers' SAP systems with the help of cloud

© Tushar Srivastava 2025
T. Srivastava, *Modernizing SAP with AWS*, https://doi.org/10.1007/979-8-8688-1579-9_2

services from AWS. And that naturally meant working not just with the customer who owned that SAP system, but also SAP, the organization itself, who provided the licenses and maintenance on that system.

Thomas quickly "slacked" his boss with the message, "Let me know if we can catch up for a coffee break in 30 ..." "For sure ...", came the reply. Thirty minutes later, as Thomas was pushing several buttons on the new fancy coffee machine in the break room (just to get a simple black Americano), Amy walked in carrying her own reusable coffee cup. Thomas glanced and felt a little guilty as he picked up his paper cup even as the black Americano poured in slowly. "Next time I will surely get my washable cup and do my bit for the environment," he quipped sheepishly.

"Congrats on your two years, Thomas. It is great to have you on the team! I hope you are celebrating in some way," replied Amy even as she ironically poured hot water and steeped some herbal tea in her cup that said "Coffee" in beautiful cursive. "Go ahead. What did you want to discuss?" she added, as the tea bag having done its job in a few dunks quickly found its way to the trash can.

Amy Penrose had been the dynamic sales leader of the SAP on AWS team. She not only charmed her customers with her passion and commitment, but her team loved her too, for her human touch in running the sales team, especially in such a high-pressure competitive environment. Having spent almost five years at AWS (which people jokingly called was like 15 at any other company), Amy was a seasoned Amazon veteran and was a poster child of the unique Amazon culture.

Thomas mentioned that he had been procrastinating on building the joint account plan with Andy from SAP and he really wanted to get a good plan in place before they decided to meet. "Essentially, I need some help and brainstorming." Amy took the discussion from the break room to a small conference room and proceeded to erase the board and lined up the colored markers neatly in front of her. She had clear intentions of making full use of them over the course of the discussion. "My next meeting is not until after lunch, so we do have some time and let's make good use of that." Amy picked the markers and proceeded to create box diagrams showing various players like AWS, SAP, customers, partners, and the like and linking them with different color-coded arrows showing interactions and relationships. Amy had a way with words and also a way with visual storytelling. Soon, an elegant picture began to emerge on the whiteboard, and Thomas stopped taking notes and just immersed himself into the discussion.

"While we build joint account plans between SAP and AWS, remember, let's always keep the customer front and center and work backward from that" was Amy's sage advice. Thomas added, *"I do have every customer's cloud roadmap and I can overlay the details of the SAP systems from what Andy can share, and we can easily find areas of synergy. That will be my initial inputs for the joint account plan."* All of a sudden it all began to crystallize for Thomas, and he started adding details to the block diagram. *"Make sure you add partner landscape and also any inputs on the transformation agenda that you may be aware of,"* Amy added. Thomas seemed very happy even as the discussion was coming to a close. He had been putting off this exercise forever, but the 30 minutes spent brainstorming on this gave him a clear direction forward. *"What would we all ever do without you, Amy!"* he added gleefully. Amy's last comments before she headed out were *"Remember, we have been in a partnership with SAP for a long time, even before we set up this go-to-market motion. That should be your starting point for any joint plans with them."* Thomas nodded in acknowledgment as Amy headed out, and he knew he had a fairly large task in front of him – putting the joint account plans to paper. He took pictures of the whiteboard before carefully erasing it even as his mind was racing through the timelines of this partnership.

Figure 2-1. *The Brainstorming Session*

Evolution of the AWS and SAP Technical Partnership

The highly evolved partnership between SAP and AWS had its beginnings in 2008.

- **2008 - Initial Collaboration**: AWS, introduced in 2006, was rapidly gaining traction by 2008 as a groundbreaking cloud service provider, and SAP saw the potential of AWS as a platform for its applications. The initial collaboration set the stage for a relationship that would shape the enterprise software and cloud computing industries. With AWS's scalable infrastructure and SAP's enterprise software prowess, the partnership promised substantial benefits for businesses.

- **2011 - SAP on AWS Officially Supported**: SAP began to officially support various solutions, like SAP BusinessObjects and SAP Rapid Deployment, on AWS. This was a pivotal moment, as it marked the endorsement of AWS as a certified platform for running critical SAP applications. By getting SAP's official endorsement, AWS positioned itself as a viable platform for enterprise-grade applications. This move validated the cloud's maturity and readiness for business-critical applications.

- **2012 - SAP HANA on AWS**: SAP HANA, an in-memory database designed for high-speed analytics and data processing, received certification for AWS deployment. Businesses could now test and deploy SAP HANA without making heavy on-premises hardware investments, thus lowering the barrier to entry and making SAP HANA accessible to a broader audience.

- **2014 - Larger Instances for SAP HANA**: AWS introduced the X1 instance family, designed with large memory footprints to cater to SAP HANA's in-memory capabilities. These specialized instances demonstrated AWS's commitment to catering to the specific needs of SAP customers, ensuring optimized performance and scalability.

- **2016 – SAP S/4HANA on AWS**: SAP S/4HANA, SAP's advanced enterprise resource planning (ERP) suite built on the HANA platform, became certified for AWS. This was a pivotal moment as enterprises could now consider transitioning their core business processes to the AWS cloud. It also underscored AWS's capability to handle complex, integrated business applications.

- **2017 – Extended Partnership and Collaboration**: SAP and AWS announced an extended strategic partnership, with SAP spotlighting AWS as a preferred, but not exclusive, cloud infrastructure provider. This deepened alliance aimed to offer integrated solutions in areas like IoT, AI, and machine learning. Such integrations enabled businesses to build more advanced, data-driven applications leveraging the strengths of both platforms.

- **2018 Onward**: Both companies focused on facilitating SAP migrations to AWS. AWS introduced tools, services, and new instance types, such as the high-memory instance, tailored for SAP workloads. As cloud adoption accelerated, these advancements ensured businesses had the means to migrate efficiently. The introduction of best practices, reference architectures, and specialized tools streamlined the migration process, reducing the time and risk involved. Also, in 2018, SAP NS2 (an independent subsidiary of SAP that provides solutions tailored for US national defense, security, and critical infrastructure sectors) and AWS announced a strategic collaboration that gave the ability to SAP NS2 customers to select AWS GovCloud (US) as a part of NS2's Secure HANA Cloud (SHC) offering, allowing for securely hosting workloads in the cloud.

Continued Commitment

Throughout this evolving partnership, SAP and AWS consistently adapted to the changing business landscape. By continually enhancing their offerings and integration points, they provided a compelling proposition for businesses seeking agility, scalability, and innovation. In essence, the SAP–AWS partnership epitomizes how collaborative efforts between industry leaders can result in synergistic solutions, providing businesses with a comprehensive set of tools and platforms to navigate their digital transformation journeys.

*Thomas knew he had a good few hours of work ahead of him over the next few days. He quickly updated his "Slack" status to a bright-red tomato indicating to his colleagues that he was doing focused **"pomodoro"** work. Over the next few days, Thomas put the customer at the focus of his planning exercise, working backward from their SAP modernization requirements and how AWS could help in achieving those. In order to do that, Thomas had to look at the systems from the customer's viewpoint. Customers running SAP view the* *systems in multiple tiers. Right at the bottom tier is the* hardware infrastructure, *which includes all the compute power, memory, storage, and related networking solutions that form the foundation elements on which SAP is installed and run. Above the infrastructure layer is the* SAP application *itself, which forms the core of the software that performs the business process transactions, and right at the top is the user interface layer, which lets users interact with the systems to enter transactions or run analytical reports. While customers can modernize at all three tiers, the journey usually starts at the infrastructure level. The common theme here is that infrastructure modernization helps to improve the performance, reliability, and security of the system. Thomas knew that AWS brought the most value in the infrastructure modernization efforts for SAP. Based on his past experience as a technology architect, Thomas built out a broad* "Hardware Infrastructure Map for SAP." *This map was to be his guiding tool as he navigated this journey for his customers.*

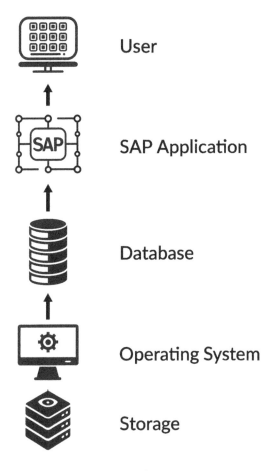

Figure 2-2. *Hardware Infrastructure Map for SAP*

Infrastructure Considerations for Operating SAP Systems

Infrastructure considerations for running SAP systems require carefully reviewing various hardware components to ensure optimal performance, reliability, and scalability. The exact requirements can vary based on the specific SAP product, the version, the number of users, and the expected workloads. However, here's a general overview of the hardware components to consider when running SAP.

Central Processing Unit (CPU)

CPU serves as the computational heart of any IT system, and this holds exceptionally true for enterprise solutions like SAP. Ensuring you have the right CPU resources is essential for optimal SAP performance. Here are some of the key considerations:

- **Architecture and Compatibility**: Contemporary SAP solutions are optimized for x86-64-bit CPU architectures. This permits the handling of larger memory addresses, an essential feature given the memory-intensive nature of many SAP operations, especially for systems like SAP HANA.

- **Cores and Threads**: Physical cores are individual processing units within the CPU. Multi-core processors can handle multiple tasks concurrently, which is pivotal for parallel processing in SAP environments. More cores generally translate to better multitasking and enhanced performance. Hyper-threading/simultaneous multithreading (SMT) technologies allow a single physical core to function as multiple logical cores. While this can improve performance in certain scenarios, it's essential to monitor real-world SAP workloads to determine the actual benefit.

- **Clock Speed**: This clock speed (measured in gigahertz or GHz) denotes how many cycles the CPU can execute per second. A higher clock speed typically translates to faster raw performance; however, it's essential to balance clock speed with other parameters like core count and thermal considerations.

- **Cache Memory**: Cache memory (levels L1, L2, and L3) is a smaller, faster type of random-access memory (RAM) directly situated on the CPU. It stores frequently accessed data and instructions, and the presence of ample cache memory can significantly boost SAP operations, especially repetitive tasks or large datasets.

- **Virtualization Support**: Hardware-assisted virtualization features like Intel VT-x and AMD-V, which are hardware extensions to support virtualization, become essential for optimal performance and stability if you are running SAP in a virtualized environment.

- **Scalability and Load Balancing**: Larger SAP deployments might necessitate multi-node setups or servers with multiple CPU sockets. This approach can horizontally scale the processing capability.

- **Load Balancing:** Distributing incoming SAP application traffic across multiple CPUs or servers can ensure optimal resource utilization and high availability.

- **Energy Efficiency and Thermal Design Power (TDP)**: Energy-efficient CPUs can lead to cost savings in the long run, especially in data centers with many servers. TDP denotes the maximum amount of heat the CPU is expected to generate. Ensuring efficient cooling solutions based on the CPU's TDP is essential for system stability.

Memory, or Random-Access Memory (RAM)

RAM is a vital component for the performance and responsiveness of SAP systems. Given the intricacies of SAP environments – encompassing databases, application servers, and various services – ensuring adequate memory allocation is paramount. Let's dive deep into the memory requirements essential for running SAP:

- **Type and Speed – DDR Generations**: Contemporary enterprise systems typically employ DDR4 or even DDR5 generation memory, boasting faster data transfer rates and improved power efficiency over previous iterations.

- **ECC (Error-Correcting Code) Memory**: Critical for SAP servers, ECC memory can detect and correct single-bit memory errors, providing a layer of data integrity that is essential for transactional and data-intensive operations.

- **Capacity**: For the initial deployment, the SAP system's baseline memory requirement encompasses the operating system, SAP software components, active user sessions, and active database contents (especially in the case of in-memory databases like SAP HANA). As your enterprise scales and data volume increases, so does the need for memory. Planning for future requirements, including SAP module additions and user increases, is pivotal.

- **Memory for SAP HANA**: SAP HANA's main advantage is its in-memory data processing capability, which necessitates large amounts of RAM, often ranging from a few hundred gigabytes to several terabytes, depending on the dataset's size.

- **Persistence Layer**: Despite being in-memory, SAP HANA requires a persistence layer to ensure data safety during events like restarts or failures. Although this is more about storage, the interplay between RAM and storage is crucial for performance.

- **Virtual Memory**: Swap space refers to a space on the storage drive where the operating system (OS) stores data from RAM that is not actively being used. While swapping helps in managing memory more efficiently, over-reliance on swap space (due to inadequate RAM) can hamper performance.

- **Buffer and Cache**: Shared memory buffers are sections of memory where SAP systems store frequently accessed data, minimizing the need to fetch data from slower storage mediums. Proper buffer configuration can significantly enhance system performance.

- **Database Cache**: For SAP systems relying on traditional databases, ample memory should be allocated for caching purposes to speed up data retrieval operations.

- **Memory for Application Servers**: Each user interaction in SAP, known as a dialog process, consumes memory. As the number of simultaneous users increases, the memory requirement for these processes also scales.

- **Background Jobs**: These are non-interactive tasks in SAP that run in the background (e.g., data backups). They also consume memory and need to be factored into total requirements.

- **Optimization and Monitoring**: Tools and utilities, both from SAP and third-party vendors, can help monitor memory usage, detect leaks, and optimize memory allocation. Regular monitoring of the system's memory performance, looking for signs of excessive swapping or memory bottlenecks, could indicate a need for additional RAM or optimization.

- **High Availability and Redundancy**: For mission-critical SAP deployments, clustered setups with failover capabilities might be used. In such setups, memory configurations should be consistent across nodes to ensure seamless failover and performance.

Storage

Implementing and running an SAP system requires thorough consideration of storage needs. The nature and scale of data processed and stored in SAP environments make it pivotal to understand and optimize storage requirements for performance, reliability, and scalability. The following are some important aspects of storage for SAP:

- **Volume and Capacity**: Even a basic SAP installation requires significant storage. This encompasses the operating system, SAP software components, databases, logs, and initial datasets. As businesses evolve, data accumulation grows, driven by increased transactions, user logs, analytic data, and backups.

- **Archiving and Backup**: Periodic backups and archiving of old data, while ensuring system functionality, will consume additional storage.

- **Performance and Speed**: Input/output operations per second (IOPS) is a critical metric, especially for database-driven systems like SAP. High IOPS ensures swift read/write operations, vital for real-time processing.

- **Latency**: Latency is the time it takes to initiate a data transfer once a request is made. For databases, low latency is crucial for responsive system behavior.

- **Throughput**: Storage throughput is the amount of data that can be read from or written to storage per second. It is measured in MB/s (megabytes per second) or GB/s (gigabytes per second) and determines how fast a system can access and process data from storage.

- **Storage Types and Technologies**: With no moving parts, solid-state drives (SSDs) provide significantly faster data access times and better reliability, making them more suitable for active databases and application servers. Hard disk drives (HDDs), while less expensive and suitable for large volumes, offer slower data access speeds compared with SSDs. HDDs are ideal for archival storage or backup. Non-Volatile Memory Express (NVMe) is an interface protocol for SSDs, and the NVMe drives offer even faster performance than traditional SSDs and are ideal for I/O-intensive tasks like databases.

- **Data Redundancy and Reliability**: Redundant Array of Independent Disks (RAID) is a way of storing the same data in different places on multiple hard disks or solid-state drives (SSDs) to protect data in the case of a drive failure. For SAP systems common configurations like RAID 5 (striping with parity) or RAID 10 (striped mirrors) offer a balance of performance and redundancy.

- **SAP HANA Storage Needs**: SAP HANA is an in-memory database, meaning primary data operations are performed in RAM. However, it still requires storage for persistence, logs, backups, and more.

  - **Persistent Storage**: While data operations are in memory, data still needs to be periodically saved to persistent storage. This ensures data safety in events like power outages or system failures.

  - **Log Volumes**: HANA continuously writes logs. High-speed storage solutions, preferably SSDs, are crucial here to ensure system stability and performance.

- **Storage Scalability**: Enterprise storage solutions often allow adding storage without needing system shutdowns (hot-add storage), ensuring uninterrupted SAP operations.

- **Storage Area Network (SAN)**: A dedicated network providing access to consolidated block-level storage. SANs are scalable and can be expanded based on requirements.

- **Virtualization and Storage**: SAP environments, when virtualized, might use storage solutions like VMware's vSAN. It pools together storage resources and delivers them on demand.

- **Management and Monitoring**: Storage management tools help in monitoring storage health, utilization rates, IOPS, latency, and more.

- **Alerts and Thresholds**: Setting up alerts for metrics like capacity, performance, and health can preempt failures or performance bottlenecks.

Network Requirements

The network infrastructure is an unsung hero in the success of any SAP deployment. Being the conduit through which data flows, it not only connects various SAP components but also links the system with end users and other enterprise IT assets. A robust, reliable, and high-performance network is essential for a smooth-running SAP environment. The network infrastructure underpins the connectivity, performance, and security of SAP deployments. Whether it is connecting a user to an application server or an application server to a database or integrating with other enterprise systems, the network plays a pivotal role. Ensuring it's robust, scalable, secure, and optimized for SAP is key to reaping the full benefits of your SAP investment. Network requirements can be understood within the following components:

- **Bandwidth and Throughput**: **Bandwidth** refers to the maximum data transfer rate of a network or internet connection, often measured in megabits per second (Mbps) or gigabits per second (Gbps). SAP operations, especially data-intensive tasks, demand high bandwidth to ensure timely data delivery. On the other hand, **throughput** is the actual data transfer rate achieved during operations, often less than the theoretical maximum bandwidth. Monitoring throughput can offer insights into network performance and congestion.

- **Latency**: Latency is defined as the time taken for a packet of data to travel from the source to the destination. For SAP systems, especially those involving real-time processing or globally distributed components, low latency is crucial. There are many factors influencing latency; physical distance, network congestion, and the number of hops (intermediate devices like routers) data must pass through can impact latency.

- **Redundancy and Failover**: To ensure high availability, critical SAP components should have redundant network connections. If one connection fails, the secondary can take over, ensuring uninterrupted operation. This can be achieved either with two Direct Connect connections or two VPNs or a combination of Direct Connect and VPN.

- **Load Balancing**: Incoming network traffic can be distributed across multiple servers, enhancing performance and ensuring system availability during high-load situations or maintenance periods. This can be achieved with either physical devices or software solutions.

- **Network Security**: Firewalls are devices or software that filter incoming and outgoing network traffic based on predetermined security policies, protecting SAP systems from potential threats. A **virtual private network** (**VPN**) is a secure, encrypted connection over the internet, allowing remote users or branches to access the SAP system safely, and with **network segmentation**, you can divide the network into smaller segments, limiting the potential impact of security breaches and improving overall performance.

- **Topology and Architecture**: Ensuring high-speed, low-latency connections within the **Local Area Network** (**LAN**), the internal network within an organization, is essential for on-premises SAP deployments, while Wide Area Network (WAN; it connects remote branches or data centers) optimization solutions can help enhance the performance of SAP systems spread across different geographical locations. Likewise, **AWS Direct Connect**, which is a dedicated network connection that links your on-premises environment to AWS, providing lower latency, secure/private connectivity, and more consistent performance than internet-based connections, is essential if parts of the SAP infrastructure are cloud-based.

- **Network Protocols and Services**: From an SAP perspective, the following components are essential:

  - **Transmission Control Protocol** (**TCP**): A reliable, connection-oriented protocol often used for SAP communications

  - **Domain Name System** (**DNS**): Resolves domain names to IP addresses, helping in locating and connecting to SAP servers

  - **Dynamic Host Configuration Protocol** (**DHCP**): Automates the assignment of IP addresses within the network

- **Quality of Service (QoS)**: QoS is a technique to manage network resources by ensuring essential data traffic gets priority. In an SAP context, certain operations or modules might require prioritization, especially during peak usage times.

- **Remote Access**: Solutions like SAP **GUI** (**Graphical User Interface**) or other remote desktop services might be used to access SAP systems, necessitating stable and secure remote network capabilities. Likewise, with the increasing use of mobile devices for SAP access, ensuring a secure and efficient mobile network connection is vital.

- **Monitoring and Management**: In order to track and monitor the health of the network, you should also invest in the following:

  - **Network Monitoring Tools**: Software solutions that provide insights into network health, performance, and security, enabling proactive issue identification and resolution

  - **Traffic Analysis**: To understand data flow patterns, identify potential bottlenecks, and optimize the network for SAP operations

High Availability and Disaster Recovery for SAP

Enterprise applications, especially critical ones like SAP, demand consistent uptime and quick recoverability after unforeseen interruptions. High availability (HA) and disaster recovery (DR) are two key strategies that enterprises employ to ensure business continuity for their SAP environments. Ensuring high availability and disaster recovery for SAP systems is not just about technology; it's a business imperative. Given the critical role SAP plays in many organizations, the stakes are high. An effective HA/DR strategy, tailored to the organization's needs and regularly tested, can make the difference between a minor hiccup and a major business disruption. Let us delve into the intricacies of these strategies:

- **High Availability (HA)**: HA focuses on minimizing system downtime, ensuring that applications are continuously operational. It's about swiftly recovering from disruptions and ensuring data integrity. Features and techniques of HA include

  - **Redundancy**: Deploying duplicate instances of SAP components on separate hardware or cloud instances. If one instance fails, the other takes over.

  - **Failover Clusters**: These are groups of servers that work together. If one server fails, the workload shifts to another server in the cluster.

  - **Load Balancers**: Distribute incoming traffic across multiple servers, preventing any single server from getting overwhelmed and ensuring continued service even if a server fails.

- **Disaster Recovery (DR)**: DR is about recovering systems and data after catastrophic events, such as natural disasters, hardware failures, or cyber-attacks. It involves a set of policies and tools to restore the application to a functional state. Features and techniques of DR include

  - **Backup and Restore**: Regularly backing up SAP data to local devices or cloud storage. In case of a disaster, the data can be restored.

- **Replication**: Continuously copying data from the primary SAP system to a secondary location. This replica can be activated if the primary system becomes unusable. The replication can be storage based or database-native replication.

- **Recovery Time Objective (RTO)**: The targeted duration of time within which a business process must be restored after a disaster.

- **Recovery Point Objective (RPO)**: Refers to the maximum age of files or data within the system that must be recovered for normal operations to resume after a disaster.

- **Integrated HA and DR Approaches**: Certain architectures configure HA and DR together. This can be achieved by the designs below:

  - **Stretch Clusters**: These are clusters where nodes are geographically dispersed. They combine the instant failover capabilities of HA with the geographic redundancy of DR.

  - **Multi-site Replication**: SAP data is replicated across multiple sites. This ensures both high availability within a site and disaster recovery across sites.

- **Testing and Validation**: This is another critical aspect of HA and DR. Testing and validation can be achieved via either regular drills, that is, periodically testing the effectiveness of HA and DR solutions by simulating disruptions, or continuous monitoring using tools to continuously monitor system health, enabling quick identification and rectification of potential issues.

- **Security Considerations**: Ensure that backed-up or replicated data is *encrypted*, both in transit and at rest, and only *authorized personnel* should be able to initiate failovers, access backups, or execute DR plans.

- **Cost Considerations**: The total cost of downtime can be calculated by measuring potential revenue losses, reputation damage, and other costs associated with SAP system downtime to gauge investment in HA/DR solutions. Leveraging a mix of solutions (like using backups for non-critical data and replication for mission-critical data) can *optimize costs* while ensuring business continuity.

With all the initial data in place, Thomas reached out to his trusted partner Ashish Kumar. While Ashish handled the business and commercial conversations, as the "SAP on AWS solution architect," Ashish was responsible for addressing the specific technical architecture needs of the customers. While not working on customer requirements, Ashish loved to spend time building little applications, answering technical queries over user forums late in the night and studying for technical certifications. Basically, as geeky as it could be!

"Ashish, buddy, remember that joint account plan work that we were supposed to do with SAP? Well, we really got to get it done," Thomas messaged Ashish over Slack. Ashish, in his usual style, responded with three grinning smileys and then added a couple more for good measure. "Well, the good news is I had a good meeting with Amy and then I worked on quite a bit of it already, so we need to get together to make sure that the specific technical details are accurate and in line with customer requirements." Exactly the kind of work that Ashish would geek out on.

In his role just before AWS, Ashish had spent 17 years with the same medical manufacturing company and was responsible for the technical architecture of their SAP systems through various acquisitions, divestitures, and growth. In his final role at his previous company, Ashish led a team of 12, running day-to-day SAP operations globally. Thomas and Ashish had hit it off almost immediately, given their shared background in SAP and almost nothing else in common. However, they formed a strong partnership together in working on SAP on AWS engagements. While on one of their customer visits together, Ashish had shared with Thomas that one of the reasons he thought of looking for a new role at 17 years was that he wanted to stay closer to technology rather than spend an extraordinary amount of time doing paperwork and performance reviews and managing egos.

"Send the draft document to me over the shared folder, and I will review and add more of the technical details," signed off Ashish. This was a chore that he would relish. Over the next few days, Thomas and Ashish worked together remotely and updated the joint account plans. Both were pretty pleased with the output. And while all this was going on, Thomas had quietly emailed Andrew asking for them to meet together to discuss the plans and also learn more about the new opportunity that Andrew spoke about. While he was poring over the finer details of his account plan one late evening, Thomas saw the familiar yellow envelope icon pop up in the corner of his computer screen. The email was from Andrew … Surely, only a sales person would reply to an email late in the night. Andrew wanted to meet

47

next Tuesday and also suggested that he would get his "cloud architect" *to participate in the meeting. As he shut down his computer, Thomas started mentally planning for the meeting already ...* I am not ordering chicken wings this time, *he thought to himself. The next day Thomas and Ashish got together to plan for this meeting.* "Well, if I am coming down to New York for this meeting, might as well stay back for a few meetings with some of the other colleagues," *Ashish added to the conversation. Being a remote employee offered flexibility, but even the usually reticent Ashish craved for face time with colleagues once in a while.* "Sure, we can squeeze in a few working sessions while you are here. Let us also ensure that we are covering the document in detail with the SAP folks, and I expect a lot of technical questions, since Andy is bringing along a cloud architect to the meeting. Minimum iterations on the document, maximum focus on pursuing opportunities." *Thomas was very clear with his instructions.*

Ashish took an early morning flight into New York and headed straight to the Amazon office in the heart of New York. The front doors still had the signage of "Lord & Taylor," *the original occupants of this New York landmark that was declared a heritage site in 2007. Though the building was built in 1914, you wouldn't be able to tell that with the reimagined interiors. With food courts, break rooms, terraces, and contemporary workspaces, JFK27 (or popularly known as* "Hank") *was the latest of Amazon's inspiring new office and collaboration space. He headed straight to* "Marketplace" *for some hot coffee and a quick snack. Sharp at 9:45 AM, Ashish was settled in the designated conference room, still waiting for Thomas to show up. About 30 minutes later, Thomas showed up. Ashish did not notice since he was engrossed in building out a large architecture diagram on the whiteboard.* "Hey, Ashish, how many software engineers does it take to change a light bulb?" *hollered Thomas across the room. Ashish turned around, smiled wryly, and said,* "None. It is actually a hardware problem." *The joke never got old even as the two buddies exchanged a high five. The two colleagues reviewed the documents and got the technical architecture color-coded on the whiteboard. They were ready to host their SAP friends and grabbed some quick lunch at the ever-buzzing cafeteria. At 2 PM, Thomas got called in the building reception with two visitors showing up to meet him, and almost at that moment he got a text from Andrew,* "We are downstairs ..." *After spending a few minutes getting visitor access and walking up to the elevators, Andrew made some introductions.* "Hi, Melanie, this is Thomas from AWS, whom I collaborate with on joint opportunities. And, Thomas, this is Melanie Richards, who is new to her role of a cloud architect at SAP" *were Andrew's quick and simple introductions. Between exchanged pleasantries, Melanie made sure she explained that while she was new to the cloud architect role, she had been with SAP for almost seven years. The three of them took the elevator and reached the conference room floor. Ashish was waiting in anticipation. "Good to see you again, brother," Andrew said while shaking hands with Ashish, and further greetings were exchanged throughout the room.*

Melanie had anticipated the question and took time to explain her role. "As you know, SAP is focused on helping customers modernize their SAP s ystems by moving to the latest version of SAP S/4HANA. SAP S/4HANA helps customers streamline business processes, reduce custom code, and run better analytics on the data. A lot of these benefits are tied to operating SAP in the cloud and leveraging cloud technologies to work with the ERP solution. As a cloud architect, *I am responsible for helping customers leverage the best from cloud solutions in context of their SAP systems. That means working with a cloud service provider like yourself, to build joint solutions for our mutual customers." Melanie did a good job of explaining her role and where she would fit in the grand scheme of things. "In a way, my role and in fact my whole team is a result of continuous partnership between SAP and AWS so that we can leverage the cloud strategically to help modernize SAP." Ashish thought to himself,* Well, that is what I am here for. *But thankfully he kept his thoughts to himself. Thomas quickly got down to business and laid out the account planning documents, while Ashish supplemented that with the architecture diagrams on the whiteboard. The conversations centered around modernizing SAP systems for the customers, with a heavy sprinkling of words like "value proposition," "business case," and "target architecture."*

As the discussion progressed, there was a clear action plan emerging on what the SAP modernization path would be for each of the mutual customers in the joint account plan. Andrew glossed over the technical details while stayed focused on the cost aspects since he was keener on building the financial business case, while on the other extreme, for Ashish, the technical details were pieces of art that kept refining over and over even during the discussion. Thomas was the glue between the two trying his best to balance the technical and commercial aspects of the customer benefits. Melanie was a keen observer and chipped in once in a while, still aware that she had a lot to learn. It was an unwritten rule in the corporate world that the newest member of the group (who had the least to contribute) would end up being the designated notetaker, even as she kept compiling a list of questions that she was looking answers for. As the conversations got more intense, with three-letter acronyms being thrown around, Melanie realized she had to get some more answers if she were to follow this discussion. She quickly raised her hand still holding her half-chewed pencil. "Ashish, you kept talking about BTP services, which I understand, but you also kept referring to the JRA. Can you explain how does that fit in and what is it actually?" Melanie posed the question thoughtfully. "Joint reference architecture ..." was Ashish's terse reply as he continued to proceed with his train of thought. Thomas sensed that while Ashish technically did answer the question, that was not what Melanie was looking for. He intervened, "Ashish, hold on ... Melanie, does that answer your question?" "Well, not really. I am curious how is the JRA relevant to our mutual customers?"

Thomas proceeded to take center stage. "Melanie, let's take a step back, and even before we talk about solving problems for our mutual customers, let me talk through about SAP and AWS as partners. I will focus on the technical partnership because that is relevant for our customers." As Thomas grabbed a couple of markers, he also said, "We can start the conversation here and continue into the happy hour that we have planned."

AWS and SAP Collaboration

At a technical level, SAP and AWS collaborate toward the success of their mutual customers. This collaboration is at multiple levels, some of which are as follows.

Engineering Collaboration

Compute

As AWS continues to build purpose-built hardware for SAP, these hardware configurations undergo a certification process by which SAP confirms that specific hardware configurations work optimally with SAP software applications. One of the key focus areas for engineering collaboration is to certify AWS hardware for SAP usage. When hardware is certified by SAP, it signifies that the hardware vendor and SAP have tested the configuration to ensure compatibility, performance, and reliability when running SAP applications. The following reasons make certification critical:

- **Compatibility**: Ensures that the hardware components and configurations have been tested and are compatible with specific SAP applications and modules. This reduces the risk of technical issues that might arise from incompatible hardware.

- **Optimized Performance**: SAP certification ensures that the hardware can provide the required performance levels for running SAP applications smoothly.

- **Reliability**: Certified hardware is tested for reliability, ensuring that it can handle mission-critical SAP applications without frequent breakdowns or issues.

- **Support**: When using SAP-certified hardware, customers are often in a better position to receive support from both SAP and the hardware vendor. Issues that arise can be addressed more efficiently because of the known compatibility between the software and hardware.

- **Reduction in Total Cost of Ownership (TCO)**: By opting for certified hardware, companies can often experience fewer technical glitches, leading to reduced downtime and IT support costs.

While there are many metrics that are used to certify, one key metric is SAPS. **SAPS** stands for **SAP Application Performance Standard**. It's a hardware-independent unit of measurement that describes the performance of a system configuration in the SAP environment. The term is often used to describe the performance capability of a given system in relation to SAP applications. The primary goal of SAPS is to offer a standardized measure that can provide a consistent comparison of system performance across different hardware architectures. Because it is hardware-independent, it allows for an apples-to-apples comparison, making it easier for businesses to make informed decisions when choosing hardware for their SAP environments.

Key technical details about SAPS are as below:

- **Measurement**: SAPS is determined based on the fully business-processed order line items per hour. Specifically, it reflects how many SAP transactions a given system can handle within that time frame.

- **Usage in Benchmarks**: SAPS values are often used in SAP standard application benchmarks, which are standardized procedures to measure the performance of hardware systems running SAP applications. Manufacturers and vendors use these benchmarks to showcase the performance capabilities of their products in an SAP environment.

- **Relevance for Customers**: For businesses that run SAP applications, understanding SAPS values can be crucial when planning new implementations or scaling existing ones. By knowing the SAPS value of a particular hardware configuration, decision-makers can ensure they select systems that meet their performance requirements.

- **Evolving Metrics**: As with many performance metrics, the exact methods and processes used to determine SAPS values can evolve over time. SAP ensures that the benchmarking processes used are up to date and reflect current technology trends and requirements.

Apart from SAPS there are other benchmarks that indicate the performance capabilities, especially for SAP HANA. The **SAP BWH (Business Warehouse HANA) benchmark** plays a critical role in evaluating the performance of SAP BW systems running on SAP HANA when hosted by cloud service providers (CSPs) like AWS. This benchmark simulates complex data processing and analytical workloads typical of enterprise data warehousing, enabling AWS to demonstrate their infrastructure's ability to support large-scale SAP deployments. By publishing BWH benchmark results, AWS provides transparency into how their compute, memory, and storage resources perform under SAP-specific conditions, helping customers make informed decisions when selecting a cloud platform for their SAP BW on HANA workloads. These results are especially important for organizations seeking high performance, scalability, and reliability in cloud-based SAP environments. That's why as part of the SAP HANA certification for VMs/instances for the cloud, CSPs actually have to run BWH benchmarks on SAP HANA systems. The BWH benchmark is extremely CPU and memory intensive and thus serves as an ideal HANA-specific performance indicator.

Storage

A key area of this partnership is storage, which plays a foundational role in ensuring the performance, availability, and resilience of SAP applications like SAP HANA, SAP S/4HANA, SAP Business Suite, and SAP BW/4HANA. The AWS and SAP collaboration around storage reflects a deep alignment to meet the demanding needs of enterprise-grade SAP environments. Whether it's delivering high-performance block storage for SAP HANA, scalable object storage for backups, or shared file systems for legacy SAP directories, AWS provides a wide portfolio of SAP-certified storage solutions.

SAP workloads demand high IOPS, low latency, and guaranteed throughput for transactional and analytical processing. Storage must support not only database performance but also backup/restore operations, high availability, disaster recovery, and long-term data retention. SAP HANA, in particular, is a memory-intensive application that also relies on fast persistent storage for log and data volumes, making storage design critical to system reliability and performance.

Amazon EBS (Elastic Block Store): Amazon EBS is the primary block storage solution for EC2 instances running SAP applications. Amazon EBS provides persistent, low-latency storage volumes with features critical for SAP:

- **Provisioned IOPS (io2 and io2 Block Express):** Optimized for performance-intensive workloads like SAP HANA, offering predictable and consistent IOPS

- **Fast Snapshot Restore**: Reduces recovery time for system backups

- **Multi-attach**: Enables shared access across instances, useful for high-availability architectures

SAP has certified Amazon EBS io2 Block Express for SAP HANA, which provides up to 4,000 MB/s throughput and 256,000 IOPS per volume, making it one of the most robust cloud-based storage options for HANA workloads.

Amazon FSx for NetApp ONTAP: AWS and NetApp, an SAP technology partner, offer Amazon FSx for NetApp ONTAP, which provides a fully managed file system that is SAP-certified for use with NetApp-based storage solutions:

- **NFS and SMB Support:** Suitable for shared SAP file systems and interface directories

- **Snapshot-Based Backups and Cloning:** Useful for non-disruptive backups and rapid system copies

- **Built-In Data Compression and Deduplication:** Helps optimize storage costs

FSx for ONTAP is especially beneficial in scenarios where enterprises are migrating SAP systems from on-prem NetApp storage to the cloud.

Amazon EFS (Elastic File System): For SAP components that require shared file systems but don't have stringent performance requirements, Amazon EFS offers a fully managed, elastic NFS file system:

- **Scales Automatically:** Adjusts capacity as files are added or removed

- **High Availability:** Automatically stores data across multiple Availability Zones

- **Simple Setup:** Useful for lower-performance shared directories in SAP environments

Amazon EFS complements Amazon EBS and Amazon S3 by serving as a middle ground for file-based storage needs with high availability and moderate performance.

SAP HANA Fast Restart with AWS: SAP HANA's *Fast Restart option*, supported on AWS, enables customers to restart HANA systems more quickly by keeping the database data in Amazon EC2 instance memory, while the persistence layer continues to reside on high-performance Amazon EBS volumes. This is particularly relevant for large HANA systems where startup times can otherwise be lengthy due to data loading.

Cross-Region and Hybrid Storage Use Cases: AWS also enables hybrid and multi-region SAP storage strategies through services like

- **AWS Storage Gateway**: Extends on-prem SAP environments to cloud-based storage

- **AWS Backup**: Centralized backup management for Amazon EBS, FSx, and Amazon S3

- **Amazon Data Lifecycle Manager**: Automates EBS snapshot creation and retention for SAP systems

Security and Compliance: All AWS storage services offer encryption at rest and in transit using AWS KMS, integrated IAM policies, logging via AWS CloudTrail, and support for SAP compliance standards including ISO, SOC, and GDPR.

Solution Collaboration

RISE with SAP

RISE with SAP is SAP's flagship offering designed to support organizations on their journey to becoming **intelligent, sustainable enterprises**. It is a **business transformation as a service (BTaaS)** solution that bundles together everything an enterprise needs to modernize its SAP landscape – including **SAP S/4HANA Cloud, business process intelligence (BPI), technical migration tools, SAP Business Technology Platform (BTP),** and **managed services** – **under a single contract and subscription model.** RISE with SAP streamlines digital transformation by delivering not just software, but a **holistic transformation service** that spans technology, business processes, and cloud infrastructure.

Core Components of RISE with SAP

- **SAP S/4HANA Cloud** (public or private edition)

- **Business process intelligence** tools (e.g., Signavio)

- **SAP Business Technology Platform (BTP)** for extensions, integration, and analytics

- **Embedded tools and services** for lifecycle management and technical migration

- **SAP Business Network starter pack**

- **Choice of hyperscaler infrastructure**, including **Amazon Web Services (AWS)**

Working together in the mutual interest of customers, AWS and SAP bring about a wide range of benefits including global reach/proven infrastructure, high performance for SAP workloads, enhanced security and compliance, innovations at scale, and operational efficiency. Customers also benefit from additional advantages from this collaboration including

- **Accelerated Cloud Adoption**: Customers migrate to SAP S/4HANA faster without managing infrastructure complexity.

- **Single Service-Level Agreement (SLA) and Contract**: SAP is the main point of accountability, simplifying vendor management.

- **Reduced TCO**: RISE bundles reduce licensing, operational, and maintenance costs.

- **Flexibility to Extend**: Customers can still innovate using AWS native services (e.g., analytics, AI) alongside their SAP landscape.

- **Hybrid and Multi-cloud Readiness**: RISE with SAP on AWS supports hybrid strategies via **AWS Outposts**, **Storage Gateway**, and **Direct Connect**.

Also, the Joint Innovation Roadmap between AWS and SAP continues to improve the RISE with SAP experience including

- Integration with AWS Graviton for cost efficiency

- Joint reference architectures for SAP workloads

- Preconfigured templates and blueprints for rapid deployment

- Collaborative security and compliance frameworks

AWS PrivateLink for RISE with SAP

AWS PrivateLink is a networking service that provides private connectivity between VPCs, AWS services, and third-party SaaS applications, using elastic network interfaces (ENIs) with private IPs in the VPC. This allows data to remain within the highly secure AWS network fabric, eliminating the need for public IP addresses and reducing the attack surface. Running SAP workloads on AWS – whether it's SAP S/4HANA, SAP BW/4HANA, or legacy SAP ECC – often involves integration with various services such as SAP Business Technology Platform (SAP BTP), SAP Fiori UI apps, SAP HANA database tools, third-party SaaS solutions (e.g., analytics, monitoring, tax services), and custom business APIs hosted on AWS. Traditionally, accessing these services over the internet introduced risks such as latency, data interception, compliance concerns, and security breaches. AWS PrivateLink addresses these by offering private, secure, and scalable connections, which is critical for enterprise-grade SAP systems that manage sensitive financial, operational, and customer data. With the growing adoption of RISE with SAP, customers often consume SAP-managed services hosted on AWS infrastructure but outside of their own VPC. PrivateLink enables customers to securely access SAP Control Plane APIs; SAP BTP services like integration, extension, or analytics tools; and SAP

S/4HANA applications running in managed SAP accounts among others. This access occurs entirely over the AWS internal backbone, avoiding exposure to the internet while enabling multi-account, multi-region deployments.

SAP Business Technology Platform (BTP)

This is again an important aspect of the technical collaboration between SAP and AWS. SAP builds some of its SaaS applications on AWS, most notably BTP. **SAP Business Technology Platform**, often abbreviated as **SAP BTP**, is an integrated platform that offers database and data management, analytics, application development, and integration into a single ecosystem. It's a **platform as a service** (**PaaS**) that facilitates the development, deployment, and management of cloud-based applications. BTP is designed to streamline business processes, enhance user experiences, and enable the development of innovative applications using data-driven insights. Core Components of SAP BTP include

- **Analytics**: SAP BTP offers a comprehensive set of analytics tools that help in processing and visualizing data. Tools like SAP Analytics Cloud allow businesses to derive insights from their data, helping in informed decision-making.

- **Application Development**: Developers can create, deploy, and manage applications with SAP BTP. It supports multiple languages and frameworks, ensuring flexibility for developers. The platform supports both the microservices approach and more traditional application architectures.

- **Integration**: The platform ensures that different applications and data sources can communicate effectively. Tools like SAP Integration Suite help streamline processes across both SAP and non-SAP applications.

Key Features and Benefits of SAP BTP

Key features and benefits include

- **Holistic Platform**: SAP BTP combines database, analytics, application development, and integration into one platform, reducing the complexities of dealing with multiple, disparate systems.

- **Flexibility and Openness**: It supports multiple programming languages and offers open standards. This ensures that developers aren't locked into a particular technology stack.

- **Extensibility**: Organizations can extend their existing solutions, be it cloud solutions like SAP S/4HANA Cloud or on-premises solutions, by developing complementary functionalities on SAP BTP.

- **Integration**: BTP's robust integration capabilities ensure that various enterprise applications, both SAP and third-party, can work cohesively.

- **Intelligent Technologies**: The platform incorporates advanced technologies like artificial intelligence (AI), machine learning, and advanced analytics, allowing businesses to create intelligent applications.

- **Secure**: With features like identity management, authentication, and encryption, SAP BTP ensures that applications are secure.

Some of the use cases with BTP are

- **Custom Application Development**: Enterprises can create tailored applications specific to their business requirements.

- **Extension of Existing Solutions**: Instead of altering core systems, companies can extend functionalities using BTP.

- **Integration Scenarios**: Linking different enterprise applications, be they cloud-native or on-premises, for streamlined operations.

- **Data-Driven Decision-Making**: With the analytics component, businesses can derive actionable insights from their data.

Field Collaboration

The third critical aspect of the technical collaboration between SAP and AWS revolves around leveraging engineering collaboration and solution collaboration to work together on customer engagements and define the target architecture for modernizing SAP on AWS. This involves field sales teams, cloud architects, solution architects, and go-to-market specialists on both sides either creating prebuilt architecture or building out custom target architecture for each customer's SAP system to suit the modernization requirements for customers' SAP systems.

The custom architecture includes key decisions around compute, storage, networking, high availability, disaster recovery, and the like. On the other hand, prebuilt architecture is something the teams collaborate on and provide as a standard "**joint reference architecture (JRA)**," which becomes a foundational solution for the customers to then build new analytics dashboards, new applications, as well as machine learning solutions.

The guiding principle behind these JRAs is to use a combination of AWS and SAP services to build a solution to solve a specific business use case. Typical use cases are around data insights and integration/app development:

- **Data Insights**: Since SAP is a transactional system, business users are always trying to gain insights from this transactional data, typically like trends of sales data, inventory levels, etc. Also in some cases, this data has to be consumed by other applications, for example, dashboards and machine learning algorithms among others, in a real-time and secure manner. In certain scenarios, both SAP data and non-SAP data have to be combined to drive insights. The JRA focuses on data federation (combining disparate data sources using a software-based meta-database management system), to bring in all this data either into SAP or from SAP into AWS (like Amazon Athena). Likewise, data from SAP can be federated into Amazon SageMaker to feed machine learning algorithms, and the output from these models (predictions) can be written back to SAP.

- **Integration and App Development**: Certain use cases require combining the features and functions of SAP BTP services and native AWS services, which are addressed by the JRA. For instance, intelligent document processing, which is the automated processing of scanned and PDF documents, can help reduce errors and improve the efficiency of document processing. Working within the SAP environment, AWS services like Textract and Translate can extract insights from documents, which can then be fed back to SAP, and users can be notified using automated alerts (Amazon Simple Notification Service), which is another example of the JRA.

The whole discussion carried into happy hours and dinner at Cairati's, the tony Italian restaurant down the street from the Amazon office, one of Thomas's favorite spots. Needless to say, Melanie was amazed, not only at the depth of the partnership, but Thomas's elegant way of explaining it all to her. She expressed her gratitude multiple times and said she was glad she came to this meeting. As Melanie continued to pick Ashish's brain on highly technical topics over red wine and pasta, Thomas pulled Andrew aside to have his own little sidebar. Andrew gushed, "Man, you folks did an amazing job today with all the detailed plans and technical input. I am very confident this would be a good starting point for our customers. And really appreciate your patience in explaining all this very well to Melanie ... That's why I love working with you guys." Thomas nodded in agreement, and as the dinner was drawing to a close, he asked Andrew the question he was anxious to ask the whole day, "What is the opportunity that you mentioned you wanted to work with me on?" "Oh, yes, definitely, man. I think there is a real opportunity there at this customer ... After all it is your favorite airline." Just as Andrew finished his sentence, the garrulous Mister Nicolo Cairati stopped by at the table talking in his heavy Italian accent, "I come to say hello to you my good friend Thomas!" Thomas always got this privilege if Nicolo was around. After all Thomas had been a regular ever since Nicolo Cairati opened at that location. After the usual small talk, Nicolo was preparing to leave when he noticed and remarked to Thomas, "You did not order chicken wings today ..."

CHAPTER 3

Day 1 Customer Conversations: Why SAP on AWS

Running an SAP system 24/7 is a massive undertaking for any enterprise. While there are many issues and challenges faced by enterprises in deploying and operating SAP, some of these issues fall under the scope of hardware and technical infrastructure. This chapter will provide an overview of some of these key hardware- and infrastructure-related challenges faced by customers and how running SAP on AWS can help address those.

"Nimbus Airlines …your friend in the skies." With these words, the screen faded ever so slowly. The roughly five-minute corporate video was the last piece of material that Thomas reviewed for the day. Ever since Andrew mentioned over dinner that Nimbus Airlines was looking to modernize their SAP systems, Thomas had been spending time on researching the company. Not that Nimbus was an unknown entity. One of the biggest airlines globally, Nimbus had been on the forefront of aviation and a pioneer in the usage of technology to keep raising the bar in the airline industry. It was a dream come true to work for Nimbus or work with them. Never shy of investing heavily in technology, Nimbus had been a trendsetter, right from being an early adopter of electronic ticketing in the 1950s to launching the first ever smartphone app by an airline, when smartphones were just a novelty. The media had also taken notice with one popular podcaster calling them "essentially a technology company who happens to fly planes."

Right after dinner at Cairati's, Andrew and Thomas had a long, animated conversation about the recent development. It was no surprise that Nimbus was an early adopter of SAP in the airline industry and had over the years grown to have one of the largest deployments of SAP across the globe. With

© Tushar Srivastava 2025
T. Srivastava, *Modernizing SAP with AWS*, https://doi.org/10.1007/979-8-8688-1579-9_3

heavy customization, global rollouts, and several third-party integrations, the day-to-day management of Nimbus's SAP systems was enough to run payroll for a few consulting companies and some. But once in a while, even trendsetters would fall behind. All this extensive growth of the SAP systems meant that Nimbus did not spend time in upgrading their systems, and like every proud company, all these years they failed to acknowledge the need to modernize. Smart consultants would come and go and present fancy charts peppered with three-letter acronyms, but Nimbus had a reputation for doing what they wanted rather than being told what they needed to do. That was when, out of the blue, SAP's North America head received a call from Nimbus, to talk about SAP modernization. The news traveled quickly down the chain, and Andrew, who had been a long-time account executive for Nimbus, received a late evening call from his leadership to start engaging with Nimbus. Everyone at SAP was ready to support and eager to engage.

"…And that is what I know, dude," Andrew recounted to Thomas. "This will be a massive engagement, and I did not want to just go by myself; I want to go in with a strong partner and tell a 'better-together' story," concluded Andrew. Ever since Thomas started off at AWS, he had been hoping for an opportunity to work with Nimbus.

As he was about to shut down his laptop for the day, Thomas noticed his phone buzz with a message. Amy would usually send a Slack message, but the text meant she had something to discuss that could not wait.

Thomas immediately called back. After the regular small talk, Amy got to the point. "I wanted to check what is our next step in engaging with Nimbus on the SAP modernization project?" "I have been doing the research, and Andrew is looking to set time with the customer team for an initial meeting. It would focus on the discovery as well as our initial conversation about cloud options," replied Thomas confidently. "Do you know who from Nimbus will be in the meeting, and do we have a date yet?" Amy was eager to make sure that all the due diligence was in place. "Andrew is still working on that, and I will let you know as soon as I hear back." Amy always liked to have all the information, but she was trusting Thomas's judgement. After all, he had the track record to have earned this trust.

Thomas waited for Andrew to book the schedules for the meeting with Nimbus, but days passed. It was almost three weeks since the dinner. All the while Thomas had been working in his head everything that he wanted to tell the executives at Nimbus on all the "value drivers" and "performance metrics*" that would drive SAP modernization. Every passing day made him more anxious even as a few texts with Andrew confirmed that he was still looking to book the date but availability of key people was a challenge.*

One fine day, as Thomas was getting ready for his weekly sales forecast call, a simple-looking email dropped in with the subject "Dates confirmed for Nimbus meeting." *As much as Thomas would have liked to check the email right then, he had to make sure he completed his weekly review with Amy on all other engagements that he was pursuing. Amy cared about Nimbus, but she cared about the quarterly numbers even more. The forecast call was uneventful, except for some missing data in the CRM that Amy was not pleased about. She did not bring up Nimbus, and neither did Thomas. He wanted to verify the contents of the email before saying anything to Amy.*

The short email from Andrew quickly confirmed the facts. SAP had secured a meeting with Nimbus for "initial discovery" around the proposed SAP modernization project, and the meeting was scheduled about a week out, at Nimbus's office. Participants from Nimbus would include members from "IT Infrastructure," "Enterprise Applications," SAP CoE ("Center of Excellence"), and a host of other supporting teams with no specific names provided.

Thomas quickly replied to Andrew letting him know that he would partici-pate and also forwarded the note to Amy, who replied with two emojis, a smiley face followed by the "thumbs-up," and plenty of exclamation marks. Over the next few days, Thomas reviewed his slides and key talking points. He knew exactly what Nimbus needed and how AWS was in the best posi-tion to help with this project. Thomas spent a fair bit of time adjusting font size, color schemes, and the right kind of icons to use and refined some of the animation. He was pretty happy about the output. A few calls with Andrew confirmed that SAP planned to bring in quite a few experts, and they discussed logistics and post-meeting dinner options to host the cus-tomer. Thomas was feeling confident about making a good first impression with Nimbus and started making some rough estimates about the size of the deal.

Thomas pulled into the drive-in line and ordered his favorite dark roast blend, all black of course. This coffee would not make much of a difference. He was already full of energy having woken up early and hit the gym, ready in his trademark "#SAPonAWS" t-shirt and crisp suit. The coffee was just a companion for the hour-long Uber ride to the Nimbus office for the big day. It was a half-a-day workshop followed by dinner, which in Thomas's mind was enough for him to convince Nimbus that AWS was the right cloud service provider for this project. Given he was traveling after the morning rush hour, the ride was pretty smooth. As his Uber ride approached closer to the destination, Nimbus's swanky office buildings were coming into full sight. Gleaming steel and glass structures with manicured lawns gave off a very contemporary vibe. The only thing that did not look modern was a restored plane from the 1960s that was proudly displayed in the sprawling lawn right at the entrance to the building. A small sign below noted that this was the plane that was used for Nimbus's first international flight from New York to London in 1962. Thomas made his way to the lobby reception where he ran into the familiar jovial Andrew. He was surrounded by about ten other people, all from SAP. For a moment Thomas was taken aback. While he knew that SAP was bringing in a team, he had not expected as many.

"There's my man!" was Andrew's cheery voice as he proceeded to high-five and "fist-bump" Thomas at the same time.

After getting a face scan and an instant photo, Thomas exchanged a few words with the people from SAP. Other than Andrew and Melanie, everyone was a new face for Thomas. Some had flown in specifically for the meeting (of course on Nimbus flights). As he settled in, Thomas could not help but admire the office, which looked as impressive from the inside as was the outside. He could see a huge reception, with an airport-themed café right next, which was in the Nimbus brand colors of red, orange, and gold. Beyond the reception, he could peek where young employees were experimenting with drones and an ample lounging space and even some "Lego" blocks to play with. It looked more like a university campus than a corporate office. Thomas also noted the serene gallery that displayed a photographic timeline of the company history, right from humble origins as a mail carrier to one of the largest airlines globally, with quite a few "industry-first" milestones along the way.

While Thomas was still silently soaking up the atmosphere, a smart-looking gentleman came from behind the glass partition of the reception and proceeded straight to Andrew offering a firm handshake. "Hey, Andrew, pleased to meet you. This is Nolan from Nimbus." Nolan escorted the entire group past the partition and past cubicles and open workspaces into a large conference room aptly named "Tarmac" (Thomas later found out that conference rooms were based on an aviation theme). Everyone settled in with Nolan being the perfect host, pointing to the restrooms and coffee machines and, most importantly, passing on the "guest Wi-Fi" password. Soon everyone was hydrated and connected. Thomas picked a couple of Nimbus's trademark in-flight cookies (freely available in the break room) and settled in his seat. The conference room doors opened for a second time, and about eight people walked in. Andrew almost bounced across the room and met with one of them and a few seconds later announced, "Guys, we have the team from Nimbus here." The murmurs in the room went up as people informally introduced themselves to their immediate neighbors. One senior executive from SAP seemed to know most of the Nimbus folks. Soon, the room fell silent again, and the senior executive proceeded to get up and said, "Thanks for coming in, everyone. I always love coming back to Nimbus, ever since I was your account executive. For those who don't know me, I am Steve Clark, the senior vice president of sales at SAP, and it is a pleasure to be here to talk about your SAP modernization program."

As customary in such large meetings, everyone introduced themselves sequentially, explaining their role and their relevance to the program. Andrew was about to take the stage to set the context of the meeting when all of a sudden, the "Tarmac" door opened. From his vantage point, Thomas was unable to see who entered but soon heard Steve Clark exclaiming, "Liz, so nice to see you! Not sure if you were coming. Oh, it's been ages." "Of course, I would not miss this." Thomas noticed the newest member from team Nimbus, dressed sharply in a gray business suit, with one hand cradling a thick binder notebook and an iPad and the other holding a coffee mug that said, "Mom, keep flying."

"Firstly, apologize for being late, but you can't help it when the company CFO wants to continue talking for 'another five minutes' and then some." The comment drew some giggles across the room. "I am Elizabeth Nelson, CIO at Nimbus, and looking forward to learning as much as possible today. Thank you, everyone, for making the time." And with those quick words, she quickly moved to an innocuous chair at the back of the room exchanging pleasantries with people she passed on the way.

Andrew resumed where he left off and took the stage. "Hello, everyone, it is a pleasure to be here, and thanks to team Nimbus for hosting us and giving this opportunity to help Nimbus on its SAP modernization journey. As you can see, we have a host of experts here, each of whom will play a role in building out the roadmap and architecture for your future SAP state. We have a packed agenda today, and we also have our partner AWS in the room." With that, Andrew flicked his remote presentation pointer, and the large screen in the room displayed the day's agenda in a large font for everyone to see. The agenda was focused on helping build a business case for SAP modernization.

Over the next couple of hours, every expert got up and talked about how Nimbus should be approaching the SAP modernization. The dialog was two-way, and each expert was asked a lot of questions, alternate approaches, and cost–benefit tradeoffs. Elizabeth was very engaged, listening intently, and taking notes but letting her team ask all the questions. Each expert focused on their own specialization; however, the overall theme emerged as follows:

Upgrade *the current SAP ECC application to the latest SAP S/4HANA.*

Review all the current customizations *and look to adopt standard functionality from S/4HANA to replace those customizations.*

Modernize interfaces *by leveraging SAP BTP (Business Technology Platform).*

Build a modern data strategy *for SAP by leveraging latest reporting features and functions (again SAP BTP).*

Move away from hosting SAP at on-premises services and instead move it to the cloud *(AWS).*

It was while talking about the move to cloud that Melanie immediately pointed to Thomas. "We have Thomas from AWS who should be able to talk in detail about the benefits of cloud and AWS specifically that would help with this project," she concluded. This was a cue for Thomas to take the stage and deliver his message. Thomas confidently moved across the room and plugged his laptop in to display his slide deck. Thomas started with listing out the key benefits, and about 45 minutes later, he was at his summary slide, which listed the benefits as below:

Large memory *instances available from AWS to host SAP*

High reliability *of AWS cloud*

Various security features of the AWS cloud

Broad set of AWS microservices *that Nimbus could leverage*

Thomas was getting a bit anxious when he did not get too many questions. Mark Chapman, Director of IT Infrastructure at Nimbus, sitting right in front, asked some basic questions about the instance sizes but nothing beyond. All the while Elizabeth was listening intently and shifting a bit in her seat. Even as Thomas was concluding, she got up and moved up closer and leaned against the wall and folded her arms and said, "Thomas, we do work a bit with AWS cloud, and I would not claim that we are experts in cloud, but I fail to see the relevance of cloud and what AWS has to offer that can help us here with our SAP project. Maybe that is why nobody is asking any questions." Even before Thomas could process the entirety of the question, she added, "Everything you mentioned that the cloud can do can be done with our very robust on-premises hardware, so why do we need the added complexity of a migration to cloud while we may already be upgrading our application stack?"

In all his time at AWS, Thomas had never felt so weak to respond. Here he was standing in front of a customer he always dreamt of working with, and his words were failing him. He had of course worked with tougher customers asking tougher questions, but today his overconfidence worked against him. He was barely paying any attention to what Elizabeth said further and did not even notice that others on team Nimbus were piling on. The saving grace came in the form of Melanie. She addressed the CIO directly, "Elizabeth, the cloud offers significant benefits toward SAP modernization; however, we did not cover everything just because we were short on time and we wanted to get the inputs from the SAP experts in. I was working with Thomas a few days ago at the AWS office, and we had detailed discussion, which addressed both the technical and business aspects of transformation and the vital role AWS plays in that. I suggest we set aside time for that separately even as we follow through with the action items from today's meeting."

Elizabeth, sharp as ever, latched on quickly, "Yes, I agree we need to give more time to the cloud topic. I can see some potential here. Melanie, can you work with Thomas and come back with more specific details? I would like to put in a date to review." As the workshop was winding down and final meeting notes were being collected and distributed, Andrew announced that dinner and drinks were being hosted at a nearby restaurant. Thomas, still too dazed from the gut punch, decided that he would head back and skip the dinner. Indeed, his cloud message failed to take off at the "Tarmac."

On his way back, Thomas continued to fidget and think about how he could have done better. Andrew texted him since he did not see him around for dinner, but Thomas chose to ignore the message. He was in no mood to talk. He was still hurting as if he had lost the whole business in one shot. Why did he not prepare better, why did he not look at additional data, and a million other questions popped in his mind. As he stepped off the "Uber," Thomas punched in the code to enter home and left a measly tip for the Uber driver. Maybe Uber should have an algorithm to predict tipping behavior based on the rider's emotional state.

Back at work the next day, Thomas had difficulty concentrating on the unread emails or Slack messages coming his way. There was one message that he kept going back to again and again: "How did it go?" was Amy's short query. After deliberating for almost an hour, Thomas replied, "I am at the office. If you are at the office and have time, we can connect and I can update you." "I am going to be at the office post lunch after my calls, so why don't you book a conference room for 2 PM and we can meet." Thomas ambled aimlessly for the rest of the afternoon, in a continuous cycle of checking his phone, his emails, and his phone again.

Amy and Thomas were settling into the conference room when he said in a resigned voice, "It did not go well, Amy …" trailing off and not offering any justifications or explanations. Amy stared at him, slowly setting aside her laptop and getting up. "Tell me what happened and start from the top." Thomas knew what she meant. Amy wanted every little detail. Over the next 30 minutes, Thomas recounted the meeting, providing details of his talk track and the poor feedback he received. The usually inquisitive Amy did not interrupt even for one question. Amy absorbed all of it even paying close attention to details that Thomas felt were not important. If anything, what Amy had learned in all these years running successful sales teams was that the devil was always in the little details. As soon as Thomas was done, Amy picked up the markers and did two things that she was really good at – telling a story visually on the whiteboard and using her sales acumen to glean information and "read the room," even if she was not in the room. "Well, you may not have been spot on with the message, but I don't think the meeting was a failure. Elizabeth did ask for a second meeting to go into details of cloud, and you have a good ally in Melanie. This situation may be a setback, but it is temporary." Thomas needed that. He had been wallowing in self-pity long enough. Amy continued, "Let's put a swat team together. I would suggest you ask Ashish to travel, and let's get Melanie also."

Meanwhile, in another part of the town, Elizabeth was heading back home after a long day. As she pulled into her garage and cut out the engine on her electric car, she stayed back staring into the windscreen and taking a moment to recap her long hectic day and what lay ahead of her. It was close to 6 PM, and that meant driving Ethan to piano practice. After a few more minutes of contemplation, Elizabeth got out of the car, walked into the house, and dropped her heavy laptop bag on the kitchen counter. The family dog "Pepper" came running and could not hold his excitement and jumped all over his "mom." Nine-year-old Ethan sped down the stairs and wanted all of Mom's attention to talk all about his day at school. In all this happy commotion, Ben walked up to Elizabeth and handing her some green tea said, "Hey, honey, how was your day? You seem tired. Do you need me to take Ethan to piano practice? You can stay home and get some rest." Elizabeth did not want to let go of this offer but knew she would feel guilty about it later. "No worries, I will take him. Gives me some time with him where I can hear all about his day," Elizabeth replied.

"Sophia, you there? Sophia …I am home," Elizabeth called out before finishing off her cup of green tea. "Hey, Sophia, do you want to come along for Ethan's piano practice? You can drive …" Elizabeth's voice trailed off. She wanted to make sure she said hello to her 15-year-old girl, whom Elizabeth still remembered as a little three-year-old running around the house in her tutu. "No, Mom, you go. I am on the phone" came the reply from upstairs. The tutu was long gone, and Elizabeth feared also her connection to her daughter. Of course, she only blamed herself.

The 20-minute drive to the music academy was a good time to catch up on the latest episode of "Adventures of Ethan in Fourth Grade," with the wide-eyed storyteller spinning tales of drama and intrigue. While Ethan was the pivotal character in most stories, Elizabeth particularly enjoyed the mystery portions, like who stole the markers from the supply box. The ride back was less eventful; however, they did stop to pick up dinner from Ethan's favorite, Chick-fil-A. Back home, after a quiet dinner, Elizabeth and Sophia had a short exchange about a school field trip and not much else. She did try telling Sophia about her day but did not get an attentive ear. Elizabeth decided it was better to hit the sack than risk starting an argument. She had a big day coming up ahead of her.

Next day back at work, Elizabeth walked into her team meeting where the agenda was specifically to debrief from the workshop on SAP modernization. Elizabeth encouraged everyone to speak, only nodding once in a while. Everyone in the room had an opinion on the project roadmap and feedback on various experts from SAP. This is not going to be easy, Elizabeth thought to herself. Amid all the chatter, Elizabeth took a deep breath and got up from her seat and prepared herself to do what she did best: "rally everyone behind a vision," a leadership quality that was noted by the prestigious Copilot Magazine *when crowning her the winner of the "Technology Leader in Aviation" award the previous year. Heading to the center of the room, Elizabeth proceeded to address everyone in the room, without the need for slides or a whiteboard.*

Gesturing animatedly, yet cool in her composure, Elizabeth proceeded, making eye contact with everyone from time to time as she spoke clearly, "Nimbus has been a pioneer in aviation specially in leveraging technology. Our business users have been demanding more from our SAP systems, and we simply cannot deliver value to the next generation of internal and external customers with the current system. At the same time, we value every dollar going into the business, so we need to make sure we have a strong business case with measurable ROI if we are to take on this massive modernization project. Lastly, we will have only one shot at doing this, so I want us to be prepared with the plan, the tools, the resources, and, most important, alignment with our business stakeholders on their commitment toward this endeavor. I will take personal ownership of alignment with business stakeholders, and I will need a specific owner for building the business case, who will look behind every nook and corner of why we should or should not be doing the project, and finally I want a strong owner for execution that will work with our partners to define technical architecture and delivery roadmap. As always, this responsibility will be in addition to our day jobs, and we will follow our standard process of 'self-nomination' and team voting for these roles." The "self-nomination" process was a key part of Elizabeth's leadership style where she would let the team nominate themselves for special projects (and she would nominate someone if no one took the lead). Her team then voted for the nominees, and the whole team was committed toward the success of the temporary leader. This self-nomination program had been a good stepping-stone for future growth and promotions.

Figure 3-1. *Elizabeth Addressing Her Team*

"Hey, Nolan, can we meet for a few quick minutes?" Elizabeth asked Nolan as the team was dispersing after the meeting, sufficiently energized. "Sure." Nolan Perez walked right behind Elizabeth as they entered her cabin and she placed all her possessions, including her favorite binder, iPad, laptop, and assortment of writing instruments, on her desk. Without waiting to take a seat, Elizabeth turned to Nolan and said, "I don't get a good feeling about this project. While SAP did bring in the experts, they are all focused on their own specific domains, and we have to figure out how we piece all of it together. Even if you leave the cost aside, I have a feeling we are not going to get internal agreement on target architecture, future operating model, and, most important, a strong business case. We all know in our gut that we have to modernize, but Nimbus does not work on gut alone. We need the numbers to back up our case. That is what Micah asked me for. In fact, that is what the board will ask me if this is going to cost over our thresh-old." Nolan listened intently. Nolan Perez, a Cuban immigrant settled in Florida with a special knack for math, was valedictorian in his undergrad-uate computer science program. So, when Nimbus came calling to hire him for the special "technology cohort," the "flight" to New York was an easy decision. The soft-spoken Nolan rose rapidly in the organization, known for his breakthrough technology innovations (resulting in many patents) and also his people management skills, a rare combination for a technology leader. Naturally, he was Elizabeth's close confidant.

After much thought, Nolan responded, "Maybe we are looking at the problem in the wrong way. We are looking at SAP modernization as a large chunky problem. We could break it down into smaller components and assign a priority score and weightage to each of it, and then it becomes easier for us to address." Nolan usually preferred a data-driven approach to problem-solving, something he had done always and deployed to good use in his current role of Information Technology Director under Elizabeth, overseeing "customer experience." While Elizabeth definitely relied on data, her strong suit was "intuition." "Well, you are right, Nolan, but what about components we are not aware of and may get totally blindsided? Apart from the technical details, I think we have a few big unknowns. Firstly, how will our SAP product licensing get impacted with this new upgrade and, second, the hosting and hardware options. I will have to work on the licensing piece with the SAP leadership and maybe get Micah involved; however, for our hosting options, I was really underwhelmed with what we heard from Thomas. I realize we have a small footprint with AWS today. Maybe that is the reason why we did not get the full picture, or maybe we did not have enough time. Whatever the case, I think if we have to buy new hardware, working contracts with our hardware vendor would be like pulling teeth. I don't want our team spending time on that." Elizabeth was laying it all out, not really expecting Nolan to provide a solution, but rather visualizing out all the pieces of the puzzle on the table.

The day progressed uneventfully, and by late afternoon the team knew who the key leaders on this major project would be. Mark Chapman would be responsible for the financial modeling and business case, while Sandeep Krishnan, Vice President of Enterprise Applications, would lead the technical execution. Both leaders enjoyed the team's trust and Elizabeth's.

Elizabeth just wrapped up a meeting with her executive assistant, reviewing her appointments for next week, when her phone buzzed with a text, "Mom, did you guys decide? I need to let my friends know. Can't keep them hanging." Elizabeth knew the urgency in Sophia's text. She had been putting off this decision for a week now. Sophia wanted to plan a trip to Europe with her friends, and while Ben was okay with it after some initial convincing, Elizabeth was the holdout. She had been delaying on this. Her logical self would not let her say "yes," but she did not want a full-blown escalation, as had become more common in the past year. "Let's talk today evening when you are back from basketball practice." Elizabeth knew she had to take a decision today evening and was thinking what would be the best way to deal with the strong-headed Sophia, as strong-headed as Elizabeth herself.

Elizabeth had been a long-time Nimbus veteran. Having excelled in roles of increasing responsibilities with top consulting firms, Elizabeth was offered a full-time position in Nimbus's technology team when she was an external consultant to them on a critical project. She had impressed the then Nimbus CEO with her research and presentation that she was eventually offered the opportunity to come in and lead the initiative that she passionately was advocating for. After spending a long time deciding, she finally asked Ben who told her to take the job without batting an eyelid. It did not matter that this would mean a relocation from Texas to New York and the fact that they had just gotten engaged a few months earlier. The eldest of five siblings, Elizabeth always displayed natural leadership, having earned the moniker of "Queen" from her father, a university professor of English literature. Elizabeth's mother always encouraged her to take risks and never held her back. As a result, young Elizabeth grew up ready to try everything, eventually excelling in both academics and sports. Tennis was her passion all through high school, and when the practical Elizabeth realized she was not cut out for professional tennis, she took up a university degree in business administration. After early roles in management, Elizabeth took up a rigorous MBA course from a prestigious university, and that was where she met Ben. The cool-headed Ben was the perfect complement to Elizabeth's bubbles of energy, he being the yang to Elizabeth's yin. On the insistence of her professors, Elizabeth took up roles in consulting and excelled at each of the firms she went to. Impressing everyone by her research, ability to rally the team, and successful customer outcomes, she was being fast-tracked to a "Partner" role at a prestigious management firm. Her mentors urged her not to throw it all away by taking up the role at Nimbus, but Ben gave her the confidence, as he always had in all 23 years they had known each other.

Consulting's loss was Nimbus's gain. Starting off in the technology team at Nimbus, Elizabeth led the charge for the project "Air-Connect," a revolutionary service that Elizabeth had originally suggested to the Nimbus leadership as a consultant. The idea was to provide air-to-ground phone service on long-haul flights, in the pre-cellphone days. Customers were willing to pay to stay connected for business or pleasure with people on the ground. Nimbus had to build a lot of the technology themselves (filing many patents along the way), since there was no real precedent to follow. The service was a huge money earner for Nimbus, and it was years before any competitor could follow suit. Customers liked the practical advantages of being able to make a phone call from the plane, while some liked the novelty factor. A businessman even claimed to have closed a million-dollar deal while in air. The last "Air-Connect" system was decommissioned seven years ago as a relic of pre smartphones and internet era. The success of Air-Connect pro-pelled Elizabeth to greater heights. She was appointed as head of all special technology projects with a focus on making the passenger in-flight experi-ence better. She took the unorthodox approach of flying on almost every sector that Nimbus flew over a one-year period collecting first-hand data. Armed with the data and her instinct, Elizabeth launched almost 200 large and small projects over a five-year period right from the quality of ink on printed boarding passes to a gesture-controlled in-flight entertainment sys-tem (that remembered a passenger's viewing history across multiple flights). It was no surprise that she had risen to the role of a CIO and some industry analysts also marked her out as a future CEO. Over the years Elizabeth had built a strong team with diverse experiences and complementary skills. Never afraid to speak their minds, the team had its fair share of personality clashes, but a common purpose always drove the team. Elizabeth had cre-ated a culture of rapid experimentation, bold ideas, and precise execution. It was a sub-culture within the larger Nimbus organization, and it made the technology team one of the most sought-after for both internal and external hires. Elizabeth was proud of what she had built.

While Elizabeth was figuring out a path forward, so was Thomas. He wrote a rather long and nice email to Melanie asking for her support in helping build the right "pitch" for Nimbus. He reasoned that a positive pitch from AWS reflected positively on SAP also. Melanie readily agreed. She was new to her role and was looking to learn as much as possible. Next, Thomas asked Ashish to make the trip to spend a few days on a collaboration ses-sion. Amy had already committed her support to this mini-project. Monday afternoon at the AWS office and all the members of "project Nimbus" were in the conference room. Andrew was informed but decided to skip and wished the team well (he was not missed). Melanie was meeting Amy for the first time and was already impressed by her energy in the room.

The seasoned sales professional Amy took a different approach to the meet-ing. She laid out a deck of index cards on the table. As everyone got curious, she wrote in big bold letters "WHY" across one of them and kept it at the center of the table. Looking at the curious faces, she smiled and spoke out making eye contact with everyone, "The first important question is, Why is Nimbus looking to modernize their SAP systems? At Amazon we always 'work backward' from a customer problem. So I ask this team, at the start of our quest, WHY?" Amy immediately had an impact, and everyone was listening with rapt attention, forgetting they had to answer. Amy did not wait and pointed to Melanie, "Thomas probably knows less about Nimbus's motivations, and Ashish was not even in the meeting. Since you represent

SAP, you are the closest to this question." That was Amy's indirect way to saying that she expected Melanie to answer. Melanie was prepared. The meticulous notetaker and technically sharp Melanie had been in many of SAP's internal meetings on Nimbus and had several sidebar meetings with the customer in the lead-up to the onsite workshop. She immediately pulled out her well-organized online notes (she was not the paper and pen type) and took to the whiteboard. Nimbus ran core financials, forecasting, HR, parts warehousing, procurement, and few other allied business processes within SAP. Over the years they had customized SAP to a large extent running all kinds of reports and unique business processes. They also ran many home-grown applications and third-party applications, which exchanged data with SAP in some way or form. They also spent a lot of efforts on day-to-day support operations, and these efforts and costs continued to grow over time. Users had also complained about the sluggishness of the system at times, and system outages had become more frequent recently.

Key Issues Faced by Nimbus Regarding Their SAP System

Nimbus has had several hardware- and infrastructure-related challenges with regard to SAP. These are detailed below:

- **Performance**: Users have been raising tickets about the time it takes to execute certain transactions. While some of these are heavy queries, many of them are routine business processes. The performance has progressively gotten worse over the years.

- **Reliability**: SAP system outages have become more frequent in the past few months. Also, the duration of outages has increased, and there is very little information about the expected time of restoration. Earlier outages were of shorter duration and were minor blips, but recently they have started to impact business operations. Some of these outages have a real cost impact, for example, inability to ship parts for aircraft repair.

- **Customizations**: The SAP system has been heavily customized over the years resulting in difficulty in maintaining and testing the code. Despite documentation, there is always dependence on the specific individuals who understand the details of the specific custom program. This is resulting in additional costs as well as delays in system upgrades.

- **Integrations**: Not all business processes run in SAP, and many run on homegrown and third-party applications. Many of these applications interface with SAP and exchange data. Over the years, many integrations have been built to support this, resulting in unwieldy integrations that sometimes break with little notice. All this adds to the overhead of managing the environment.

- **Application Modernization**: The current version of SAP that Nimbus runs (SAP ECC) was implemented over ten years ago. Since then, SAP has upgraded the application significantly (the latest release being SAP S/4HANA), and Nimbus's business users are looking to leverage the latest functionality.

- **Day-to-Day Support**: Nimbus started off with a small team doing SAP support; however, this has grown over a period of time consisting of both internal and external teams. While growth is expected, the turnaround for issues has gone up with no one team able to take ownership and identify why this has happened.

- **Data Insights**: A key issue is the ability to gather intelligence from the data within and outside SAP. There are many data sources, and teams have built their own data warehousing solutions. Business users then use a number of tools to query this data to build their own dashboards and insights. Many times this data is not current, while some reports are delivered as attachments in emails, and there are even times there are no patterns being drawn between correlated data because they reside in different silos. Also, if a business user has a new query, it takes a lot of resources and coordination across teams to build the report, validate it, and deliver it to the business user.

- **Hardware**: SAP is hosted in-house on hardware procured through a vendor. Since SAP requires very specific hardware, there are long lead times to procure new hardware. As a result, there are delays in new projects and specifically the ability of the team to experiment.

By the time Melanie was done, Amy was smiling ear to ear. "Great job, Melanie. You have pleasantly surprised me. I was not expecting you to have such an in-depth analysis. I was thinking we would have to assume and extrapolate." Thomas, quick not to miss any details, snapped a picture of the whiteboard on his phone, while Ashish was staring intently at the whiteboard and lost in thought. Amy walked up to the board and stuck the WHY index card right on top of Melanie's output. Pleased with the work so far, they decided to take a coffee break. Melanie, fresh from her success, stuck to green tea. The team headed back to the room and documented all the output. Amy was quick to erase the whiteboard when the team ended for the day. They headed out to dinner. Where else but Cairati's?

The team assembled early the next day. Amy had ordered breakfast, since she clearly wanted to make the most of the whole day. She had canceled her earlier meetings and was fully dedicated to this planning session. Clearly this was very important to her. Just like the previous day, Amy took charge and opened the session. "After hearing from Melanie and documenting everything, we have fair understanding of the reasons why Nimbus is looking to make a change. Each stakeholder group at Nimbus has their own view of this project; however, one thing is very clear. This is a very large project with a far-reaching impact on different parts of their business, and it would need heavy investments from Nimbus. When there is so much at stake, Nimbus would evaluate all risks possible associated with the change. They would like to do it once and do it right. If there are too many unknowns, it means that there are many variables that Nimbus can't control, which in turn increases the risk. So right now, I am sure they are spending a lot of time learning as much as they can. Most likely internal meetings, meetings with partners (like us), and learning from other customers who have executed a similar project in the past." Amy had everyone's attention. She proceeded to write out the keywords on the whiteboard.

Amy let the room soak in everything she said. She proceeded to put in an extra layer of cream cheese on her bagels and poured herself out a large cup of black coffee. A short while later, Amy again took charge of the proceedings. "If we are to put ourselves in the customer's shoes, over the next few months, this project is going to be 'a journey.' The customer has a starting point, they sort of know their final destination, but what they don't have right now is the path to that destination, a map, way points, the right partners to take along this journey and who are the ones who may have completed a similar journey in the past." Melanie was absolutely enthralled at this analogy while Amy kept going. "There are some known needs, and then there are unknown needs. Things that Nimbus is not planning for yet or is not aware of available options for. We need to build a case around both, the known and unknown needs. It is very important that we win trust with Nimbus over the next few interactions. While there would be many partners who will be critical to the success of this project, AWS has to earn the role of being a 'trusted guide' on this journey. The only way we can do this is we focus on educating the customer about all the knowns and unknowns and make the path much clearer and more visible to them." *There was a long moment of silence as no one was in any position to react. Ashish finally cleared his throat to speak, and the wall of silence came crashing down. "Amy, the education that we are talking about needs to happen over a series of technical workshops with Nimbus's technical team. I can surely lead those, but do we have commitment from the customer for this?" Being the practical technical geek, Ashish was always focused on actual execution. "Yes, you are right. We do have to deliver the technical workshops, and we do not have the commitment from the customer, yet. We are going to earn that right only by demonstrating to the customer that the workshops actually help with their journey rather than a checkbox item for AWS," quipped Amy. The seasoned sales executive drew from her many years of experience helping clients.*

Thomas marveled at Amy's clarity of thought and the ease with which she was able to break it down for the group. He always thought of his boss as a role model to learn from, and today was again one such masterclass. Over the next few hours, the team brainstormed all the ideas together and wrote and rewrote the plans, the approach, and the overall message. Melanie focused on the SAP angle and specifically on the application-side benefits, Ashish focused on the technical benefits that AWS could provide toward this project, while Thomas focused on the overall execution, looking around nooks and corners for possible omissions and misses. The team continued the meeting into the third day with Amy reviewing most of the plans and nudging the team to look at multiple options. "This is frankly one of the most in-depth exercises I have done in preparation for a customer project. I feel very confident about the overall message that AWS is putting together. This will also amplify SAP's own message about application modernization, and together the two messages will resonate well," Melanie shared her feelings with the team. She was quick to the point that SAP was equally invested, if not more, in this engagement. "We definitely like to dive deep here at AWS," Ashish chuckled even as Amy's eyes lit up and she let out a broad smile.

As the day was wrapping up, Thomas made sure that the next steps were clearly outlined. Exhausted from all the work, he looked around and said, "I will create a final document and supporting material and share it with everyone for feedback and review. After about a week, I will incorporate all the feedback and lock the files. Melanie will update her team at SAP about the progress that we have made and make sure that the AWS message is aligned with the SAP message. If we need to review with other team members at SAP, Melanie will reach back out, and we can set some time. Ashish on his part will start working on future-looking items, after we have had our next meeting with Nimbus, things like architecture workshop, technical sessions, design documents, and related items. That brings us to the most important action item, securing time back again with Nimbus. I will craft a message and go back to Nimbus with a request for a meeting that will be focused on the cloud and specifically how AWS would be relevant to this project. Once the meeting is secured, we can plan again for us to get together and prepare. The next step would be the meeting." Thomas was oozing with confidence, not only after a grueling three days of work, but also the pep talk that Amy had given him privately, essentially saying that the first meeting was not a total failure, but they had an opportunity to build upon that now. Ashish was headed back to catch his flight the same evening, and Amy and Melanie also called it a day. Thomas was left with his own thoughts. He had to send an email to Elizabeth, and he was working the content over and over in his head.

The next morning Thomas decided to work from home and spent 45 minutes crafting a short email. He was not happy with the outcome and kept changing it over and over again. Finally, he hit "Send." The message was straightforward. AWS did not have enough time to present in the previous meeting since, firstly, it was SAP's meeting and, second, AWS did not fully understand Nimbus's needs. Now that they better understood their needs, AWS would like to present again to help educate Nimbus and explain how AWS could help in this project. Thomas went back to refining the documents and sharing them for review.

It had been a week since the email had gone to Elizabeth, and Thomas had yet not received a reply. He was getting a bit nervous and decided to call Andrew. "Well, I know they have been 'super busy,' but I usually get a response from the Nimbus team." That made Thomas's heart sink even further. He immediately followed up on his email. Late afternoon, Thomas got a text, "Hey, it's Nolan from Nimbus. Can we talk?" Thomas remembered, Oh, yes, Nolan, he escorted us to the conference room. *He quickly responded to the text. As Nolan was ready to call it a day, he got a call and he recognized the number; it was the same one he had texted with earlier in the day.*

A cheerful and warm voice on the other end said, "Hey, Thomas, this is Nolan here. Hope you are well …"

"Doing well, Nolan. How are you? Thanks for the call."

"Yeah, I thought I would catch you before the end of the day. Elizabeth forwarded me your email, and I wanted to connect with you on that. We at Nimbus definitely think we need to connect with AWS in the context of our SAP project. We have quite a few questions on our end."

"Yes, and that is my goal too, to answer as many questions so that you can make an informed decision as you move forward."

"Okay, cool. Please send me a detailed agenda; even a draft would work. I want to review, and we can then pick a date based on calendar availability."

Thomas did not wait for the next day, but rather worked on a draft agenda over the evening and sent it over to Nolan. He was elated. This was a small victory.

Over the next few days, Nolan added some more items to the agenda before it was finalized. Nolan then suggested a date three weeks out. Thomas felt this would be ideal. It was not too far out and gave enough time to coordinate schedules and prepare for the meeting. Thomas informed the core team. There was palpable excitement in the team. Thomas also decided to include Andrew as part of the customer meeting. It was time for Thomas to call for a prep meeting, and he thought that virtual would do. About three days later Thomas got everyone on a virtual call bridge. Amy and Andrew did some quick introductions, since they were the only ones who did not know each other. The agenda was reviewed, and speaking roles were discussed and assigned. Everyone agreed that the agenda looked good, and the talk track was well aligned with Nimbus's needs. Now it was just a matter of two weeks before the meeting would take place. The longest two weeks of Thomas's life.

On the appointed day, Melanie and Andrew from SAP and Thomas, Amy, and Ashish from AWS converged at the Nimbus office at the appointed time. Others had been here earlier, but for Ashish and Amy this was their first visit, so they soaked in the views. Ashish in fact flew on a Nimbus flight coming in for this meeting. Nolan met the team in the lobby, and after the customary face scans, the team moved into the designated conference room, named "Takeoff," much smaller than the previous one, "Tarmac." Elizabeth, Mark, and Sandeep were already in the conference room. Pleasantries were exchanged, and Nolan explained, "We have a much smaller group, because we want to dive deep into the details. It will only be Elizabeth (CIO), Mark (Director of IT Infrastructure), Sandeep (Vice President, Enterprise Applications), and me (Nolan, Director of IT, Customer Experience) in this meeting. We are a core group that is going to be leading the SAP modernization project and will work on the initial planning and direction." Nolan very succinctly laid out the expectations and direction. Thomas was already at the front of the room and pressed on his wireless remote clicker. The large screen in the meeting room came to life.

"When I was here a few weeks ago, I was part of a larger workshop being managed by SAP. Given the strong partnership that SAP and AWS have, Andrew called me in and asked to participate in the workshop. I will be the first to admit I did not do a good job. I did not understand the gravity and context of the transformation project and shared only high-level information, which may or may not have been relevant to you." The candid admission was receiving approving nods already. "I went back to the drawing board, and with the support of Melanie from SAP and my colleagues Amy and Ashish, I reviewed everything we know about your initiative and built out a point of view that we would like to share. We are not here simply to sell, but to educate you and answer questions that will help you in your decision-making." By now Thomas knew he had everyone's attention, and he could see a few people close down their laptop lids. "What you have in front of you is a journey, where you know your starting point, but not the roadmap to reach your final destination. Today we want to talk about that journey and how AWS can be a part of that journey and help you along the way. SAP modernization is a multifaceted program, and today we want to cover core infrastructure and hardware aspects of the program. This is where AWS would have maximum impact." Over the next two hours, supported by his team, Thomas walked through the key reasons why migrating SAP from on-premises hardware to AWS on the cloud would help in this modernization journey. The Nimbus team stayed engaged throughout asking questions along the way.

Key Reasons Customers Look to Modernize SAP Systems

As discussed before the key reasons for any customer (including Nimbus) to modernize SAP are

- **Better Performance:** Make sure that users are getting a fast response when running SAP transactions.

- **Better Reliability:** Make sure SAP does not have an outage and any outage has minimal downtime.

- **Reduce Customizations:** Replace customizations with standard product features.

- **Optimize Integrations:** Simplify the management of integrations between SAP and third-party applications.

- **Application Modernization:** Upgrade SAP from ECC to S/4HANA.

- **Automate Day-to-Day Support:** Look at ways to automate day-to-day management of tasks and system operations.

- **Gain Data Insights:** Create a more unified view of the data within SAP and non-SAP systems and gain insights.

- **Hardware:** Review options to modernize hardware on which SAP is hosted.

Why Run SAP on AWS

AWS is able to support these needs (and more) in the following way. In the dynamic landscape of cloud computing, AWS stands out as a prime choice for hosting SAP systems. The reasons for this preference are rooted in AWS's pioneering spirit, robust infrastructure, and deep focus on innovation.

- **Reliable Global Infrastructure**: SAP is one of the most critical applications that a business runs to manage its day-to-day operations. Given that SAP runs transactions like sales orders, payroll, inventory, and procurement among others, businesses want

SAP systems to be running smoothly with near-zero interruption. As a result, businesses spend a lot of resources on making sure that the platform for hosting SAP is very robust and not prone to failures, especially unplanned failures. In that context, one of the key considerations when running SAP on AWS is the reliable global infrastructure that AWS offers. The AWS cloud infrastructure is foundationally built around "regions" and "Availability Zones." A region is a physical geographic zone that consists of multiple Availability Zones (AZs). Each AZ in turn is made up of one or more "data centers" that are connected with each other via low-latency, high-throughput, and highly redundant networking. As of August 2025, AWS global infrastructure consists of 37 regions and 117 AZs. Each region is designed to be completely isolated from each other, thus providing the highest level of stability, reliability, and fault tolerance. AZs are physically separated within a metro region, are placed in lower-risk flood plains, and are connected with each other via low-latency links. Finally, the data centers within the AZs are supplied power by discrete UPS (uninterrupted power supply), onsite backup power generators, and independent sub-stations to reduce impact in case of power grid failure. From an SAP standpoint, it means that running SAP on AWS automatically provides built-in reliability and fault tolerance that ensures that the SAP systems face near-zero unplanned downtime.

- **Security and Compliance:** Another critical aspect when hosting SAP is the security and compliance considerations. SAP is a transactional system and thus stores a lot of sensitive information about the business operations including sales order details, payroll, customer information, financial information, and product information among others. Likewise, given the sensitive nature of data stored within SAP, there are different compliance rules and regulations that apply to SAP that businesses have to consider (which may vary by region of operation). AWS offers a comprehensive security model to safeguard SAP applications, emphasizing the protection of databases and data in transit and at rest.

- **Network Security**: AWS recommends that direct user access to databases for SAP applications should be restricted. Network traffic to the Amazon EC2 instance should only be permitted from instances running SAP application servers. Security groups, network access control lists (NACLs), and route tables should be configured to allow necessary traffic, with communication to the database server.

- **Encryption**: AWS advises encrypting data stored within its storage services. This includes data at rest and in transit, ensuring that sensitive SAP application data remains secure. AWS provides specific documentation on encrypting data for Amazon FSx, protecting Amazon S3 objects using encryption, and Amazon EBS encryption.

- **Security Services and Capabilities**: To run SAP applications securely on the AWS platform, one can utilize services such as Amazon VPC, AWS Virtual Private Network, AWS Direct Connect, and specialized services like AWS WAF, AWS Network Firewall, AWS Shield, AWS Config, and AWS CloudTrail among others. These services offer mechanisms to control access to databases and ensure secure connections.

- **Compute Instance Types for SAP**: Amazon EC2 provides a variety of instance types that are optimized for different use cases, including those suitable for SAP workloads. These instance types offer various combinations of CPU, memory, storage, and networking capacity to meet the requirements of different SAP applications. Each instance type includes one or more instance sizes, enabling the user to scale resources according to the requirements of the workload. AWS has collaborated with SAP to test and certify certain EC2 instance types specifically for SAP solutions on AWS.

  - **For SAP NetWeaver–Based Solutions**: For SAP NetWeaver on AWS, a range of EC2 instance types is supported, spanning different categories to cater to various workload requirements:

    - **General Purpose**: Instances like *m4.large* to *m4.16xlarge* offer a balanced CPU to memory ratio, suitable for a variety of applications.

- **Compute Optimized**: Instances such as *c3.large* to *c4.8xlarge* provide high compute power and are ideal for compute-intensive applications.

- **Memory Optimized**: The *r3* and *r4* families, like *r3.large* to *r4.16xlarge*, are designed for memory-intensive applications. Additional memory-optimized instances include *r6idn*, *r6a*, *r7a*, *r7i*, *x1*, *x1e*, *x2iezn*, *x2idn*, and *x2iedn*.

- **Storage Optimized**: The *i3en* and *i4i* families offer high disk throughput and I/O and are ideal for high-performance databases.

These instances are fully supported for SAP NetWeaver and come with different configurations of vCPU, memory, and network performance, allowing users to select the most appropriate instance type based on the specific requirements of their SAP NetWeaver workloads.

- **For SAP HANA–Based Solutions:** The current generation of Amazon EC2 instances certified for SAP HANA includes various families optimized for different performance needs, such as *r4*, *r5*, *r5b*, *r6i*, *r7i*, *x1*, *x1e*, *x2idn*, *x2iedn*, and high-memory instances. These instances are designed to support both OLTP (Online Transaction Processing) and OLAP (Online Analytical Processing) workloads, with configurations ranging widely in terms of vCPU, memory, and network performance capacities. For scale-out scenarios, specifically for SAP HANA OLAP workloads, instances like *r5*, *r6i*, *x1*, *x1e*, *x2idn*, *x2iedn*, and high-memory instances are used. These are particularly suitable for larger deployments that require horizontal scaling to manage larger databases or increased load by distributing the workload across multiple servers. When selecting an EC2 instance for SAP HANA, it's crucial to consider the specific requirements of the workload, including the size of the in-memory database, the expected performance, and the network throughput requirements.

- **Cloud Elasticity**: A key feature of AWS is the elasticity offered by the cloud, which means that the infrastructure can scale up or scale down very easily with little planning. This is especially useful in the context of SAP since this allows quick scale-up of systems to meet additional demands (typically during period end closing). Specifically, elasticity allows the following:

  - **Flexibility**: Elasticity ensures that businesses can quickly adapt to changes in workload demands, such as during peak business hours or promotional periods or when running resource-intensive SAP reports.

  - **Performance Optimization**: With the ability to scale resources, SAP applications can maintain optimal performance levels even as demand fluctuates, ensuring consistent service levels and user satisfaction.

  - **Innovation**: Elastic resources allow companies to experiment and innovate with their SAP systems without the need for large up-front investments in hardware.

- **Pay-As-You-Go Pricing**: AWS provides pay-as-you-go pricing models for SAP workloads, meaning businesses pay only for the resources they use. Additionally, AWS offers cost reductions for commitments over a certain period and volume-based discounts, which can further enhance savings as usage scales up. These benefits underscore why a significant number of businesses opt to run their SAP workloads on AWS, leveraging the cloud's scalability, agility, and cost-effectiveness.

- **Cost Savings**: AWS has been proven to provide tangible business benefits like cost savings, flexibility, and speed, which have been experienced by a wide range of customers. This encompasses the ability to quickly deploy SAP solutions and a reduction in the total cost of ownership (TCO) of SAP systems by up to 71% compared with traditional on-premises infrastructure.

- **Automation for SAP**: AWS continues to invest in building tools and automation that can help reduce manual work in managing SAP infrastructure operations. These tools provide a host of options including the following use cases:

  - **System Provisioning**: This is the process of setting up infrastructure in the cloud, including establishing user, system, and service access to the applications, data, and cloud resources. Using Launch Wizard, the user can automatically provision systems by providing inputs including application requirements on the service console, SAP HANA settings, SAP landscape settings, and deployment details. Launch Wizard identifies the appropriate AWS resources to support the application, which can then also deploy the resources to operate the SAP application directly from Launch Wizard.

  - **System Monitoring**: Using Amazon CloudWatch the SAP system engineer can monitor the SAP application clusters, HANA database clusters, and HANA replication and SAP application core services without any need for servers or agents. All the metrics can be accessed through a custom CloudWatch dashboard.

  - **SAP Serverless Refresh**: SAP systems are refreshed from time to time to support needs like testing and production operations. Instead of performing refreshes manually, serverless AWS services can be used to perform the SAP system refresh.

  - **Auto-start and Auto-stop**: Typically, SAP systems consist of multiple components including database servers, application servers, core services, external systems like tax solutions, and job scheduling systems among others. The starting/stopping of such integrated systems requires a very specific sequence of tasks. This sequence can be automated using a combination of AWS services like AWS Systems Manager, Lambda, and CloudWatch.

  - **Auto-scaling**: As noted earlier, elasticity is a key benefit of the cloud for running SAP systems. As a result, the SAP Basis administrators have to scale the infrastructure up or down as per the demands on the system. This activity of scale-up and scale-down can also be automated to adapt to spikes/dips in user logins, period end closing, and other planned and unplanned peaks and troughs. This can be achieved via a combination of AWS services like Amazon EventBridge, Lambda functions, and AWS Systems Manager.

- **Extension and Innovation Beyond Infrastructure**: While moving SAP systems to AWS drives benefits, customers can also realize benefits beyond just infrastructure, but innovating and extending SAP with AWS solutions and services. These innovations complement customers' existing SAP environments by providing new capabilities for industry, line of business, and technical use cases. These solutions are focused on the areas of specialty like data analytics, IoT, DevOps, apps, APIs, and AI/ML. For instance, when leveraging SAP data for building a data lake on AWS, a customer can

  - Bring together disparate and siloed data through a templatized architecture across SAP and AWS services for extract, transform, and load (like Glue, Lambda, Kinesis).

  - Store the data using services like Amazon S3 and analyze the data using services like Redshift and Athena.

  - Consume the data either using AWS services like QuickSight or third-party solutions for visualization.

  Likewise, customers can build solutions around IoT and AI/ML among others, which would all be innovations and extensions beyond the traditional infrastructure modernization.

- **Mature Customer Base**: Over the years more than 6,000 customers have adopted AWS as the cloud service provider for hosting their SAP environment. These include customers across public and commercial sectors and across industry verticals, representing both large customers and small- and mid-sized customers. Many of these customers have provided public testimonial and references, which has further inspired confidence in other customers to invest in AWS as the cloud platform of choice for running SAP workloads.

Figure 3-2. *Why SAP on AWS*

Thomas was in a different zone by the time he finished his case as to how AWS could help Nimbus in this modernization journey. The Nimbus team was completely engaged in the discussion, and Elizabeth was the first to speak up, "That was an awesome presentation. This is a great starting point for what we are looking for." Others from Nimbus, including Nolan, Mark, and Sandeep, all added their complimentary feedback. Thomas was on cloud nine, given how disastrous his previous visit to Nimbus went. Amy, the seasoned professional as ever, soaked in the success but was the first to snap out of it. She quickly brought everyone back on to the agenda at hand saying, "Let us plan appropriate next steps. My recommendation would be to a much detailed 'Immersion Day' where we walk your extended technical teams through each of these topics in detail and make them sufficiently educated on the AWS options as you move forward with SAP modernization. The Immersion Day would be more technical and include hands-on sessions also."

"I would love for my team to review that," Mark said, looking at it from an IT infrastructure lens. "I think the SAP Applications team would want to sit in on those, specifically the extension and innovation use cases," added

Sandeep. Thomas was quick to take note and said he would plan the Immersion Day very soon and coordinate with the Nimbus team. Elizabeth made it a point to shake everyone's hands and complimented them on the good job done. As the team was exiting the Nimbus office, they quickly debriefed and exchanged congratulations all around. "That was a great meeting. Good job, Thomas," said a smiling Melanie. "It is all a collaborative effort," Thomas replied. As everyone got into their respective Uber rides, Thomas did not forget and took out his phone and texted Amy. "Thank you …boss." All he got in reply was a thumbs-up and a smiley face.

CHAPTER 4

Design of the AWS Cloud

This chapter will cover the design of the AWS cloud infrastructure including concepts of regions, availability zones, data centers, connectivity, and other related concepts. The chapter outlines how this design is relevant for SAP deployments.

It had been more than a week since the meeting at Nimbus's office had concluded. Thomas had received a short email from Nolan, thanking him for the great job done and how it had been a good learning for Nimbus. However, having not heard back from Nimbus in all this while made him nervous. Thomas had been planning for a follow-up Immersion Day and getting his internal resources lined up for that, but unless he had details nailed down with the customer, it would just delay the process. Thomas knew it was time for action. He was going to reach back out to Nolan and show the urgency for next steps. "Amy, I think we have been waiting long enough. I will reach back out to Nolan," Thomas sent this message over Slack. *"They are probably still digesting all they heard, or maybe they are talking to our competition,"* Amy slacked back adding a few "smileys" to soften the message. *Thomas composed a short email, asking Nolan about the next steps and how AWS could continue to help and stay engaged. Another three days went by.*

Elizabeth was getting ready for an important evening. Nothing fancy, but she wanted to make efforts. It was an evening out with Sophia for some mother–daughter time. It was Elizabeth's idea since most of her interactions with Sophia would be short and simple or turn into mini-arguments. This was Elizabeth's way of staying 'relevant.' "Sophia, dear, I am ready, waiting downstairs," hollered Elizabeth, knowing well Sophia would take still more time to come down. While waiting, she was tempted to check her work emails, but avoided it, another habit she was trying to break. Ben had taken Ethan to shoot some hoops, while Pepper cuddled at Elizabeth's feet. Sophia was still not down. Another 15 minutes and Sophia came bustling down, and it did not look like she put in any efforts to get dressed for this dinner date. I am sure you were just texting with friends while I was waiting here, *words that Elizabeth thought but did not utter. She just smiled and said, "I have reservations at the new Moroccan restaurant. Hope that works." "Yeah sure." Sophia was cool with the choice.*

© Tushar Srivastava 2025
T. Srivastava, *Modernizing SAP with AWS*, https://doi.org/10.1007/979-8-8688-1579-9_4

"How was your day at school?" Elizabeth ventured into some small talk during the drive to the restaurant. "It was okay. Nothing much happened." Sophia kept the 'small talk' really small. Few words were spoken till they reached the restaurant. The new restaurant had a fancy menu and even fancier interiors. The décor spoke of the owner's Moroccan heritage and life struggles of making it in America and finally opening a restaurant. As they wrapped up dinner with a final bite of the meskouta, *Sophia was texting on her phone, and Elizabeth looked like she had given up trying to make a conversation. The evening did not go as per plan, but Elizbeth was thankful for whatever time she got to spend with her young daughter. Back home Elizabeth and Ben stayed back in the kitchen for a round of green tea while the kids got ready to sleep. "I am not sure if I am losing my connection with Sophia day by day. She just would not share with me, Ben." Ben smiled and drew a large sip of tea and said, "She is your daughter. It is just a phase. Don't overthink this." Just then Elizabeth saw her phone buzz with a text message, "Micah wants to meet tomorrow." Elizabeth knew what Nolan's message meant. "Do you need to take care of something at work, honey?" the ever-supportive Ben queried. "I will take care of it tomorrow." Elizabeth was learning to draw a boundary between work and home, a line that had been blurred a long time ago. As they headed upstairs, she did text back, "Let's meet at my office at 8 AM. Order breakfast."*

Nolan picked some drive-thru breakfast as he headed to work. As he entered Elizabeth's office, she looked up from the laptop to say a quick hello. Nolan quickly glanced at his digital watch; it was 7:55 AM. "I guess Micah saw the license cost and blew a fuse. I have seen that happen before," Elizabeth ventured. "Well, I may agree with him. Did you see the numbers yourself?" Nolan responded. Elizabeth continued, "Yes, I did see the numbers, but we have to see the numbers in the context of the benefits and ROI and not just line items by themselves. Mark is still working on the overall financial business case, so we will use those inputs too. Reminds me, have you heard from Mark yet? We need a draft business case soon." Nolan knew Elizabeth's mind was running in many directions. He had seen her in action, and there was always a method to her madness. Instead of responding he pivoted, "We also need to look at the cloud capabilities, and we have not set up the Immersion Day with AWS as we had discussed. I am still stalling them." "Nolan, I think we have enough inputs from AWS, and I think we all really liked what we heard. While I agree that the Immersion Day will be useful, I want to make sure we have other key items addressed, and then we can come back to the AWS workshops. From what I see, the cloud is one less of an unknown now. Can you please check with Mark on the business case draft?"

The meeting was scheduled at 11 AM at Micah Brown's office, Chief Financial Officer at Nimbus and a numbers person like no other. He also happened to be Elizabeth's boss. Elizabeth and Nolan were already there in the office at 10:55 while Elizabeth was still going over her material in her head. Micah arrived five minutes late to the meeting and promptly apologized. "How are you doing, Nolan?" The man good with numbers was as good with names. Nolan smiled back and confirmed everything in his life was as beautiful as it could be even as his head swirled with the thought, How else do you respond to your CFO whom you may have met once or twice in passing? *Micah did not waste much time and got to the point, "Well, Elizabeth, I am not sure what to make of these numbers. This is the license cost of upgrading our SAP systems. I thought we already paid for all this, so why are we doing this again?" "We are going in for a brand-new version of SAP called* **S/4HANA***, which would require a new implementation," Elizabeth protested weakly. "I assume you are then going to put together a business case for the benefits and how quickly we recoup the cost and start seeing the benefits. Right?" Micah could shake the best leader's confidence with his line of questioning. He was not done yet. "I need the business to sign off on the benefits before we upgrade to a new fancy system." Elizabeth was prepared. All these years, she understood Micah's style. He would place all his tough questions up front and then give the other party a keen listening.*

"Micah, there is more to this program. It is a complete SAP modernization program. We are looking at upgrading SAP to the latest version S/4HANA that will provide many of the functions that the business has been looking for, including your own finance teams. We are looking at eliminating customizations, thus reducing the cost to maintain the systems in the long run, and we are also looking at leveraging the cloud as an option for hosting SAP and extending its capabilities. The numbers you saw were raw costs just for the licensing of SAP." Elizabeth was not done yet, and Micah kept listening. "We are already working on building the financial business case with all the cost–benefit analysis, and we also expect to save additional costs by leveraging the cloud. Those also will need to be quantified. The license numbers were sent your way since I wanted to make sure you had a view of what we are working with. It does not look good …yet." Elizabeth closed her arguments with a matter-of-fact look. Nolan thought that both she and Micah kind of enjoyed this little sparring match. "Well, I would definitely like to see the business case and make sure you negotiate hard. You really don't want me to negotiate on your behalf. Also, I am curious about your cloud angle. I thought the cloud was more for experiment and research for our innovation teams." Micah made all his asks known, and the Nimbus veteran always insisted on highest standards. Others had found out the hard way.

"Why did you share the raw numbers? We should have presented the water-tight business case," was Nolan's query as the two headed back out after the meeting. *"Micah needed to see the raw numbers, so he would know how much better we get over time, and he would have asked for the raw numbers anyways,"* Elizabeth answered from her experience. Nolan just nodded. *"Nolan, let's get with Mark to review the status of the business case, and by the way, I would like for us to get the Immersion Day planned with AWS, since, I think, it is going to become a relevant topic of discussion with Micah also."* Nolan was silently admiring Elizabeth's farsightedness, realizing he still had a lot to learn from her. Back on his desk, Nolan prioritized the items in his head. This is going to be a long day, *he thought to himself.*

Thomas was beyond excited. He quickly created a group message to both Ashish and Amy. "Nimbus wants to plan for the Immersion Day. They are committing their team to participate and see this as critical to the success of their SAP modernization program," *he typed out quickly. Ashish was the first to respond,* "That is more work for me." *He added a few emojis to make sure everyone understood the sarcasm. Amy instead created a group call to take stock of the situation.* "We need to plan really well for this. There are no second chances. Ashish, of course you will lead the discussion, but if you need some experts to support you, get going on that right away. Let's focus on hands-on labs to support the slideware." *Thomas added his thoughts,* "We can personalize the content to Nimbus's specific case. Also, I will find out the roles of the key participants, and we can tailor content to the specific roles." *Ashish took in all the feedback and knew this was a critical customer. He had done an Immersion Day many times, but there was always something different about each customer. He instinctively knew that Nimbus was going to be a tough customer, and he needs to prepare for all the tough questions.* "Don't worry, guys. I will keep it personal and interactive. You set a pretty high bar, Thomas." *Ashish meant it.*

Meanwhile back at Nimbus, Mark Chapman and Nolan were huddled in a conference room pretty much the whole day. Downing his third cup of coffee, Mark said, "I don't think we have all the details to be able to build the financial business case. I have looked at SAP's provided report of standard processes that will replace our custom programs and also looked at benefits of simplified interfaces, and we have converted all that to a dollar amount. Of course, we have made some assumptions, which can be defended. What I don't have is the cost of the change, except SAP provided license numbers. And if there are other benefits and cost that we are not looking at." *Nolan sympathized, but they needed to move forward.* "I suggest we do more 'field work.' Let's interview the business teams and talk to our partner teams including SAP and probably AWS. Once we have collected the data points, we can then convert them into benefits and cost. Micah is looking at this *project with an eagle eye, and unless the business case proves otherwise, this will be a no-go. Elizabeth herself is not completely convinced, so essentially this is a 'truth-seeking' exercise as to whether this modernization project would reap the desired benefits at all or not." Mark knew that was the go-forward path but wanted to hear from Nolan. "And oh by the way, we are finally getting to do the Immersion Day with AWS, so please nominate the people on your team who you think will benefit from this technical deep dive," Nolan said even as Mark was mentally figuring out how much more work still needed to be done. "Sure, I will send my best people. Just send me the dates," confirmed Mark. Given the heavy focus on infrastructure from AWS, Mark saw this as a good opportunity to get his team up to speed and take the lead on the cloud in the context of SAP. Over the next few days, Nolan confirmed with Sandeep on his team's participation in the Immersion Day and sent out the list of attendees to Thomas. He listed himself as an attendee too, not just because he was an integral part of the decision-making team, but the nerd in Nolan wanted to understand the technical details of the cloud as it applied to SAP.*

*The **Immersion Day** at AWS had evolved over years of customer engagement and education. As a customer got ready to leverage AWS in their organization, the Immersion Day became a good starting point for them to dive deep into AWS services and deploying them and learn key best practices. Over the years the Immersion Days had become even more focused, concentrating on specializations like SAP on AWS. The Immersion Day offered hands-on labs, presentations, and live demos. Ashish had become an expert on leading SAP on AWS Immersion Days and had led many customers through their technical journeys on the cloud. Over the years he had become a trusted advisor, and many of them kept coming back to him for advice. However, even the confident Ashish was a tad nervous about presenting to a large audience at Nimbus. Thomas set up internal review sessions in the lead-up to the Immersion Day, and Ashish with his attention to detail kept refining the content over and over. Amy dropped in once in a while to check on the progress and offer her sharp insights. As the date approached closer, Thomas confirmed the logistics with Nolan. The day before the Immersion Day, Amy took Ashish and Thomas out for a quiet dinner, just to calm nerves and, importantly, get them 'game ready.' "I will not be traveling to Nimbus for the Immersion Day, and I trust that between the two of you, primarily Ashish, the Immersion Day should be in good hands. I want us to make sure we are addressing all technical needs, and that opens up the clear pathway to the commercial discussion. Remember, Ashish, this is the opportunity where you turn into their trusted advisor." Amy made sure both Ashish and Thomas understood the plan well. Amy had a good knack for walking the tight rope between giving her team independence and getting involved herself. Nimbus was a good example.*

On the appointed day, Ashish and Thomas showed up at Nimbus about an hour before the scheduled appointed time. Nolan was already there to pick them up at the lobby. Nolan offered to have some coffee and snacks before heading to the conference room since they had time. Thomas, ever so alert to the opportunity of building relationships, readily agreed. Over coffee the trio exchanged small talk over each other's professional and personal interests. Nolan and Ashish quickly bonded over a shared love for technology, while Thomas listened twice as much as he spoke. A mentor had told him a long time ago, 'You can build stronger relationships using your ears rather than your mouth.' "If you guys like, you can grab a quick refill as we head to the training room," Nolan remarked looking at his oversized watch. The three of them trooped to a large training room that had capacity to hold at least 50 people. Ashish quickly unpacked his bag and took out all sorts of gadgets, much like a soldier getting his weapons ready for a battle. All matters of cables, a Bluetooth 'clicker,' and a wireless keyboard were just some of Ashish's elaborate gadgetry. He could deliver an Immersion Day on the moon if needed.

People started rolling in slowly, and Thomas shook everyone's hands, making it a point to ask and register everyone's names mentally. Somewhere in the mill of people, Mark Chapman and Sandeep Krishnan walked in, and Thomas gave them some extra attention. Ashish was done with his technical setup and joined Thomas. "Always nice to come back and meet familiar faces. Hope you have been doing well, Mark and Sandeep," Thomas quipped. Nolan knew how important this workshop was and did not want to lose any precious time. He quickly grabbed the microphone and tapped it a few times to make sure it worked and said, "Hi, everyone, thanks for coming in today. We have a couple of friends from AWS here today to deliver an 'Immersion Day' on the topic of SAP on AWS. Most of you are members of Mark's and Sandeep's teams, representing IT Infrastructure and the Applications team, respectively, and we also have a few participants from other teams. As you all know, we at Nimbus are looking to modernize our SAP systems, and over the past few weeks, we realize that the 'cloud' will play an important role in this modernization effort. In true Nimbus fashion, we want to do our own research before deciding a path forward. Our goal through this Immersion Day is to learn enough about AWS's solutions that can help make our SAP modernization journey even smoother." Nolan was articulate and to the point. Mark and Sandeep were nodding in agreement from the back of the room.

Thomas introduced himself quickly and made way for the 'expert.' Ashish surveyed the room and saw about 25 pairs of eyes looking inquisitively. "This is not an Immersion Day, but rather days," and the room filled with feeble laughs. "Nolan put it really well, and if I have to add anything, it would be that over the next few sessions, I want to take the opportunity to educate you on technical aspects of how to modernize SAP with AWS and more importantly answer any questions you may have. Almost every customer that I have worked with, has initial difficulty in fitting the pieces together, since cloud for SAP is a relatively modern concept, and I would encourage all of you to ask plenty of questions during the session or offline even after the session is over. My goal is to prepare all of you well for a much bigger journey in front of you, which is SAP modernization, where AWS is only one milestone, albeit an important one." Ashish had calmed his nerves and in the process acquired the full attention from his audience. Ashish clicked through his initial slides and said, "Since many of you may be new to cloud and new to AWS, I want to start from the basics and talk about the basics of AWS and the design of the AWS cloud. We will discuss how this design helps us architect SAP on AWS in a robust manner."

Understanding the Design of the AWS Cloud

The building blocks of Amazon Web Services (AWS) infrastructure are designed to provide a flexible, secure, and resilient environment for deploying applications and services. From a physical infrastructure standpoint, the AWS global infrastructure is divided into regions, Availability Zones, and data centers.

Data Centers

An **AWS data center** is a highly secure physical facility that houses computer systems and associated components, such as telecommunications and storage systems for AWS. These data centers are the foundation of AWS cloud services, providing the necessary infrastructure to host and run the services offered by AWS, including storage, computing power, and networking capabilities. AWS data centers are designed with multiple layers of security, power redundancy, cooling, and networking equipment to ensure high availability and reliability of the services provided to AWS customers globally. Each AWS data center entails:

- **Infrastructure**: The physical infrastructure includes servers, storage units, network gear, and advanced security devices. This equipment is supported by redundant power supply systems, cooling systems, and backup generators to ensure continuous operation.

- **Security**: Multiple layers of security controls include physical barriers, surveillance systems, secure access protocols, and continuous monitoring to protect against unauthorized access and potential threats.

- **Data Protection**: Inside the data centers, AWS deploys advanced network security and encryption methods to protect the integrity and confidentiality of customer data.

- **Environmental Controls**: Data centers are designed with environmental sustainability in mind, using energy-efficient technologies and systems to reduce their carbon footprint.

- **Location Strategy**: AWS strategically selects locations for their data centers to minimize risks from natural disasters while also considering the proximity to customers for reduced latency.

- **Compliance**: These data centers adhere to strict compliance standards, undergoing rigorous certifications and audits to meet global security and privacy requirements.

- **Global Network**: AWS data centers are interconnected via a high-speed private network, allowing for efficient data transfer and redundancy across global locations.

AWS data centers, the backbone of their cloud infrastructure, are designed with a multi-layered security approach to protect against various risks and ensure high levels of security and compliance including:

- **Perimeter Layer**: Physical security is the first line of defense, including features like security guards, fencing, security feeds, intrusion detection technology, and other measures.

- **Data Layer**: This critical layer, where customer data is held, has restricted access and threat detection devices to ensure data protection.

- **Infrastructure Layer**: Consists of the building itself and the supporting systems, including power backups, HVAC, and fire suppression systems.

- **Environmental Layer**: Site selection and construction take into account environmental risks like flooding and seismic activity to ensure sustainability and operational integrity.

These layers collectively ensure that AWS data centers are secure, resilient, and capable of supporting the vast array of AWS cloud services provided globally.

AWS does not expose or identify its individual data centers to customers. So there are no naming conventions for AWS data centers specifically.

Availability Zones

An **AWS Availability Zone (AZ)** is a single data center or a group of data centers located within a region. Each AZ is designed to be redundant and isolated from failures of other AZs, with independent, redundant power supply and networking.

In addition, the AZs within a region are separated by a meaningful distance from each other, up to 60 miles (approximately 100 kilometers) from each other, to prevent related failures. At the same time they are close enough to provide low-latency synchronous replication.

Also, the AZs are designed in a way so they are not impacted simultaneously by a large-scale scenarios like a fire, earthquake, flood, or utility failure. Common points of failure, like generators and cooling equipment, are not shared across Availability Zones and are designed to be supplied by independent power substations. All these design features provide customers with the ability to run production applications and databases that are more highly available, fault-tolerant, and scalable than would be possible from a single data center.

The concept of Availability Zones is central to the design of AWS architecture, ensuring that the cloud infrastructure is robust and able to handle various scenarios that could lead to potential outages. This allows businesses to operate continuously and without interruption, providing peace of mind that their applications and data are secure and available when needed. Key features of Availability Zones are:

- **Isolation and Redundancy**: AZs are geographically separate, minimizing the risk of a single event impacting multiple AZs. Each AZ is typically miles away from any other in the same region, yet close enough for business continuity applications that require rapid failover.

- **Connectivity**: Availability Zones (AZs) are interconnected using high-bandwidth, low-latency networking through fully redundant, dedicated metro fiber, ensuring high-throughput and low-latency communication between AZs.

- **Security and Compliance**: Just like AWS regions, AZs are compliant with the highest security standards, offering encrypted communication and rigorous physical security.

- **Fault Tolerance**: By architecting solutions across multiple AZs, AWS customers can achieve higher fault tolerance. Services such as Amazon RDS and Amazon EC2 can be configured to replicate across AZs to ensure high availability.

- **Flexible Architectures**: AZs allow for complex architectures that balance load, segregate environments, and allow for disaster recovery plans that can tolerate the failure of an entire data center.

Naming Convention

AZs are named with the following format structure in order to provide information about the AZ: AZs are named using the region code followed by a letter identifier. For example, an AZ in the US East (N. Virginia) region might be labeled as `us-east-1a`. This naming convention helps to identify the AZ's location within its respective region and maintain orderly infrastructure management.

AWS Region

At the top of the AWS infrastructure hierarchy is the region. An **AWS Region** is a geographical location around the world that consists of multiple Availability Zones. Each Region is isolated and independent of each other. This separation between the Regions limits failures to a single Region in case of service disruptions. Additionally, the resources and data that users create in one region do not exist in any other region unless the users explicitly use a replication or copy feature offered by an AWS service or replicate the data themselves. AWS Regions are foundational components in the architecture of AWS's global cloud infrastructure. They represent the broadest geographical categories within AWS's network, defining the physical geographical areas where clusters of data centers are located. In essence, AWS regions are designed to offer a balance between widespread geographical coverage, high availability, compliance with local laws and regulations, and network performance optimization, all of which are critical to the diverse needs of AWS's global customer base. Key features of regions are as below:

- **Geographical Spread**: AWS's global infrastructure is divided into regions that cover major geographic areas across the Americas, Europe, Asia, and more, allowing users to deploy applications and store data in locations chosen for proximity to end users or compliance with jurisdictional regulations.

- **Availability Zones**: Each region comprises multiple Availability Zones, which are distinct data centers with their own power, cooling, and security, operating independently of each other to provide fault tolerance and stability.

- **Data Residency and Sovereignty**: Regions address the need for data residency, allowing organizations to meet local compliance and data sovereignty requirements by keeping data in a specific territory.

- **Service Selection**: While AWS offers a vast array of services, not all services are available in every region. Customers must select regions based on the services they plan to utilize.

- **Performance Optimization**: Regions allow for performance optimization, with customers choosing regions closest to their user base to minimize latency and maximize application performance.

- **Scalability and Flexibility**: The multi-region approach provides scalability and flexibility, as customers can deploy applications across multiple regions for increased resilience and geographic spread.

- **Pricing Strategy**: The pricing of AWS services may differ by Region, influenced by the cost of operating and maintaining the data centers in each area.

- **Expansion and Growth**: AWS continually expands its global network by establishing new regions and AZs, enhancing global reach and capacity.

- **Compliance with Standards**: AWS ensures that each Region adheres to specific certifications and standards, which can vary based on local laws and regulations.

Naming Convention

AWS Regions are named in a standardized format that provides intuitive information about their geographical location:

- The first part (us, eu, ap, etc.) indicates the continent or a general global area.

- The second part usually refers to a specific area or city within that continent or area (east, west, central, etc.).

- The third part is a number that differentiates between regions in the same area.

For example, *us-west-1* is the first AWS region on the west coast of the United States, whereas *eu-central-1* refers to the central region of Europe, specifically in Frankfurt.

Other Infrastructure Deployments

Apart from regions, AZs, and data centers, AWS also offers additional infrastructure deployment options as below.

AWS Local Zones

AWS local zones are a type of infrastructure deployment that extends AWS Regions by placing select AWS resources closer to large population centers. AWS local zones thus serve to augment the existing AWS infrastructure, providing a way to meet specific geographical and performance requirements of various applications and users.

- **Purpose**: Local zones are designed to bring AWS services near to end users, significantly reducing latency and providing high-speed access to applications.

- **Use Cases**: They are ideal for running applications that require low latency, like real-time gaming, live streaming, and interactive experiences such as AR/VR. Local zones also support hybrid cloud migrations and enable compliance with data residency regulations.

- **Management**: Resources in local zones can be managed through the AWS Management Console, AWS **Command Line Interface** (**CLI**), and AWS **Software Development Kits** (**SDKs**), just like other AWS services.

- **Cost**: Enabling a local zone does not incur additional charges. However, the pricing of resources within a local zone may differ from those in the parent AWS Region.

AWS Outposts

AWS Outposts is a fully managed service that brings AWS infrastructure, services, APIs, and tools to virtually any data center, colocation space, or on-premises facility for a truly consistent hybrid experience. AWS Outposts is meant for situations where customers need to keep their applications close to on-premises data and applications while still benefiting from the scalability, elasticity, and innovation that AWS provides. AWS Outposts is a hardware in an enclosure that can be deployed at a customer site but is supported fully by AWS in installation and operation. Here are some detailed aspects of AWS Outposts:

- **Integration and Management**: AWS Outposts seamlessly integrates with AWS Regions, allowing customers to manage their on-premises applications using the same AWS Management Console, CLI, and SDKs.

- **Resource Support**: Outposts supports various AWS resources such as Amazon EC2 instances, ECS clusters, EKS nodes, RDS databases, and more, to run low-latency workloads on-premises.

- **Configuration and Pricing**: Customers can select from different Outposts configurations, which include a mix of EC2 instance types and storage options. The pricing model includes options like all up-front, partial up-front, or no up-front payments, with a typical commitment term of three years.

AWS Points of Presence (PoPs)

These are sites distributed globally that host Amazon CloudFront, Amazon Route 53, and AWS Global Accelerator, providing a **content delivery network** (**CDN**), DNS resolution services, and edge networking optimization, respectively. These PoPs are designed to deliver AWS services with lower latency by being closer to end users. AWS PoPs are crucial for the high-speed, secure, and reliable delivery of AWS services to users worldwide, reducing latency and improving the user experience by processing data closer to end users. The PoPs have the following characteristics:

- **Network Composition**: Over 400 PoPs are part of the global edge network, including more than 400 edge locations and 13 regional mid-tier caches, located in over 90 cities across 48 countries (as of September 2025).

- **Isolation and Capacity**: Each PoP operates independently, ensuring that issues in one location do not affect the network's overall integrity. The AWS network interconnects with thousands of different network carriers globally and boasts hundreds of terabits of capacity for optimal performance. Edge locations are interconnected with AWS Regions through a fully redundant fiber network backbone.

Networking

The next important component of the AWS global infrastructure is the **networking**. At a fundamental level, the networking provides the connectivity between AWS sites as well as access to users providing patterns for traffic flow and scalability across different components.

AWS Network Backbone

The **AWS network backbone**, a core part of AWS's global infrastructure, is a high-capacity, high-speed network that interconnects all the AWS Regions, edge locations, and data centers across the world. Given below are details about its functionalities and features:

- **Redundancy**: The network is fully redundant, utilizing 400 GbE fiber links, which helps in maintaining service continuity even if one or more network components fail.

- **Capacity**: It is designed to handle massive amounts of data transfer with many terabits of capacity, facilitating the high-performance requirements of modern applications.

- **Latency**: The backbone is optimized for low latency, essential for time-sensitive applications. AWS achieves this through a combination of geographically dispersed regions and local zones, designed to bring AWS services closer to end users.

- **Quality of Service**: With low packet loss and high network quality, AWS ensures reliable and consistent network performance, which is critical for all online services, especially those requiring real-time data transfer.

- **Global Reach**: AWS's global network infrastructure allows for rapid scaling and deployment of resources, supporting the launch of servers in multiple regions quickly and efficiently.

- **Local Zones and Wavelength**: To further reduce latency, AWS local zones provide AWS services close to large population centers, and AWS Wavelength brings AWS services to the edge of telecommunication networks.

- **Scalability**: The backbone supports scalable architecture designs, allowing for seamless increases in traffic and workload without significant re-architecting.

This backbone is an integral part of AWS, enabling the delivery of a broad set of advanced services with the performance, security, and reliability that its customers require.

Physical Networking Equipment

Within the AWS infrastructure, the **physical networking equipment** underpins the global network that powers the extensive range of cloud services. While specific models and configurations are proprietary, the types of hardware typically used in such environments include:

- **Enterprise-Grade Routers**: Used to route traffic at scale, these devices handle the ingress and egress of massive amounts of data between the AWS global network and the internet.

- **Network Switches**: Critical for intra–data center communication, switches handle the traffic within AWS data centers, connecting servers, storage systems, and other network components.

- **Load Balancers**: Both physical and software-based, these distribute incoming network and application traffic across multiple servers to balance the load and ensure reliability and availability.

- **Fiber-Optic Cabling**: AWS uses a vast amount of cabling within and between data centers, relying on fiber-optic technology for its high-speed and low-latency characteristics.

The equipment used is designed for redundancy, reliability, and scalability to meet the high standards of performance and security that AWS customers expect.

Amazon Virtual Private Cloud (VPC)

In the context of SAP on AWS, an **AWS account** serves as the foundational unit for managing and operating SAP workloads in the cloud. Each AWS account provides isolation, billing boundaries, and access control, enabling organizations to design secure and scalable SAP landscapes. For large enterprises, a multi-account strategy is often recommended – using separate accounts for development, testing, and production SAP environments to enhance security, simplify governance, and support compliance. AWS Organizations and AWS Control Tower can further help manage multiple accounts efficiently, enforce policies, and automate account provisioning, making it easier to operate SAP workloads in a controlled, enterprise-grade environment. As a customer starts using AWS, they create a logically isolated section of the AWS cloud. This is known as the **Virtual Private Cloud** and is the cornerstone of AWS networking. Within a VPC, you can define your own IP address range, create subnets, configure route tables, and set up network gateways. This virtual network closely resembles a traditional network that a user would operate in their own data center, with the benefits of using the scalable infrastructure of AWS. The VPC has the following components:

- **Subnets**: Subnets within AWS are subdivisions you can create within a **Virtual Private Cloud** (**VPC**) that allow you to segment and organize your resources. Each subnet is located within a single Availability Zone and is associated with a specific range of IP addresses. Subnets enable the user to group and isolate resources, manage public and private environments within the same VPC, control access to instances and resources, and design network architecture that spans multiple Availability Zones for high availability. A user can set up public-facing subnets for servers that need to communicate with the internet and private-facing subnets for backend systems that don't need internet access:

  - **Public Subnet**: Instances have direct access to the internet via an internet gateway. An internet gateway allows resources in public subnets (such as EC2 instances) to connect to the internet if they have a public IPv4 or IPv6 address. Additionally, resources on the internet can initiate connections to resources in the subnet using their public IPv4 or IPv6 address.

  - **Private Subnet**: Instances do not have direct access to the internet but may access it through a **NAT** (**Network Address Translation**) gateway. The NAT gateway allows instances in a private subnet to connect to services outside the VPC, but external services cannot initiate a connection with those instances.

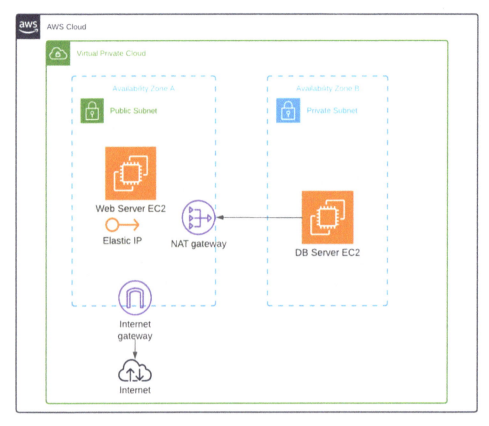

Figure 4-1. *AWS Network Architecture*

- **AWS Route Tables**: These contain a set of rules, called routes, that determine where network traffic from the VPC subnets or gateways is directed. Each subnet in a VPC must be associated with a route table, which specifies the allowed routes for outbound traffic leaving that subnet. Route tables can direct traffic to different targets like an internet gateway, a virtual private gateway, a NAT device, a VPC peering connection, a network interface, or an AWS Transit Gateway (TGW). There are two types of route tables in a VPC:

  - **Main Route Table**: Automatically created with a VPC and controls the default routing for all subnets that are not associated with any other route table

  - **Custom Route Tables**: Created by users and associated with specific subnets to define different routing rules for those subnets

- **Connectivity Patterns**: Once the VPC and subnets are created, there are multiple connectivity options either for external users to communicate with the VPC or multiple VPCs to communicate with each other. Some of the common patterns are

  - **Site-to-Site VPN**: This is a service that allows the customer to connect on-premises network to their VPC over a secure and encrypted VPN connection. It essentially extends the on-premises networks to the cloud as if they were part of the same private network. Data transferred between the customer network and VPC is encrypted by the VPN connection, providing a secure bridge between customer infrastructure and AWS. AWS provides two components for this purpose – a virtual private gateway, attached to the VPC, which serves as the VPN concentrator on the AWS side of the site-to-site VPN connection, and a customer gateway, which is a physical device or software application on the customer side of the site-to-site VPN connection.

  - **AWS Direct Connect**: This is a preferred option for private and dedicated connectivity. AWS offers a dedicated network connection from the customer premises to AWS, bypassing the internet for more reliable and consistent network performance. It can reduce network costs, increase bandwidth throughput, and provide a more consistent network experience for applications running in the AWS cloud. Direct Connect is particularly beneficial for large data transfers, such as dataset uploads to Amazon S3, database replication, or disaster recovery scenarios.

  - **VPC Peering**: If a customer has multiple VPCs, there is a need for communication between the VPCs. This can be achieved via VPC peering, which is a networking connection between two VPCs that routes traffic between them using private IPv4 or IPv6 addresses. Instances in either VPC can communicate with each other as if they were within the same network. VPC peering connections can be established between a customer's own VPCs, with a VPC in another AWS account or with a VPC in a different AWS Region. VPC peering provides a direct network route between the VPCs, avoiding the use of the public internet or a VPN connection and thereby maintaining the privacy and security of the communications.

- **AWS Transit Gateway**: The VPC peering method does not scale well if the number of VPCs is large (due to the non-transitive nature, individual connections have to be established between each pair of VPCs). AWS Transit Gateway addresses that and acts as a network transit hub that simplifies the process of connecting multiple VPCs, on-premises networks, and remote offices together. It centralizes the management of routing and enables the customer to scale connectivity across thousands of Amazon VPCs, AWS accounts, and on-premises networks. This service simplifies the network and puts an end to complex peering relationships, streamlining how services across multiple environments communicate with each other.

- **AWS PrivateLink**: AWS PrivateLink enables private connectivity between SAP workloads and AWS services without exposing traffic to the public internet. In the context of SAP, this is particularly valuable for securing data exchange between SAP systems and integrated AWS services like Amazon S3 or Amazon RDS or third-party services hosted on AWS. By using PrivateLink, enterprises can enhance their security posture, maintain compliance, and reduce the risk of data breaches while ensuring low-latency, reliable communication for mission-critical SAP applications.

All these components enable AWS customers to build scalable, flexible, and highly secure network architectures tailored to their specific application and business requirements.

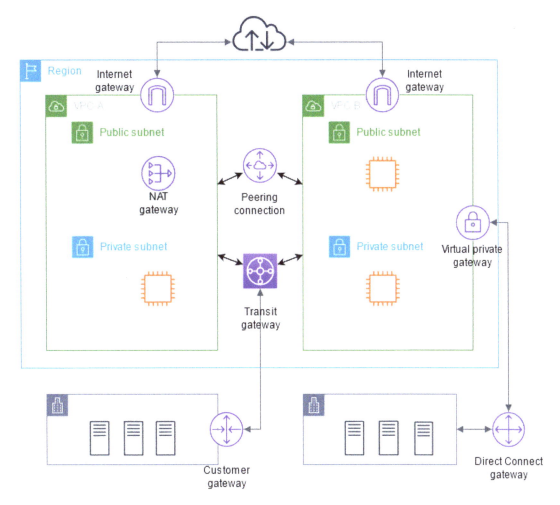

Figure 4-2. *AWS Connectivity Patterns*

By the time Ashish was done for the day, a lot of the participants came up to him asking follow-up questions, asking for his email to continue the discussion offline. The ever-smiling Ashish obliged. As the participants dispersed, Nolan came up to Thomas and Ashish and said, "That was a great session, Ashish. I learned so much. And judging from all the questions during the session, looks like everyone was totally engaged. I look forward to the survey results. I am assuming we would get the slides from the session today?" "Yes, of course, I would be putting all the content in a shared folder and will send you the link," Ashish said as a matter of fact. Nolan escorted Thomas and Ashish back to the lobby. Thomas, wanting to make sure the plan stay on track, said, "Nolan, as you know there will be multiple sessions, so I will reach out to you as we plan subsequent sessions. In the

111

meanwhile, we will continue to answer email queries from the participants." "Thanks, Thomas," Nolan acknowledged. As Thomas and Ashish walked out, they silently "high-fived" each other. They both knew that they made great progress with Nimbus today, but it was just the beginning. The plane had taken off smoothly, but they still had the whole flight to navigate.

The next day Nolan dropped by Elizabeth's office. "I can come by later if you are busy." "No worries. Come over. I have time before my meeting. What's up?" Elizabeth was curious. "The AWS workshop went well yesterday. We had about 25 folks across Infra and Apps, and AWS did an amazing job. That guy Ashish knows his stuff. Lots of good questions, and I see that cloud literacy would be a key part of our success." "That is good to hear." Elizabeth was very pleased with the outcome. "However, we still need more work on our business case. Mark is not making much progress, and he needs help." Elizabeth took a deep breath. "I think we are going to help him help us. Let us get the leadership team together to do a quick status review and move this forward quickly. I hope to have a good update for Micah's weekly staff meeting." Just as Nolan was walking out, Elizabeth's phone buzzed with a text, "Mom, is it okay if I stayed back at Stella's place today?" "Sweetie, remember we have a family dinner planned for weeks now. Are you sure you can't move it to another date?" Elizabeth replied. Elizabeth called after ten minutes but got no answer. She tried a few more times, but the call kept going to voicemail.

Early next week the leadership status review meeting was set up at Elizabeth's office. Mark and Sandeep walked in almost together. "How is the business case coming along?" asked Sandeep politely. "I have made some progress, but definitely some ways to go," Mark stated. "Let me know if I can help in any way," offered Sandeep out of courtesy. Nolan walked into the room just holding onto his favorite black notebook; however, Elizabeth was still not around. "I am not sure where she is, though she specifically asked for this time," Nolan wondered loudly, ensuring that Sandeep and Mark did not blame him for any scheduling faux pas. A few minutes later Elizabeth walked in hurriedly and apologized immediately to the team waiting for her, "Sorry, guys. Was taking care of a family situation." Elizabeth wasted no time and got into the agenda right away. "Mark, I know we are a bit behind on the business case. What is the situation there?" "We have the data regarding standard processes that will replace customizations, details about simplified interfaces, and also SAP provided license cost," Mark repeated the status from a few days ago. Elizabeth listened intently and continued, "By the way, what is your feedback from the AWS session from last week?" "It was very useful and gave us a new way to think about SAP modernization and how the cloud can play a role," Sandeep shared his opinion. "I agree. Specifically from my infrastructure lens, it was very useful to think of cloud providing the reliability and stability we would expect for SAP systems," added Mark.

Elizabeth addressed her team, "Well, that is great to hear. And what I also understand is that as you engage more with the key stakeholders, there are new insights that help us see the whole picture. Mark, I think you should spend some time with the business users documenting the key areas of improvement that we will see from their perspective, if we modernize SAP. Sandeep should be part of the conversations since he is responsible for deployment of that new solution."

In the same breath she continued, "Also, continue with the sessions with the AWS team and get details on the benefits they can add to our program and any associated costs. Finally, also look at the overall deployment cost, both internal and external. That should help us to get to a well-rounded business case. I will continue the negotiations with SAP on the license costs and whatever benefits we can accrue that will get added to the business case. Mark, in all my years working in technology, my big learning is that you have to be good at both technology and 'selling.' Finally, don't simply look at the cost of change, but importantly, also look at the cost of 'not changing.' It will completely change your perspective and how you sell the business case to the stakeholders." In a little over 20 minutes, Elizabeth left the leadership team in awe and demonstrated why she was one of the most successful technology leaders in corporate America.

CHAPTER 5

Designing the AWS Infrastructure for SAP

This chapter covers how to architect the optimized AWS infrastructure (compute, network, storage, and other services) for running SAP workloads on AWS.

Thomas had called for a virtual meeting to keep Amy updated on the progress at Nimbus. Amy kicked things off. "I guess it went well; else, I would have already heard from you guys," she said all the while adjusting the camera to get the best angle on the screen. "Yes, I think it went really well, and Ashish did an amazing job, as always," Thomas added. "Yes, we got an engaged audience and some very good questions. I have also been getting emails from them with queries on specific topics. There is a definite buzz around cloud, and the Nimbus team is eager to learn more," Ashish shared his insights.

Over the next 20 minutes, Thomas reviewed the overall session, key questions asked, and other important observations from the session. Amy seemed quite pleased but did throw in a question, "So what is next?" – exactly the question that Thomas was prepared for. "As I see it, we will continue the sessions for Nimbus covering all the aspects including technical architecture, SAP operating model in the cloud, working with SAP data in the cloud, as well as migration options. This should give the Nimbus team enough insights regarding AWS in the context of their SAP modernization. However, we do need to continue to build a relationship with the Nimbus team. The core team in charge of this decision is of course Elizabeth, the CIO; Mark Chapman, Director of IT Infrastructure; Sandeep Krishnan, Vice President of IT Applications; and Nolan Perez, IT Director. Nolan seems to have a more direct engagement with us, and I think it is important we invest time in building a relationship with him as we work toward building with others."

Amy liked Thomas's foresight and added, "While we educate the customer and build a relationship, we also have to be mindful of the competition. Let's take this one step at a time." Ashish knew right away this meant more travel, which of course he did not mind. He of course would be flying Nimbus exclusively.

© Tushar Srivastava 2025
T. Srivastava, *Modernizing SAP with AWS*, https://doi.org/10.1007/979-8-8688-1579-9_5

Meanwhile, Mark was all charged from the meetings with Elizabeth and had a newfound vigor in dealing with the business case for SAP modernization. Having spent his entire career building IT infrastructure, Mark intuitively knew how to build a good foundation that would help the structure last for years. He started his career during the early days of mainframes and had personally laid out cable lines for primitive local networks within Nimbus, trying to emulate what research facilities and universities were doing at that time. Of course, no one imagined at that time that these local networks were precursors to the internet. Mark brought that intuition and discipline to his team and insisted on a strong foundation, often at the cost of speed, a philosophy that sometimes clashed with the approach of the new generation of executives.

Mark was, however, universally respected for his technical thoroughness, and when he got the 'Unsung Champion' award from the then Nimbus CEO, the citation read 'the work done by you and your team is unseen by most, but lets our customer-facing teams sleep better, much like the contribution of soldiers on the frontlines.' The little trophy still found its place of pride in Mark's office after all these years. Having spent all his professional life at Nimbus, it was easy for Mark to secure meetings with internal business stakeholders.

Over the next few days, Mark met with the business unit heads to explain the SAP modernization initiative, but spent more time with the rank and file asking all sorts of questions, looking at how users used the SAP system, and collecting general feedback. Some of the insights in Mark's own words were 'mind-boggling.' For example, a set of users in 'Customer Services' did not use the native reporting capabilities of SAP that were rolled out with a lot of investment; rather, they simply downloaded the data and manipulated it in spreadsheets. The reason was that there was no proper training on the new features. Another aspect that amazed Mark was the innovative thinking displayed by the teams. Mark listed a few new features available in the new S/4HANA system and shared that with the team. Within three days, he received about 40 suggestions of how these new features could make life easier for the teams. Encouraged by this experiment, Mark worked with Sandeep to list out some key new features of S/4HANA and distributed them to the team asking how all these could be adopted and benefit the team. Mark created a structured way of collecting all the feedback and ranked them on priority and benefits. He was then able to create a benefit matrix by the department and by individual team that each of these new features would bring in. After making some assumptions about cost, Mark was able to convert almost all the features into dollar values. Taking an extra step, Mark also documented time and cost spent in the current process and again converted it to a dollar value, getting to a closer picture of 'cost of not changing.'

After days of detailed data collection, review, and scoring of the cost models, Mark had an early draft ready to review with the teams. Based on his learnings from recent days, Mark took a different approach. Instead of meeting just with the business unit heads to review the findings, he invited a select group from the actual teams he had been working with. "Over the past few days, I have been collecting data on how the SAP system is being used by the end-users, what challenges they see in the current processes, and what new features they could benefit from. Even though I am an old-timer at Nimbus, I could not have predicted the kind of insights I received," Mark said even as there were smiles breaking out in the room.

He continued, "I collected data around benefits from new business processes and, importantly, the cost of continuing with the same processes and not changing. When you start adding up all the small and large benefits across teams and across individuals, you slowly start to see the whole elephant," and the screen flashed an animation of an elephant being built out of the jigsaw pieces. "This literally is the elephant in the room, which is currently invisible because we view issues at team levels, rarely at the business unit level, and never at an organization level. But this elephant represents the inefficiencies or rather opportunities that lie in front of us in terms of business improvements if we are to take on the SAP modernization project," concluded Mark. Mark preferred working in the trenches and was never a natural orator; however, the conviction on the backing of data shone through his entire presentation. Mark highlighted the key issues and invited team members to present their specific improvement ideas. By having each business team present their own contributions, the group could better understand how these ideas benefit the team as a whole. The passion in the room was palpable.

Mark's presentation overran by 45 minutes, but everyone stayed glued to their seats. As Mark put out a summary slide with the benefits, costs, and pros–cons, he could see the excitement in the room. "That was awesome, Mark," "Thanks for considering all our feedback," "Best discussion with IT I ever had," and many other congratulatory messages echoed in the room. The usually reserved Mark could not help but sport a beaming smile and took the time to thank everyone as they were leaving the room.

As people milled out of the room, Troy Harris, the head of the Customer Service business unit, came up and gave Mark a hug. "Good to see you after such a long time. And great job. It was evident that you took the pains to dive deep into the issues and come back with substantial findings, and I loved how you backed everything with relevant and easy-to-understand data," Troy shared his observations with Mark. "Good to see you too. It has been what... seven years now? Glad that this presentation was useful," Mark quipped.

Several years ago, when Troy did a stint in IT, he and Mark had been on the same team. "Oh definitely, very useful. And you have full support from my team toward the SAP modernization project. Just let me know how we can help. I am excited and look forward to the benefits," Troy said as a parting note. That evening before shutting down for the day, Mark drafted a succinct email detailing the success of the presentation to the business units and the research work that went into it over the past few days. He addressed it to Elizabeth and Nolan and quickly hit 'Send.' Before shutting down his laptop, he made sure that the email left his 'Outbox.'

While Mark was busy sending out the email, Elizabeth was busy dealing with a 'situation' of her own. "Sophia, dear, I think you should reconsider. You have been doing good in math all through your schooling. Science or business-focused subjects would be good for you, and I think you will do well in those. Why do you want to pick up visual arts?" Elizabeth wanted to know. "Mom, you never trusted my choices, you never wanted me to go to Europe, and now you don't want me to pick subjects of my choice …" Sophia's voice trailed off. "Sweetie, of course, I trust you, but do you trust me? I have been through this and seen what happens when people make wrong choices. You are talking about your career," Elizabeth implored.

The discussion ended without a resolution, with Sophia picking up her phone and heading to her room. "Ben, I can deal with anything at work or in life. I just don't know how to deal with my own daughter. I am just looking out for her and don't want her to make choices that she will regret later. It is just so hard for me to swallow that she would trust her own friends over her mom," Elizabeth sighed to Ben, who was watching rather calmly as the drama unfolded. "She is only in high school, honey. You are taking this too seriously. I am sure she will come around, and anyways, she has your instincts. She is not one to back down!" Ben responded. "Let's get dinner," Ben said, trying to change the topic. "I just don't get it. Why is every conversation turning into a confrontation? Was I like this when I was her age?" Elizabeth just could not let go. She had just lost appetite for dinner.

Nolan re-read Mark's email and could not help smiling. He was early in the office to get focused work done before the start of all his meetings for the day. He knew that Mark's email was a significant progress toward building the business case, and finally Mark had found the right thread to pull to get the business case moving fast in the right direction. Nolan shut down his email application and logged out of 'Slack.' He wanted to work on an important task, essentially the reason why he was in the office at that hour. About 90 minutes later people started streaming into work as Nolan was putting the finishing touches on his task, feeling very satisfied with his work output. Nolan had just coded a prototype application that would let passengers finish their in-flight movies and shows on their personal devices even after the completion of the flight. He would pass on the code to his team to make it 'production ready,' and then it was up to the 'In-Flight Experience' business unit how to roll it out and monetize it. Even though he was in a management role, nothing gave Nolan more satisfaction than getting his hands dirty with code. Nolan knew Elizabeth would want to meet to discuss Mark's mini-success, even though nothing was scheduled on the calendar. He expected to hear from Elizabeth's executive assistant anytime soon.

Sure enough, an unscheduled meeting was underway at Elizabeth's office. A smiling Mark and Nolan were present. Elizabeth seemed a bit preoccupied, so there were moments of awkward silence. Realizing her error and the fact that she had called for this meeting, Elizabeth started off, setting aside her laptop and phone, "Thanks for coming in at short notice. Mark, I read your email, and I am very pleased with the progress. I reviewed your presentation at a high level, and I think the numbers you present support the business case. All the interviews you did with the team and getting ground-level data were very impactful. And I especially loved the idea of letting the individuals come up and talk about the ideas they proposed. You also specifically mentioned how Troy came up to you and shared his support for the modernization initiative. All in all, I think this has been significant progress toward not just the business case but the overall modernization project." "Thanks to your idea," Mark was quick to share credit where it was due.

Elizabeth smiled and nodded in acknowledgment and continued to make a point, "Whenever we talk about a large initiative, we are talking about a significant change, especially for people who use the system on a day-to-day basis. There are a couple of ways to deal with the change. One is top-down where 'we' decide what is best for the business and ask them to adopt. The second is to make the business users a part of the discussion early on and value their opinions. Our biggest phase of this project would be leading the 'change management' with the business users and their buy-in. What you have done, Mark, is beyond just early discussions, but rather 'involve' the user community, by asking them to come up with ideas of how they would use the new system. In a way, you have cleared the path for this significant change, and instead of resisting, the business is actually going to show ownership of this change. I would encourage you to keep the different business unit leaders updated and make Troy your business champion."

Mark nodded in complete agreement, and Nolan who had been watching the proceedings just had an epiphany. This was a brilliant observation from Elizabeth, and he had been getting it wrong all along. He thought of his 'brilliant new app' and realized he had to talk to the business unit first, share the idea, and involve them. He had to make sure they were as excited about this as he was and get buy-in from them – almost make it seem like it was their idea. He immediately slacked his development team not to work on the app just yet. As Mark and Nolan headed out, with key action items, Elizabeth could not help but ponder over this conversation around change management and user involvement. Though she kept work and home separate, she thought maybe she had something to learn from work and apply in her personal life.

It had been a few days since Thomas had the status review meeting. It was an opportune time to follow up on one of his key action items. Thomas pulled out his phone and composed a short text, "Hi, Nolan, it has been a while since we had the AWS workshop. Thought it would be good for us to connect and discuss the future sessions and also grab dinner. Let me know." Thomas was mentally prepared for a few more follow-ups; however, he got a reply ten minutes later. "Sure, that would be great. Yes, we need to plan the next workshop session, and let me know what cuisine are you thinking?" Thomas did not waste a minute. Dinner was set for two days out at where else but Cairati's. Nolan arrived sharp on time at 6 PM on the appointed day and was escorted to the reserved table by the smiling wait staff. Thomas who was already there 15 minutes before the appointed time got up and warmly shook hands.

"Hope it was not a long drive for you, Nolan, and anyways the traffic is sparse around this time."

"Oh yeah, it was fine. I had some early afternoon meetings, so this worked out well. This seems like a pretty nice restaurant. Do you come here often?"

"Yeah, I like this place, and I am a regular here. Glad you liked it. They are an Italian restaurant, but the specialty is Tuscan cuisine. The food will not disappoint you."

Thomas ordered some Tuscan red wine, while Nolan took time to study the menu. Thomas opened up the discussion, "So, Nolan, how long have you been with Nimbus?" "It will be 11 years next month," Nolan responded with a smile. The two warmed up to each other over some great-tasting wine and Italian bread dipped in olive oil with a few laughs and chuckles thrown in. As the main course arrived, Thomas asked casually, "Nolan, what were your impressions from the Immersion Day workshop?" As Nolan served himself some steaming hot Alfredo pasta, he said, "It was actually pretty good. A lot of us were not aware of the basic nuts and bolts of the cloud, so the AWS session was actually very helpful. And your solution architect, Ashish, did an amazing job to lay out the foundation blocks and then build upon that. I am personally a technology geek, and I learned a lot that day." Thomas nodded in agreement, and Nolan continued, "I think we need to get the next session scheduled where we can now get into the specifics of how the cloud can support the SAP modernization project and some key features around SAP on AWS."

"Absolutely, and that is exactly what the next part of the Immersion Day would focus on. We will build upon the foundation elements and focus on how these foundation elements can support the SAP environment and some important tools available from AWS," Thomas responded as he savored the delicious pasta.

The rest of the dinner proceeded uneventfully, with jokes and anecdotes shared. Initially hesitant, but then Nolan ordered desserts on Thomas's insistence. Nolan asked the waiter for some recommendations and went in for the restaurant's signature dessert dish, the tiramisu. "Excellent choice," the waiter smiled and took back the dessert menus. "Oh, by the way, Thomas, a quick update is that we are making some very good progress with the business case. We met with the business unit teams and got some really valuable input. I am expecting us to move fast on this," shared Nolan thinking it would be appropriate to share with Thomas the urgency. "That is good to know. I will work on the dates that we discussed and will plan the next session." The tasty tiramisu was wiped clean, and Thomas left a generous tip. As the valet rolled in Nolan's car, they shared a quick parting "armwrestle"-style handshake and a side hug, much like players would do after a tennis match. Thomas instinctively pulled out his phone and texted Amy, "Great dinner with Nolan. We are building a strong relationship." Amy texted back, "Awesome," with a couple smiley faces, and "I hope you left them a good tip."

The next morning Nolan passed by Elizabeth's office hoping to grab a few minutes of her time. Luckily, she was just getting back from a coffee run and bumped into him. Thankfully, the coffee did not spill. "Sorry, Elizabeth," Nolan started apologizing sheepishly. "Hey, no issues. I should have not been in such a rush," Elizabeth responded, still getting the coffee cup firmly back in her grip (she would not let a perfect cup of her favorite brew go to waste). "I just wanted to let you know that I met Thomas, for dinner, and we had a pretty good discussion. The guy is a good listener and genuinely cares about our project's success. Plus, he has a good nose for some nice Italian food," Nolan reported on his previous evening meeting. "Well, that is good. We need the right partners for this endeavor. What would be our next step with them, Nolan?" Elizabeth was quick not to lose sight of the bigger picture. Nolan was prepared for this and said, "I am glad you asked. We will continue with the workshop sessions. After the success of the first session, I think we will see a lot of benefits from the next set of topics. Secondly, I let him know about our progress on the business case, and at the right time, I will ask Thomas to work with Mark, to add the AWS perspective to the business case."

"Awesome, Nolan. That is some great foresight."

"Thanks, Elizabeth, and talking of the business case, I wanted to remind you that you need to talk to the folks at SAP also, to review timelines and, most importantly, talk about the new licensing terms that they proposed," Nolan added, knowing that this had been pending with Elizabeth for a while. "Well, yes, I really don't like negotiations, but I guess I can't push it out much longer," Elizabeth said with a roll of her eyes.

Meanwhile, Thomas called Ashish the next day asking him to plan his travel soon. "The meeting with Nolan was great. We have to get ready for the next session of our workshop. I will email the dates out to you, and remember, we are now getting into the nuts and bolts of SAP on AWS, which means we have to spend extra time on some key concepts," Thomas said thoughtfully. "Yes, I know. I am already working on the right content to present and some tailor-made hands-on workshops. I have been getting email queries already from the participants, and I have incorporated some of their requests into the next session." Ashish was already ahead of the game.

Across the town, as Elizabeth was wrapping up her day, she quickly called her executive assistant asking to confirm a meeting with SAP to 'discuss license terms for the S/4HANA modernization' project. "Apart from Andrew, our SAP account executive, please also ask for Steve Clark, their senior vice president, to also participate. I have known Steve for a while, and I think it will be very valuable for him to join the discussion. Oh, remember, let's have the meeting at SAP's office and not here."

The meeting with SAP was secured quickly. Being one of SAP's largest customers and the fact that they were actively looking to modernize to S/4HANA, it was an easy task. On the day of the meeting, Elizabeth tagged along with Nimbus's Director of IT Procurement given the strategic nature of these conversations. They were welcomed warmly by Andrew Grant. As they made their way to the small conference room, Elizabeth stopped by the fancy coffee machine to brew herself some dark roast. Settling into the conference room, Elizabeth looked around. A lot of posters of successful SAP customers lined the walls. Apart from Andrew, there were a couple of other SAP employees, with specific roles to play in the licensing discussion. The team was engaging in small talk, but Steve Clark was still not around.

"I will look for Steve. I did see him in the morning though," an anxious Andrew offered. As he was heading out, Steve came rushing in taking his earphones out and placing them in its case. "Sorry, everyone. I was just on a call that kept going over," Steve offered as an apology. He immediately made his way to Elizabeth, and the two exchanged a hug and a huge smile. Steve had worked with Elizabeth a long time ago when he was covering Nimbus as an account executive and she was an up-and-coming executive in the IT ranks.

*"It is always nice to see the Nimbus team coming over to the SAP office once in a while,"
chuckled Steve. "I think we should visit more often, Steve; I don't see a Nimbus in any of
your customer posters on the walls. I guess we are not big enough for you guys," Elizabeth
joked. She had fired her first salvo even before the negotiations had started. "Hey, Liz, you
are our biggest customer, and we don't need a wall poster for that. Everyone knows that,"
Steve cracked a joke of his own.*

*As the discussions progressed, Andrew offered, "I can have the team now run us
through a slide deck on the benefits of S/4HANA and …" "Sorry for cutting you off, but
if we were looking to understand benefits, then the CIO and procurement team from
Nimbus would not be here. We have done our research, and today we want to talk about
how SAP is in the cockpit with us and not a passenger in first class," Elizabeth cut off
Andrew while offering an aviation analogy. Steve chuckled. She continued, "My team is
building a business case, and we have done our best to convert the benefits of S/4HANA
into dollar benefits for our business users. Remember, this is going to be a long journey
for Nimbus, and we would like SAP to be a part of this. I am looking for SAP to invest
in this transformation. Both in terms of effort to help us succeed and in terms of the
best financial model that will ensure that the business case is justified. We have still not
crossed the financial hurdle, and I have meetings coming up with our stakeholders to
discuss." Steve was looking for an opening and here it was. "Of course, we are committed
to your success since Nimbus is a strategic customer of SAP. We did share an initial cost
estimate for new licensing, and I hope Nimbus has reviewed it." "Yes, we did," the Nimbus
procurement director responded dryly. Over the next hour or so, both parties laid out their
case in trying to reach a common agreement. Andrew's phone buzzed with a message, and
he proclaimed, "Lunch is delivered." A break that everyone was thankful for. Everyone
lingered out for a break and to dig into lunch.*

*Steve and Elizabeth were on a corner spot savoring the lunch. "Steve, we have known
each other for a while. I trust you will work on getting Nimbus the right pricing. I will
be happy to do as many case studies and marketing events based on the success of our
program," Elizabeth said, offering an olive branch. "Hey, Liz, for sure. I appreciate the
offer. Nimbus is way too important for us to let fail. I will work with Andrew and our other
teams, and we can see what we can do to make sure that we are meeting your financial
goals," Steve said enthusiastically. "I truly appreciate that," Elizabeth thanked Steve as she
wrapped up lunch. Her dessert was left untouched. The rest of the meeting went on without
much fuss. Some key data points and next steps were discussed. As Elizabeth was getting
back into her car, she texted Steve saying, "Thank you, Steve. This was very helpful, and I
look forward to your support." Steve replied with a "thumbs-up" emoji.*

Soon the appointed day came again. Thomas and Ashish were back at the Nimbus office in the same large conference room. By now they were quite familiar with the Nimbus office even knowing where exactly the better coffee machine was. Ashish was busy with the rigmarole of getting his laptop connected to the screen and the Wi-Fi network, making sure everything worked. Familiar faces were pouring into the room, stopping to say hello and exchanging a few words. Nolan walked in "high-fiving" Thomas. "Nice to see you back here. I hope you have some good content today. Ashish set a very high bar last time. Just saying …" Nolan joked. "You bet," Thomas quipped.

Mark and Sandeep came in too and occupied pretty much the same seats they did last time. Without wasting time, Thomas took center stage and said, "Hello, glad to see everyone back. I hope you are as interactive as you were last time. Last time the session was foundational, dealing with the elements of the AWS cloud. In this session, we will cover designing the AWS infrastructure, including compute, network, storage, etc., specifically for SAP. And now I turn it over to the most knowledgeable person on this topic in the room, Ashish. No one wants to listen to me, the second most knowledgeable person on this topic in this room." There was some mild laughter in the room as Thomas sprinted back to his seat. Maybe stand-up comedy when I retire, *he smiled at his own thought. Ashish took the stage and quickly clicked forward to the agenda for the session. Soon, the room fell silent. Ashish had the audience totally tuned in.*

Introducing RISE with SAP

Before going into the design of SAP architecture on AWS, it would be good to review RISE with SAP. **RISE with SAP** was officially launched by SAP on **January 27, 2021**, as a strategic initiative to help businesses accelerate their digital transformation journey and move to the cloud. The offering emerged in response to several evolving market needs: a growing urgency for business resilience, rising interest in cloud adoption, and the complexity many customers faced in transitioning to SAP S/4HANA and modernizing legacy systems. Before RISE, customers typically had to manage multiple contracts across different vendors – for infrastructure, ERP software, managed services, and business process tools – leading to fragmented responsibilities, higher costs, and longer implementation times. There was also no unified framework for analyzing, optimizing, and transforming business processes. SAP recognized the need for a simplified, holistic transformation as a service offering that could reduce complexity, bundle tools and services into a single subscription, support a modular, scalable cloud transformation path, and enable businesses to become 'intelligent enterprises.'

RISE with SAP is a comprehensive, subscription-based offering introduced by SAP to help businesses transform into intelligent, cloud-enabled enterprises. It bundles together the essential components required for digital transformation – offering business process intelligence, cloud infrastructure, platform services, and SAP-managed services – all under a single contract. The aim is to simplify the journey to SAP S/4HANA Cloud while reducing complexity, cost, and time.

Key Components of RISE with SAP

- **SAP S/4HANA Cloud**

    - The core of RISE with SAP is SAP S/4HANA Cloud, which provides next-generation ERP capabilities with built-in AI, machine learning, and advanced analytics.

    - It supports both **public** and **private cloud** deployment models to fit varying customer requirements for flexibility, customization, and control.

- **Business Process Intelligence (BPI)**

    - RISE includes tools such as **SAP Signavio** for analyzing and optimizing business processes.

    - It helps customers benchmark, visualize, and continuously improve their operations by identifying inefficiencies and recommending automation or redesign.

- **SAP Business Technology Platform (SAP BTP)**

    - SAP BTP provides a unified platform for data management, analytics, application development, and integration.

    - Customers can extend SAP applications, build custom apps, or integrate third-party systems in a secure and scalable way.

- **Embedded Tools and Services**

    - Includes tools for lifecycle management such as **SAP Readiness Check**, **Custom Code Migration**, and **SAP Cloud ALM**.

    - Customers get access to SAP's **lifecycle management** and **cloud operations services**, including patching, updates, and backups.

- **SAP Business Network Starter Pack**

  - Enables basic connectivity to the **SAP Business Network** (Ariba, Asset Intelligence Network, Logistics Business Network), enhancing supply chain visibility and collaboration.

Benefits of RISE with SAP

- **Simplified Contracting**: One contract for software, infrastructure, and managed services from SAP, reducing procurement and negotiation complexity.

- **Accelerated Transformation**: Tools and services bundled to speed up the move to SAP S/4HANA Cloud.

- **Lower Total Cost of Ownership (TCO)**: Subscription-based pricing, optimized infrastructure usage, and managed services reduce the burden of up-front investment and operational costs.

- **Business Agility**: Ability to adopt innovations rapidly, scale as needed, and respond to market demands with cloud-native flexibility.

- **End-to-End Responsibility**: SAP acts as a single point of accountability, covering software, SLAs, cloud infrastructure, and technical operations.

RISE with SAP + AWS

In partnership with AWS, SAP provides a jointly engineered and validated infrastructure environment that meets the performance, compliance, and security needs of enterprise SAP workloads. Key integrations include

- **SAP-certified AWS instances for HANA and S/4HANA**

- **High-performance storage and networking**

- **AWS security and compliance services**

- **Automation through AWS Launch Wizard and AWS Systems Manager**

This partnership ensures that SAP customers benefit from the global scale, resilience, and innovation of AWS while enjoying SAP's end-to-end managed experience.

RISE with SAP is not just a technology upgrade – it's a business transformation offering. By combining cloud ERP, platform services, business process insights, and cloud infrastructure, RISE empowers companies to modernize their operations, become more agile, and embrace a future-ready digital foundation, all managed under a single SAP-led agreement.

Designing SAP Architecture on AWS

AWS provides the infrastructure to run SAP workloads. In order to achieve the optimized and secure architecture that meets the needs of SAP, a lot of thought needs to be given to various choices and options that the customer has. Of all the AWS services available, the core services relevant for an SAP deployment are compute, storage, networking, operations management, security, identity, and compliance. Customers use a self-service model (managed by either the customer or a partner) to deploy AWS resources and services. While AWS manages its own global infrastructure, the customer (or partner) is responsible for managing everything above that. This includes infrastructure services like operating system administration, patching, backup, recovery, network security, and monitoring. It also includes SAP hosting services like SAP Basis administration, SAP installation, operation, SAP upgrades/patching, and SAP monitoring.

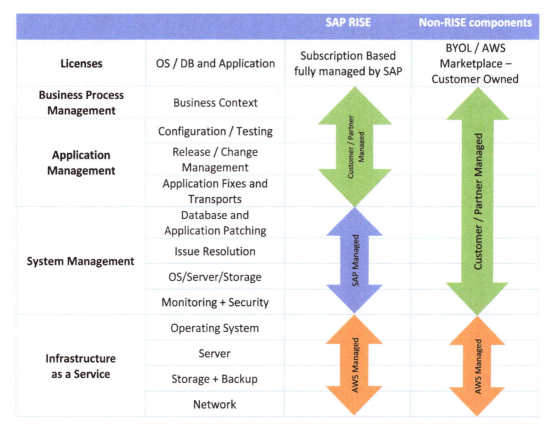

Figure 5-1. SAP on AWS Responsibility Matrix

Let's delve into the key topics as below.

Foundational Considerations

Even before getting into the architecture design, there are a few planning considerations that need to be reviewed. Primary among them are discussed below:

- **Licenses**: Most SAP solutions available on AWS operate under a model where you **bring your own software and license** (**BYOL**). You don't need unique or additional SAP licenses to run SAP systems on AWS. If you already have SAP licenses, you can utilize them for SAP on AWS. It's your responsibility to secure a valid SAP license and to ensure compliance with SAP's licensing policies. AWS does not offer or sell SAP licenses.

- **Deployment**: The deployment of SAP solutions on AWS can be done in one of the following three ways:

  - **Manual Deployment**: The most basic option where the solution can be set up by first manually setting up the necessary AWS infrastructure resources and then adhering to the appropriate SAP installation guide for AWS.

  - **Automated Deployment**: AWS provides a tool, "AWS Launch Wizard for SAP," that can be used for automated provisioning of AWS infrastructure for SAP. The user has to input the SAP HANA settings, SAP landscape settings, and deployment details on the console, and Launch Wizard identifies the appropriate AWS resources to deploy and run the SAP application.

  - **Prebuilt Images**: Certain SAP solutions on AWS come as ready-made system images, featuring a preinstalled and preconfigured SAP system. These prebuilt SAP system images allow for quick deployment of a new SAP system, saving the time and effort typically needed for a manual SAP installation. The prebuilt images are available from SAP **CAL** (**Cloud Appliance Library**). The SAP CAL offers access to an online collection of the most recent preconfigured SAP solutions. Many of the solutions in the SAP Cloud Appliance Library come with complimentary trial or developer edition licenses.

- **Choosing a Region and Availability Zone**: Choosing the right region for deploying SAP on AWS involves several considerations:

  - **Proximity to Users**: Select a region closest to the majority of your SAP system users to reduce latency. This ensures faster response times and better performance.

  - **Compliance and Data Residency Requirements**: Consider legal and regulatory requirements related to data residency and privacy. Some regions may be more suitable than others depending on these requirements.

  - **Availability and Service Options**: Not all AWS regions offer the same services. Ensure the region you choose supports all the AWS services you plan to use with your SAP deployment.

- **Network Performance**: Analyze the network performance between your users, other dependent systems, and the AWS region. Good network performance is crucial for SAP systems.

- **Cost Considerations**: Pricing can vary between regions. Consider the cost implications of running services in different regions and choose accordingly.

- **Resource Availability**: Some regions may have limitations on resource availability (like specific EC2 instances). Ensure the region you select can accommodate your resource requirements.

- **Long-Term Strategy**: Align your choice with your organization's long-term IT and business strategy, including expansion plans, which might influence future region selection.

It's advisable to conduct a thorough assessment considering these factors and possibly consult with AWS support or a consultant specializing in AWS infrastructure for a more tailored recommendation.

As for the Availability Zone within a region, no specific technical considerations are required when choosing an AZ for running SAP. The only guidance is that all SAP applications and systems should be deployed in the same AZ.

- **Architecture Patterns**: The "**SAP All on AWS**" architecture refers to a comprehensive setup where all components of an SAP landscape are deployed and managed on the AWS cloud platform. This architecture leverages the cloud capabilities of AWS to provide scalability, flexibility, and robustness for SAP environments. The "**Hybrid AWS Architecture for SAP**" refers to a computing environment where an organization's SAP systems are distributed across both the AWS cloud and on-premises data centers. This architecture is designed to leverage the benefits of both cloud and on-premises environments, offering flexibility, scalability, and the ability to meet diverse operational and compliance requirements. This architecture is useful for running trials, training, **proof of concept** (**PoC**), non-production landscapes, and other scenarios. A comparison of the two architectures is shown in Table 5-1.

Table 5-1. *All on AWS vs. Hybrid Architecture Comparison*

Parameter	All on AWS	Hybrid
Deployment	In this architecture, all SAP components and related systems are fully hosted and managed on AWS.	Mixes AWS cloud resources with on-premises data centers. SAP systems are distributed across both environments.
Complexity	Since everything is on AWS, there's uniformity in technologies and platforms used, which can simplify management and operations.	Generally, more complex to manage due to the coexistence of cloud and on-premises resources, requiring synchronization and integration.
Scalability and flexibility	Leveraging AWS's vast resources, it offers significant scalability and flexibility, especially useful for fluctuating workloads.	While it provides scalability, it's limited by the on-premises infrastructure's capacity. Useful for meeting data residency requirements or when certain data or applications need to remain on-premises.
High availability and disaster recovery	Utilizes AWS's global infrastructure, ensuring high availability and effective disaster recovery solutions.	Can be achieved but requires more intricate planning and implementation across both cloud and on-premises environments.
Security	Benefits from AWS's robust security model.	Needs a comprehensive approach that covers both cloud and on-premises infrastructures, often leading to more complex security management.
Integration	Easier integration with other AWS services and solutions.	Integrating cloud services with on-premises systems can be challenging and might require additional tools or middleware.
Use cases	Ideal for organizations looking to fully migrate to the cloud, startups, or businesses without significant existing on-premises infrastructure.	Suited for organizations with significant existing on-premises investments, those with specific compliance or data residency requirements, or those adopting a phased approach to cloud migration.

Network and Connectivity

Network and connectivity are very important design considerations for hosting SAP on AWS. The sections below cover them in detail.

Network

As noted previously in *Chapter* 1, *Amazon VPC (Virtual Private Cloud)* enables the user to create a virtual network that is uniquely yours, situated within the AWS cloud. This virtual network is essentially your private section within AWS, where you can deploy AWS resources. It mirrors the functionality of a conventional network in your own data center while leveraging AWS's scalable infrastructure. In your VPC, you have the flexibility to choose IP address ranges, set up subnets, and define route tables, network gateways, and security configurations. It's possible to link instances in your VPC to the internet, as well as integrate your VPC with your corporate data center, effectively extending your data center into the AWS cloud. For enhanced security in each subnet, you can implement various layers of protection, such as security groups and network access control lists. Specifically for SAP applications, there are recommended subnet zoning patterns within VPC.

To determine the appropriate subnet for an application, it's crucial to understand its accessibility requirements. Here are various access scenarios for SAP applications:

- **Internal-Only Access**: Applications in this category are strictly accessed within the organization. External access is not permitted, except by SAP support teams. In order to access these applications, the user is required to be on the corporate network, either directly or through a VPN. Applications like SAP Enterprise Resource Planning (ERP), SAP S/4HANA, SAP Business Warehouse (BW), and SAP BW/4HANA typically fall under this category, necessitating internal-only access in most organizations.

- **Internal and Controlled External Access**: These applications are primarily accessed internally, but limited external access is granted to pre-approved external entities. For instance, SAP **Process Integration** (**PI**) or SAP **Process Orchestration** (**PO**) might be accessible from internal networks, while select external parties might have access from pre-authorized IPs. Integration with external SaaS solutions, such as SAP SuccessFactors and SAP Ariba, is often included to enhance the functionality of SAP solutions on AWS.

- **Internal and Uncontrolled External Access**: Applications like SAP Hybris (Commerce Cloud) or an externally oriented SAP Enterprise Portal belong to this group. While they are mostly publicly accessible, certain components are reserved for internal use only, like those for administration, configuration, and integration with other in-house applications.

Based on the above access patterns, the subnet zones and network architecture can be designed as per the below recommendation:

- **Internal-Only Access**: For this set of applications, it is recommended to create three (or four) subnets as below:

  - **Public Subnet**: This subnet is to place the SAP Router and the NAT gateway. The SAP Router is a software used by SAP that provides a remote connection between the customer's network and SAP. This is primarily used by the SAP support team to access the customer's SAP system in case of troubleshooting an issue raised by a customer. The NAT gateway is a Network Address Translation service. The NAT gateway helps applications in the private subnet (see below) access the internet.

  - **Management Private Subnet**: Management and administration tools like jump hosts are placed in this subnet. These applications are not accessed by end users directly but are used by system and network administrators to provide support to end users. These applications, though placed in a private subnet, can still access the internet via the NAT gateway that is placed in the public subnet (above).

  - **Apps and Database Private Subnet**: Finally, the SAP application and databases are placed in this subnet, and the end users can access the application using SAP GUI or via HTTP(S) request to the SAP Web Dispatcher (a software web switch that can either accept or reject a connection). A fourth private subnet can be created to store just the database to provide an additional layer of protection by means of separate route tables and network ACLs.

- **Controlled External Access**: SAP **PI/PO (Process Integration/ Process Orchestration)** is a middleware tool provided by SAP for integration between SAP and non-SAP applications. This is a good example of controlled external access. There are two primary options for controlled external access:

  - **VPN**: A VPN (virtual private network) connection can be established between trusted external parties and AWS (where SAP is hosted), by means of either VGW (virtual private gateway) or a software VPN server placed in a public subnet. The method allows both ingress and egress network traffic.

  - **ELB and NAT Gateway**: ELB (Elastic Load Balancing) is an AWS service that automatically distributes incoming application traffic across multiple targets and virtual appliances in one or more Availability Zones. Either the Network Load Balancer (NLB) or Application Load Balancer (ALB) can be used for ingress network traffic. The NLB operates at the "layer 4" of the OSI (Open Systems Interconnection) model, making it ideal to distribute the TCP traffic, while the ALB operates at "layer 7" making it an ideal choice for HTTP or HTTPS traffic. For egress, NAT gateways can be deployed.

  - **Other Options**: NAT devices and reverse proxies can be other alternatives; however, the ELB option is recommended since it is a managed service, but these would need the overhead of managing.

- **Uncontrolled External Access**: In some cases, external users need access to SAP systems without a VPN, for instance, Fiori applications, SAP Enterprise Portal, etc. The traffic is usually limited to HTTP/ HTTPS. In this case, an **ALB (Application Load Balancer)** placed in a public subnet can be used as the entry point for the network request, and the ALB sends a request to the SAP Web Dispatcher. AWS Shield and AWS WAF (Web Application Firewall) are also deployed to protect from web exploits including DDoS (Distributed Denial of Service).

Subnets are not the only way to separate applications. Applications can also be restricted by placing them in different VPCs altogether. In that case, the network area (VPC and subnet) hosting the application components is defined as a "network zone." Typical zones are "Restricted Zone," Intranet Zone, Management Zone, Extranet Zone, External Zone, and Internet Zone. It is not recommended to split closely related components across different VPCs. The various VPCs can be connected via VPC peering.

In all cases, security groups, network access control lists, and route tables can be deployed to set up specific access control as needed per business requirements.

Connectivity

While the easiest way to provide access to end users to SAP systems on AWS is by placing the SAP system in a single VPC with a single public subnet and an internet gateway to enable communication, it is not a practical or recommended approach. More robust and scalable solutions exist as follows.

Site-to-Site/Hardware VPN

A **hardware VPN for SAP** on AWS refers to a physical device that provides a secure and encrypted connection between your on-premises network and your AWS infrastructure, specifically for your SAP applications. This setup is particularly relevant when deploying SAP systems in an AWS environment. The hardware VPN is a physical piece of equipment, like a VPN concentrator or a router with VPN capabilities, installed in your data center and creates an encrypted tunnel between your on-premises network and the VPC where your SAP systems are hosted. The VPN device can be configured with the necessary settings (like IP addresses, encryption standards, and authentication details) to establish a secure connection to AWS. AWS offers a VPN service that integrates with your hardware VPN providing the other end of the tunnel in the AWS environment.

Key Benefits of a Hardware VPN:

- **Security**: Provides a high level of security by encrypting data in transit between your on-premises SAP environment and AWS, which is crucial for sensitive business data handled by SAP systems.

- **Reliability**: Hardware VPNs are often more reliable for consistent network performance compared with software VPNs, which is important for mission-critical SAP applications.

- **Control**: Allows more control over the network infrastructure, which can be important for compliance with specific industry regulations.

- **Consistent Performance**: Offers more consistent network performance and lower latency compared with internet-based connections, which is beneficial for high-throughput SAP applications.

- **Scalability**: While it is a physical setup, it can be scaled as per your organization's requirements in tandem with AWS's scalable infrastructure.

Considerations:

- **Cost and Maintenance**: Hardware VPNs involve additional costs for the physical device and its maintenance.

- **Setup Complexity**: Setting up a hardware VPN can be more complex compared with a software-based solution.

- **Scalability Limits**: While scalable, there are limits compared with fully cloud-based solutions, especially in terms of rapid scaling up or down.

AWS Client VPN

AWS Client VPN is a managed client-based VPN service that enables secure access to AWS resources and on-premises networks. When used in the context of SAP on AWS, it allows users to securely connect to SAP applications hosted on AWS from any location. Unlike a hardware VPN that connects entire networks, an AWS Client VPN connects individual clients (like laptops or mobile devices) to the AWS network. It establishes a secure TLS connection from any location to the AWS network, which provides access to AWS resources and, if configured, to on-premises networks.

AWS Client VPN integrates with various authentication methods (like Active Directory, SAML 2.0, and mutual authentication) and allows fine-grained authorization control. You configure a Client VPN endpoint in your VPC and associate it with subnets in your VPC, and users can connect to the Client VPN endpoint to access SAP systems. It works with OpenVPN-based clients, which are available for a wide range of devices and operating systems.

Benefits of AWS Client VPN for SAP on AWS:

- **Remote Access**: Enables secure and easy remote access to SAP systems hosted on AWS, which is vital for users who need to access these systems from various locations.

- **Security**: Offers a high level of security by encrypting the data in transit, which is essential for protecting sensitive SAP data.

- **Scalability and Flexibility**: Being a managed service, AWS Client VPN scales automatically to accommodate user demand and allows flexibility in access control.

- **Ease of Management**: As a managed service, it reduces the overhead of managing the underlying infrastructure and is integrated with AWS management tools for monitoring and logging.

- **Global Reach**: Users can connect to SAP systems from any location, making it suitable for global teams and remote workers.

Use Cases for SAP:

- **Remote Work**: Particularly useful for remote workers who need to securely access SAP systems

- **Global Teams**: Beneficial for teams spread across different geographies needing access to a centralized SAP system on AWS

- **Business Partners and Contractors**: Allows secure access for external parties who require temporary access to the SAP environment

Considerations:

- **Client Software**: Requires users to install VPN client software.

- **Costs**: There are costs associated with the use of AWS Client VPN, based on the number of connections and the amount of data transferred.

AWS Direct Connect

AWS Direct Connect is a cloud service solution that allows you to establish a dedicated network connection between your on-premises infrastructure and AWS. When used for SAP on AWS, it facilitates a more reliable, consistent, and high-capacity network connection for running SAP applications. AWS Direct Connect provides a dedicated network link from your premises (data center, office, or colocation environment) to AWS. This connection bypasses the public internet, offering a more private and consistent network experience, and supports high-bandwidth capacities, which can be crucial for data-intensive SAP applications. Overall, Direct Connect can reduce network costs, increase bandwidth throughput, and provide a more consistent network experience than internet-based connections. Setup of Direct Connect involves working with an AWS Direct Connect partner to establish the connection.

Benefits of AWS Direct Connect for SAP on AWS:

- **Performance**: Offers lower latency and higher throughput, which is beneficial for performance-intensive SAP applications

- **Reliability**: Provides more reliable and consistent network performance compared with typical internet connections, crucial for enterprise-grade SAP solutions

- **Security**: Enhances security by providing a private, dedicated network connection, which is essential for handling sensitive business data in SAP systems

- **Cost-Effectiveness**: Potentially more cost-effective than internet-based connections for large volumes of data transfer

- **Scalability**: Easily scales with your business needs, allowing you to increase or decrease bandwidth as required

Use Cases for SAP:

- **Large Data Transfers**: Ideal for scenarios with large data transfers between on-premises environments and AWS, such as SAP HANA migrations or data warehousing

- **Hybrid Environments**: Suitable for hybrid cloud environments where SAP systems are distributed across on-premises data centers and AWS

- **Business Continuity**: Ensures a stable and reliable connection for business continuity and disaster recovery scenarios

- **Compliance and Security**: Useful for organizations with strict regulatory compliance requirements for data privacy and security

Considerations:

- **Setup and Maintenance**: Requires initial setup and ongoing maintenance of the physical connection

- **Costs**: Involves costs for the dedicated connection, which may vary based on the required capacity and distance

AWS Direct Connect offers a high-performance, reliable, and secure connectivity option for SAP on AWS, especially suitable for enterprises with large-scale SAP deployments, significant data transfer needs, and strict compliance requirements. It provides an alternative to traditional internet connections, emphasizing lower latency, higher throughput, and enhanced security for critical SAP workloads.

Compute

The role of compute in cloud computing is central and multifunctional. Compute resources in the cloud refer to the processing power provided by virtualized servers or physical servers made available over the internet. Compared with the traditional model of on-premises compute hardware, the key roles and benefits of compute in cloud computing are

- **Scalability**: Cloud computing offers unparalleled scalability. You can easily scale computing resources up or down based on demand. This flexibility is crucial for handling varying workloads, like sudden traffic spikes or scaling down during off-peak times.

- **Cost-Effectiveness**: With cloud computing, you typically pay only for the compute resources you use. This can be more cost-effective compared with maintaining an in-house data center, where you have to invest in hardware that may not be used to its full capacity.

- **Elasticity**: Cloud compute resources can be quickly provisioned and released, providing elasticity. This means that resources can be dynamically allocated to match the demand without the need for up-front investment in infrastructure.

- **Performance**: Cloud providers invest in the latest, high-performing computing hardware, which means you can benefit from the latest technologies without having to constantly upgrade your own hardware.

- **Global Reach**: Cloud providers have data centers worldwide, allowing you to deploy applications close to your users. This reduces latency and improves the performance of your applications.

- **Diverse Offerings**: Cloud providers offer a variety of compute options, from virtual machines with different capabilities (CPU, memory, storage) to serverless computing where you don't need to manage the underlying servers.

- **Focus on Core Business**: By using cloud compute resources, companies can focus on their core business activities without the hassle of managing IT infrastructure. This is particularly beneficial for small- to medium-sized businesses.

- **Disaster Recovery and Redundancy**: Cloud computing provides tools for backup, disaster recovery, and redundancy. This ensures business continuity even in the event of hardware failures or other disruptions.

- **Innovation and Speed**: Cloud computing enables faster development and deployment of applications. Organizations can quickly set up and dismantle test and development environments, leading to faster innovation.

- **Security**: Although cloud security is a shared responsibility, cloud providers typically offer a high level of security for their compute resources, including physical security, network security, and operational security measures.

In essence, compute in cloud computing provides a flexible, scalable, and efficient way to handle computing tasks, enabling organizations to adapt quickly to changing needs, reduce costs, and focus on strategic work rather than on managing IT infrastructure.

Compute Offering from AWS

AWS offers a wide range of compute services to meet the diverse needs of its users. These services can be broadly categorized into three main types:

- **Virtual Machines**:

  - **Amazon EC2 (Elastic Compute Cloud)**: The most popular AWS compute service, EC2 allows you to launch virtual machines (instances) with various configurations of CPU, memory, storage, and networking resources. You can choose from a wide variety of instance types, including general-purpose, compute-optimized, memory-optimized, and storage-optimized instances.

  - **Amazon Lightsail**: This is a simpler and more affordable alternative to EC2 for running small web applications and static websites.

  - **AWS App Runner**: This is a service for deploying and managing web applications in containers without having to manage the underlying infrastructure.

- **Serverless Computing**:

  - **AWS Lambda**: A serverless compute service that lets you run code without having to provision or manage servers. You simply upload your code, and Lambda takes care of running it in response to events.

  - **AWS Fargate**: A container orchestration service that allows you to run Docker containers without having to manage a container cluster. Fargate works seamlessly with AWS Lambda for running event-driven containerized applications.

- **Batch Computing**:

  - **AWS Batch**: A service for running large-scale batch jobs on a managed compute infrastructure. Batch is ideal for running scientific simulations, data analysis, and other computationally intensive workloads.

  - **AWS Elastic Beanstalk**: A service for deploying and managing web applications in the cloud. Elastic Beanstalk automates many of the tasks involved in deploying and managing applications, such as provisioning servers, configuring software, and scaling resources.

Additional EC2 Services:

- **Amazon EC2 Auto-scaling**: Automatically scales your EC2 instances up or down based on demand

- **Amazon EC2 Image Builder**: Creates and manages custom Amazon Machine Images (AMIs) for use with EC2

- **Amazon Linux**: A free and open source operating system for use with EC2

Instance Naming Convention: Since AWS offers a variety of EC2 instances, they are named with a unique naming format allowing for easy identification. This convention typically consists of a combination of letters and numbers, each part signifying specific attributes of the instance. Here's a breakdown of the naming convention:

- **Instance Family**: The first part of the name, consisting of letters, indicates the instance family. Each family is optimized for specific types of workloads, for example:

  - **c**: Compute optimized

  - **d**: Dense storage

  - **f**: FPGA

  - **g**: Graphics intensive

  - **hpc**: High-performance computing

- **i**: Storage optimized

- **im**: Storage optimized with a one to four ratio of vCPU to memory

- **is**: Storage optimized with a one to six ratio of vCPU to memory

- **inf**: AWS Inferentia

- **m**: General purpose

- **mac**: macOS

- **p**: GPU accelerated

- **r**: Memory optimized

- **t**: Burstable performance

- **trn**: AWS Trainium

- **u**: High memory

- **vt**: Video transcoding

- **x**: Memory intensive

- **Generation Number**: The number following the instance family letter indicates the generation of the instance. For instance, m5 is the fifth generation of the m (general-purpose) family.

- **Processor Family**: The letter following the generation number indicates the processor family:

  - **a**: AMD processors

  - **g**: AWS Graviton processors

  - **i**: Intel processors

- **Additional Qualifiers**:

  - **d**: Instance store volumes

  - **n**: Network and EBS optimized

  - **e**: Extra storage or memory

- **z**: High performance

- **q**: Qualcomm inference accelerators

- **flex**: Flex instance

- **Size**: The size of the instance (like large, xlarge, 2xlarge, etc.) indicates the scale of resources allocated to the instance. For example, large usually signifies a baseline level of resources for the family, xlarge is a step-up, 2xlarge is larger still, and so on. This size typically correlates with factors like the number of vCPUs, amount of RAM, and network performance.

- **Specialized Instances**: Some instances have unique naming conventions to reflect their specialized nature, for example:

  - **High-Memory Instances**: Names like u-6tb1.metal indicate ultra-high-memory instances (u), with 6tb indicating the memory capacity and metal indicating a bare metal instance.

So, to illustrate, an instance named **c7gn.xlarge** indicates a "compute optimized, seventh-generation, Graviton processor, network- and EBS-optimized, xlarge" instance.

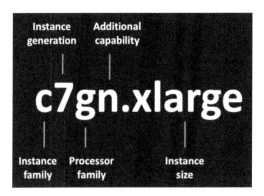

Figure 5-2. *Instance Naming Convention*

Compute in the Context of SAP

The role of compute in SAP systems is crucial and multifaceted. Compute, in this context, refers to the processing power required to run SAP applications and handle the data they manage. Here are some key aspects of how compute plays a role in SAP systems:

144

- **Data Processing**: SAP systems handle large volumes of data, including transactional data, analytical data, and more. The compute resources ensure that this data is processed efficiently, allowing for real-time analytics and quick transaction processing.

- **Performance and Scalability**: The compute power determines the performance of the SAP system. It needs to be scalable to handle varying loads, which can fluctuate based on the number of users, the complexity of tasks, and other factors. High compute capacity ensures that the system performs well even under heavy loads.

- **Integration and Communication**: SAP systems often need to integrate with other systems and applications. Adequate compute resources are necessary to manage these integrations smoothly, ensuring seamless data exchange and communication.

- **Support for Advanced Technologies**: Modern SAP systems leverage advanced technologies like machine learning, artificial intelligence, and IoT. These technologies require significant compute power to function effectively.

- **System Reliability and Uptime**: Adequate compute resources contribute to the overall reliability and uptime of SAP systems. This is critical for businesses that rely on SAP for their core operations.

- **Backup and Recovery**: Compute resources are also important for backup and recovery operations. They ensure that these processes are completed swiftly to minimize downtime in case of system failures.

- **Upgrades and Maintenance**: Regular upgrades and maintenance of SAP systems require compute resources to implement changes without affecting the system performance.

In summary, compute resources in SAP systems are fundamental for ensuring that the system runs efficiently, scales effectively, and supports the advanced functionalities that modern businesses require.

Another important parameter in the context of compute selection for SAP is SAPS. In order to help customers run SAP systems on optimized and performant hardware, SAP has defined **SAP Application Performance Standard (SAPS)**, a hardware-independent unit of measurement used to describe the performance of a system configuration. It essentially helps quantify the workload a system can handle based on its CPU, memory, and other resources. SAPS is derived from the Sales and Distribution (SD) benchmark, where 100 SAPS is defined as processing 2,000 fully business-processed order line items per hour. SAPS is an important measure that helps compare performance across different hardware platforms, enables sizing and planning for SAP implementations, and provides a basis for capacity planning and resource allocation.

Compute Offerings for SAP on AWS

In the context of designing the SAP on AWS architecture, it is important to select the right compute instances. Though AWS offers a variety of compute options, in the context of SAP, Amazon **EC2 (Elastic Compute Cloud)** is the relevant service. While these virtual machines with EC2 have many components, the core components relevant for SAP architecture are

- **Central Processing Unit (CPU)**: The CPU, often referred to as the processor, is the primary component responsible for executing instructions and processing data. It performs the basic arithmetical, logical, and input/output operations of the system. CPUs come with varying numbers of cores and threads, impacting their ability to perform parallel processing. Higher clock speeds and advanced architectures enhance performance.

- **Memory (RAM)**: Random-access memory (RAM) is used to store data that is actively being worked on as a temporary storage that allows data to be accessed quickly by the CPU. RAM is volatile, meaning its contents are lost when the power is turned off. The amount of RAM influences a system's ability to handle multiple tasks simultaneously and impacts overall performance.

Since SAP cannot be run on any regular hardware, AWS and SAP engineering teams work together to certify the EC2 instances that can be used to run SAP (for HANA, non-HANA DB, App Server, NetWeaver, etc.). A lot of parameters go into the certification process including the output SAPS provided by the instances. The list of certified instances is provided by SAP in an SAP note.

Whenever a solution architect starts to design the SAP on AWS architecture, they review a number of parameters and considerations before picking the right instance type. Some of the important parameters are as below:

- **SAP Application Requirements**: Understand the specific needs of your SAP application. This includes the SAP module being used (like SAP HANA, SAP NetWeaver), its version, and any specific requirements it has.

  - **Specific SAP Module and Version**: Different SAP modules, like SAP HANA, SAP S/4HANA, or SAP Business Suite on HANA, have unique resource demands. The version of SAP you are running may also dictate certain hardware requirements or optimizations.

  - **Application Workload Characteristics**: Analyze the workload characteristics of the SAP application. Some workloads might be more transactional (requiring faster CPUs and more IOPS for storage), while others could be analytical (requiring more memory for processing large datasets).

  - **Customizations and Integrations**: If the SAP environment is heavily customized or integrated with other systems, this can impact performance and resource requirements. Customized modules might require additional compute or memory resources.

- **Compute Power (CPU)**: Evaluate the CPU requirements based on the workload. SAP applications, especially those like SAP HANA, can be CPU-intensive. Select an instance type that provides sufficient compute power to handle the workload without unnecessary over-provisioning.

  - **Core Count and Performance**: Determine the number of cores and the performance of each core required by SAP applications. More cores are generally beneficial for parallel processing, but core performance (frequency, cache size) is also crucial.

  - **Workload Distribution and Multithreading**: Understand how the SAP application distributes its workload. Some applications benefit more from multithreading and can efficiently utilize CPUs with a higher thread count.

- **Sizing and Benchmarking**: Utilize SAP-specific benchmarks and sizing tools (like SAP Quick Sizer) to estimate the CPU capacity needed. This helps in choosing an EC2 instance that matches the compute requirements without over-provisioning.

- **Memory (RAM)**: SAP systems, particularly SAP HANA, are memory-intensive. Ensure that the instance has enough RAM to support your database's size and performance requirements. Amazon offers instances with large memory sizes specifically for SAP HANA workloads. Typically, the SAP "Early Watch Alert" report or the "Utilization" report is a good place to look for peak and average memory requirements.

  - **Database Size and Growth**: For applications like SAP HANA, the size of the in-memory database is a critical factor. You need to account not just for the current database size but also for projected growth.

  - **Performance Considerations**: The memory size directly impacts the performance of in-memory databases. Insufficient memory can lead to increased disk I/O, which degrades performance.

  - **Memory-Intensive Workloads**: Some SAP modules or custom applications may be particularly memory-intensive. In such cases, choosing instances with a higher memory-to-CPU ratio might be beneficial.

Based on the criteria above, and the SAPS provided by the SAP-certified EC2 instances, the architect can then pick the right type of instance, say "compute-optimized, c-series" for Web Dispatcher and SAP Router (where extra CPU may be needed) or "memory-optimized, r-series" for the HANA database server or "general-purpose, m-series" for application servers. AWS offers SAP-certified instances from the lowest end at 256 GB memory up to high-memory instances of 32 TB *(current as of September 2025)*.

- **Scale-Up vs. Scale-Out:** 'Scale-up' and 'scale-out' are two strategies for increasing the capacity and performance of SAP systems on AWS, each addressing different aspects of scalability:

- **Scale-Up:** Scale-up refers to the process of increasing the resources (CPU, RAM, storage) of an existing server or instance to enhance its performance and capacity. This approach is commonly used for applications like SAP, particularly for databases like SAP HANA, where increasing memory and CPU resources directly impacts performance. In the context of AWS, this translates to

  - **Increasing Instance Size**: This involves moving to a larger EC2 instance within the same family or to a different family that offers higher specifications, for example, upgrading from an x1e.xlarge instance to an x1e.2xlarge instance.

  - **Advantages**: Simplified management as it doesn't involve architectural changes, immediate improvement in performance due to increased resources, beneficial for workloads that are memory- or CPU-bound.

  - **Limitations**: There's an upper limit to how much you can scale up, defined by the maximum size of instances available in AWS. Also, it can be more costly as larger instances are generally more expensive.

  - **Use Cases**: Ideal for SAP HANA databases where performance is directly tied to memory and CPU and for applications that don't distribute well across multiple nodes or servers.

- **Scale-Out:** Scale-out involves adding more instances or nodes to an existing system to distribute the workload and increase capacity. This method is particularly effective for handling increased user loads or parallel processing requirements. In AWS, this translates to

  - **Adding More EC2 Instances**: Deploying additional EC2 instances to distribute the SAP workload. This can be within the same AWS region or across multiple regions for better geographical coverage.

- **Advantages**: Offers potentially unlimited scalability by adding more nodes as required, can enhance resilience and availability, often more cost-effective than scaling up for large-scale deployments.

- **Limitations**: Requires a distributed architecture that can efficiently split workloads across multiple nodes, can introduce complexity in management and maintenance.

- **Use Cases**: Suitable for SAP application servers where workloads can be distributed across multiple instances, beneficial for achieving high availability and disaster recovery objectives.

The choice between scaling up and scaling out depends on several factors:

- **Application Architecture**: Some SAP components are designed to scale better vertically (scale-up) like SAP HANA, while others can efficiently distribute workloads across multiple nodes (scale-out), such as SAP application servers.

- **Cost Considerations**: Scaling up might be more straightforward and less costly in the short term but could become expensive as you reach the upper limits of instance sizes. Scaling out can be more cost-effective for long-term scalability.

- **Performance Needs**: Scale-up is typically faster to implement for immediate performance needs, while scale-out might be better for gradual increases in workload or user base.

In practice, a combination of both strategies is often employed to balance immediate performance needs with long-term scalability and cost-effectiveness. AWS provides the flexibility to dynamically adjust your infrastructure to meet the evolving demands of your SAP environment.

Storage

AWS offers various storage options to meet different needs of customers. Broadly, AWS offers the following storage services (apart from a few others):

- **Amazon Simple Storage Service (S3)**: Amazon S3 is a service that provides classic object storage, where data is stored as discrete 'blobs' or 'objects.' Each 'bucket' holds the data (object) as well as the metadata associated with it. This service works well for unstructured data like photos, videos etc., typically non-transactional data. Key aspects of Amazon S3 are

  - **Object Storage**: Amazon S3 stores data as objects within resources called buckets. An object can consist of any kind of data in any format, and each object is stored with a unique identifier, its metadata, and an optional access control policy.

  - **Durability and Availability**: Amazon S3 provides high durability, storing copies of objects across multiple systems. It is designed to deliver 99.999999999% (11 9s) durability and has a robust infrastructure to ensure data availability and reliability.

  - **Scalability**: One of Amazon S3's primary benefits is its scalability. Users can store and retrieve any amount of data, at any time, from anywhere on the web. This makes it ideal for applications that need to scale up or down based on demand.

  - **Security**: Amazon S3 offers comprehensive security and compliance capabilities that can meet even the most stringent regulatory requirements. It allows for encryption of data both at rest and in transit and offers integrated tools like AWS Identity and Access Management (IAM), access control lists (ACLs), and bucket policies for managing access.

  - **Performance**: Amazon S3 is designed for high-speed performance, especially when integrated with other AWS services. It also supports transferring large volumes of data through AWS Direct Connect or other transfer acceleration features.

  - **Data Management Features**: Amazon S3 provides a range of tools for managing data, including lifecycle policies for automatic archiving to Amazon S3 Glacier, versioning, cross-region replication, and detailed logging.

- **Cost-Effective Pricing Models**: With Amazon S3, you pay only for what you use. There's no minimum fee, and various storage classes are available for different use cases, ranging from frequently accessed data to infrequently accessed but rapidly retrievable data and to long-term archiving at lower costs.

- **Use Cases**: Common use cases include website hosting, data backups, disaster recovery, archiving, and serving as a data lake for big data analytics.

Amazon S3 is widely used due to its reliability, scalability, and flexibility, making it suitable for businesses and applications of all sizes and types.

- **Amazon Elastic Block Store (EBS):** Block Store is the approach of dividing data into blocks of equal size. Each of these data blocks is then stored on underlying physical storage, thereby providing fast access and retrieval. Key aspects of Amazon EBS are

  - **Block Storage**: Unlike object storage like Amazon S3, Amazon EBS provides block-level storage volumes. Block storage is suitable for scenarios where you need to treat your storage like a raw, unformatted hard drive. Amazon EBS volumes can be attached to EC2 instances and are used similarly to physical disks.

  - **Persistent Storage**: Amazon EBS volumes are persistent, meaning they do not depend on the life of an EC2 instance. Data on an Amazon EBS volume persists independently of the lifespan of the instance it is attached to, ensuring data durability.

  - **Scalability and Flexibility**: You can scale your usage up or down within minutes, and you only pay for what you use. Amazon EBS volumes can also be resized, and their performance can be changed dynamically to meet evolving storage needs.

- **High Availability and Reliability**: Amazon EBS volumes are automatically replicated within their Availability Zone to protect from component failure, offering high availability and durability.

- **Snapshots**: Amazon EBS allows you to create snapshots (backups) of any volume, which are stored in Amazon S3 for long-term durability. These snapshots can be used to quickly create new Amazon EBS volumes.

- **Security**: Volumes can be encrypted with AWS Key Management Service (KMS) keys. Encryption and access control capabilities ensure the security of data, both at rest and in transit.

- **Integration**: Amazon EBS is designed to work well with Amazon EC2, offering tight integration. When used with EC2 instances, EBS volumes perform like network-attached storage.

- **Use Cases**: Amazon EBS is commonly used for workloads that require a persistent storage solution, such as databases, file systems, and containers, or for applications requiring raw block-level storage.

In summary, Amazon EBS offers a reliable, scalable, and high-performance block storage solution that is integral to a wide range of applications running on EC2 instances. Its versatility makes it a popular choice for a variety of AWS-based storage needs.

- **Amazon Elastic File System (EFS)**: File system storage is a hierarchical data storage methodology that stores data in files, organizes files in folders, and organizes folders in directories and subdirectories. Amazon EFS is a cloud-based file storage service designed to offer scalable, elastic, and integrated file storage for use with both AWS cloud services and on-premises resources. Here are some key aspects of Amazon EFS:

  - **Elastic and Scalable File Storage**: Amazon EFS automatically scales up and down as you add or remove files, so you only pay for the storage you use. It can grow and shrink automatically to petabyte scale, removing the need to provision and manage capacity to accommodate growth.

- **Fully Managed Service**: As a fully managed service, Amazon EFS eliminates the need to manage file storage infrastructure, allowing you to focus on your applications rather than on managing and scaling a file system.

- **Compatibility with Standard File Protocols**: Amazon EFS is compatible with all the Linux-based workloads that use standard file system interfaces and semantics (such as Network File System (NFS)). This makes it easy to integrate with existing applications and tools.

- **High Availability and Durability**: Amazon EFS file systems are designed to be highly available and durable, automatically replicating data across multiple Availability Zones in an AWS Region.

- **Performance and Use Cases**: Amazon EFS is optimized for a broad spectrum of use cases, including web serving, content management, data analytics, and enterprise applications. It supports high levels of throughput and IOPS, low latencies, and many file operations per second.

- **Shared File Access**: Amazon EFS can be used by thousands of Amazon EC2 instances simultaneously, as well as by on-premises servers via AWS Direct Connect or AWS VPN, providing a common data source for workloads and applications running on more than one compute instance.

- **Security and Compliance**: It integrates with AWS Key Management Service (KMS) for encryption, supports access point permissions for application-specific access, and integrates with IAM for identity-based access, ensuring robust security and compliance.

- **Cost-Effective Solutions**: Amazon EFS offers a simple, pay-as-you-go model and also provides cost-saving options like the Amazon EFS Infrequent Access (IA) storage class, which automatically moves files not accessed according to the lifecycle policy to a lower-cost storage tier.

- **Integration with AWS Services**: Amazon EFS integrates with other AWS services like Amazon EC2, AWS Lambda, and AWS container services, making it a flexible option for various application architectures.

In summary, Amazon EFS provides a simple, scalable, fully managed elastic NFS file system for use with AWS cloud services and on-premises resources, suitable for a wide range of applications and use cases. Its scalability, ease of use, and integration capabilities make it a popular choice for file storage needs in the AWS ecosystem.

- **Relevance of IOPS**: In the context of SAP deployment on AWS, the storage service used will depend on the use case and storage requirement. Another common design consideration for storage is the throughput metric IOPS (input/output operations per second), which refers to a performance measurement used to benchmark the speed at which a storage system (like hard drives, SSDs, or storage area networks) can read from and write to a storage medium. IOPS is a crucial factor in the performance of SAP systems, especially those running high-demand databases like SAP HANA. IOPS in SAP is important in terms of

  - **Database Performance**: SAP applications, particularly database-intensive ones like SAP HANA, require high-speed data access. The IOPS metric is critical in determining how quickly the database can perform read and write operations, which directly affects the overall performance of the SAP system.

  - **System Responsiveness**: Higher IOPS can lead to quicker data retrieval and faster transaction processing, enhancing system responsiveness. This is particularly important in real-time analytics and transactional processing systems.

  - **Storage Selection**: When configuring storage for SAP, particularly for databases, selecting storage hardware or cloud storage options (like Amazon EBS) with the appropriate IOPS rating is essential. The required IOPS for an SAP environment depends on the specific workload and the size of the database.

- **Sizing and Scaling**: Understanding the IOPS requirements is crucial for correctly sizing the storage infrastructure for SAP. It ensures that the storage system can handle the peak load without causing performance bottlenecks.

- **Cost Considerations**: Higher IOPS typically comes at a higher cost. Balancing the IOPS requirements with budget constraints is a key part of designing an SAP infrastructure.

- **Considerations for Storage for SAP**: When setting up the SAP system on AWS, the general approach is to set up the ABAP SAP Central Services (ASCS), SAP kernel, application servers, and database server. There could be multiple application servers per SAP S-ID. All these components can be on one single EC2 instance at one extreme or each on its own EC2 instance on the other extreme. In practical scenarios it lies somewhere in between – for instance, for 'production' and 'quality' systems, the ASCS and SAP kernel on a separate EC2 instance, the database server on a separate EC2 instance, and the SAP application servers on an EC2 instance (or multiple EC2 instances) of their own. However, the Central Services and SAP kernel are accessed by all the applications servers as well as the database server. Based on the above, the use cases for storage for SAP on AWS are as below:

- **Shared File System**: This is relevant when sharing the data across multiple application servers. The right storage service would be Amazon EFS, which is scalable and supports NFS (Network File System), a distributed file system protocol that is commonly used to share files over the network, typically for the data stored in the ASCS and SAP kernel.

- **Database Storage**: Any typical database used for SAP including HANA when deployed on an EC2 instance would use Amazon EBS. This storage is not shared across EC2 instances. All the app servers would point to the database server, and the database would access the data from the Amazon EBS storage and process the transaction with the app server. Amazon EBS offers different storage options including GP3, GP2, IO2 Block Express, and FSxN, providing peak performance ranging from 16,000 IOPS to 256,000 IOPS. Users can choose the right option depending on if they expect low volume of transactions or higher.

- **Backup and Recovery**: When backing up SAP HANA databases, as well as other SAP application data, Amazon S3 is often used due to its durability and scalability.

- **Data Archiving**: When storing infrequently accessed data for compliance or historical analysis, Amazon S3 Glacier or S3 Glacier Deep Archive is suitable for long-term data archiving, offering a secure, durable, and cost-effective storage solution.

- **Analytics**: When storing and analyzing large datasets for business intelligence and analytics, Amazon S3 can be used to create data lakes. It integrates with AWS analytics services like Amazon Redshift, Athena, Amazon QuickSight, and EMR for big data processing and analytics.

- **SAP Content and Document Management**: When managing documents and digital content within SAP applications, Amazon S3 for storing unstructured data such as documents, images, and media files can be used or Amazon EFS for content that requires a file system interface.

- **Hybrid Storage Scenarios**: When integrating on-premises SAP environments with AWS, AWS Storage Gateway can be used, which facilitates hybrid storage scenarios, connecting on-premises environments with AWS cloud storage.

Figure 5-3. *SAP on AWS Architecture*

As the session came to an end, Ashish was surrounded by eager participants, who had so much to absorb and so many questions. Ashish was patient with everyone, answering questions, pointing to further reading material, and asking for longer questions to be discussed offline. Nolan walked up to Thomas, "I was only joking when I was talking about raising the bar, but clearly I see that Ashish took it seriously. This was an amazing session. How easily Ashish took complicated chunks and broke them out was a treat to watch. I think even I can now set up SAP on AWS!" Thomas laughed and added, "Nimbus is an important customer, and you got the best team from AWS. I think Ashish is a celebrity now. Look at all the crowd around him." As Nolan and Thomas were exchanging banter, Mark walked up to them. Sticking his hand out to Thomas for a formal handshake, he said, "Thomas, this is Mark Chapman. I am Director for IT Infrastructure and also responsible for building the business case for SAP modernization. The AWS sessions have been amazing. I would like to spend time with you and your team to gather inputs for our business case and add the AWS perspective on how the cloud can drive benefits and reduce costs for this large project." Mark was very clear in his ask and rarely wasted time on small talk. "For sure, Mark, it would be my pleasure. I will be your point person and will set up time with you to go through some of the details, which I am sure you will find valuable in your business case," replied Thomas, equally clear and succinct in his response. Another session by AWS at Nimbus and another text between Thomas and Amy. "The flight is cruising at 30,000 feet! Great session again today. We are definitely in a position of trust." Amy came back with a very "Amy-like" response, "Love it! It's time to serve snacks on board …"

CHAPTER 6

Designing the Operating Model

This chapter covers details on the day-to-day operating model of SAP systems on AWS. Once you have a good understanding of the infrastructure concepts, this chapter will delve into concepts of the SAP operations including high availability, disaster recovery, security, automation of ongoing tasks, and monitoring.

While the AWS team was basking in the success of their second session of the workshop, the SAP team was working fervently to put together a revised proposal for Nimbus. Steve valued his relationship with Elizabeth and was pulling out all the stops to make sure that the new proposal met Nimbus's needs. Andrew on his part was taking care of all the finer details that would go into the business justification section.

"Hey, Melanie, can you please help with a few additional data points on additional SaaS products that would go into the new proposal bundle," Andrew 'slacked' Melanie. "Yes, I think I have some of the information and can work with a few others to compile all of that together," replied Melanie. It started to feel like everyone at SAP was working on this important Nimbus deal. Andrew was keeping track of all items on a spreadsheet. Every other minute, someone or the other was looking for some piece of information to be able to complete their own assigned tasks. Steve would check in with the team every hour.

It had been almost two weeks since the proposal revision was underway, and even as Andrew, Melanie, and the extended team were tired and fatigued, the revised proposal was shaping up well. Steve called for one final team review since he intended to deliver the proposal back to Elizabeth before the end of the week.

"I see that we are finally able to revise the total bundle of products that aligns with the Nimbus's roadmap. That is a good start. How close are we to the target pricing?" Steve opened the discussion, ending with a query. After some long silence, Andrew's voice crackled on the virtual meeting, "Sorry, I was on mute. Yes, we were able to make

© Tushar Srivastava 2025
T. Srivastava, *Modernizing SAP with AWS*, https://doi.org/10.1007/979-8-8688-1579-9_6

significant adjustments, and we are now about 13% over the customer's expected target price. However, we have added some additional products to the bundle, which I think would be well suited for the modernization project."

Steve thought for a while and addressed Melanie directly, "Melanie, our goal has always been to make the customer successful. Do you have substantial data that shows that the additional products would justify being 13% over the target price?" The ever-organized Melanie responded, "Yes, Steve. We are not only committing to modernize their SAP landscape but also future-proof it and add additional capabilities around analytics and code simplification. Given that these are two vital areas of concern for Nimbus, I think that the revised proposal definitely has a strong value proposition for them." Steve was impressed with Melanie's confidence. He went around the virtual conference room and took feedback from all participants. Satisfied with the outcome, he said, "I will text Elizabeth today and secure some time to informally let her know about the revised proposal. And, Andrew, you can deliver the new proposal formally to both Elizabeth and the Nimbus procurement team." "Absolutely, Steve." This time Andrew had no trouble in getting off mute.

While Andrew was putting the final touches on his revised proposal, Thomas was re-reading the email from Mark. He quickly dashed off a Slack message to the trusted AWS 'tag-team,' "Hey, Amy and Ashish, Mark wants to discuss AWS inputs to the SAP modernization business case." Amy's sage observation came through, "I think they are getting serious about this project and are likely going to get into finer details and make a procurement decision soon." Ashish came up with his usual laconic response, "I agree." "I will ask Mark for a meeting. I think Ashish and I will be able to handle the request." Amy as usual gave a "thumbs-up" before exiting the group chat. Without wasting time, Thomas got back to Mark, offering dates for the meeting. Within the hour Mark responded, and they had the date locked down, though a virtual meeting per Mark's preference. Not much to prepare, except to listen to Mark's questions and have a productive discussion, *Thomas thought to himself as he prepared to pack up for the day. It was his 'no-dinner' day, per the new fad diet he had just started following.*

A few days had just passed when Thomas received a text, "Hey, buddy, we submitted a revised proposal to Nimbus last week, so thought it might be a good idea to catch up." Thomas re-read the text from Andrew and smiled to himself. Looks like Nimbus is definitely getting serious. *He replied back to Andrew and offered to meet in person. Taking off early the next day, Thomas entered the new coffee shop in downtown, the designated spot for the meeting. Andrew and Melanie were already waiting. Thomas ordered a dark roast and avoided any of the delicious baked snacks. He was still following his diet. Settling down on the small table, the trio exchanged greetings and light fist bumps. "Where is Ashish?" Andrew enquired in his usually chirpy self. "Well, he is not local here and did not have any specific meeting in the area," Thomas stated more as a matter of fact than an excuse.*

Gulping down the last remnants of his caramel mocha, Andrew came down to business, "We submitted a revised proposal late last week, and oh man, it was so much of rework." Thomas looked on as if asking for more details. Melanie jumped in, "We revised some of the product mix and adjusted some pricing, and Steve was able to secure a better discount from the leadership. Overall, we are still over budget, but I think the new proposal has a strong value proposition, helping Nimbus simplify the SAP modernization. I am sorry but I can't share any additional commercial details." The astute Melanie was quick to make sure no financial numbers were exchanged with a partner, especially concerning a customer transaction.

Thomas perked up and shared, "Well, that is some great news. Mark has asked us for input to his business case. With revised pricing from you and asking for inputs from us, I think Nimbus is taking this SAP modernization program seriously." Heads were nodding and everyone seemed to concur. "Oh also, we had a couple of great technical sessions at the Nimbus office, and the audience was very engaged. I think these are all good signs," Thomas added, almost as an afterthought. The discussions continued on some peripheral items as Andrew continued to order some snacks and additional coffee. As the informal meeting progressed, sensing that they could split sometime soon, Melanie spoke up, "Thomas, we need to continue to partner together for the success of Nimbus. SAP modernization is a long and tough journey. You have been winning the trust of the customer by getting them cloud-ready for SAP, while we have focused on the new features and functions and addressed the new licensing costs. All these are important inputs toward the business case, and the Nimbus leadership will probably be reviewing a go–no-go decision on this initiative. Needless to say, there is a lot at stake for SAP and I guess for AWS also." Thomas was caught slightly off guard by this sudden somber tone, but gathered himself and said, "Yes, absolutely. All three teams, Nimbus, SAP, and AWS, have to work closely together to make sure that the technical and commercial benefits are strong leading to a successful modernization program." "There's my man," Andrew only said, as he backslapped Thomas and ordered a couple more biscotti 'to go' as they all got up to leave.

It was a bright day, and unusually for the middle of the week, Thomas had a pretty light workload. He messaged Ashish reminding him of the virtual meeting with Mark and double-confirmed that Ashish had the meeting bridge details. A couple of minutes before the meeting, Ashish logged in, just to make sure there were no technical glitches. Thomas was already on the call. "Hello, Thomas. Hello, Ashish. How have you been? Good to see you both," Mark politely enquired as he adjusted his headset.

Staring into the little face tiles, Thomas waved and exchanged polite greetings. Ashish followed suit. Without wasting any more time, Mark got to the agenda, "As you are aware, we are making some good progress on our SAP modernization project. I am tasked with putting the business case together. As you can imagine, the business case itself has many components and variables, and we are addressing it one at a time. We had some good meetings with the business stakeholders and are also expecting revised numbers from SAP. As we are also looking at SAP running on the cloud, I wanted to get some inputs from you toward the business case." Mark ended right there even though it seemed like he wanted to add more. "Of course, that is no problem at all. I am assuming you are looking for total cost estimates for running SAP on AWS. We can definitely provide that, once we have reviewed the current hardware sizing, utilization, and some other key details," Thomas replied eagerly. He was quick to add, "However, apart from the AWS cost estimates, we have seen that customers also look at savings accrued by replacing current hardware or not renewing your data center lease. To get a more comprehensive view, you can look at costs like heating, cooling, physical security, insurance, and other costs associated with running your own data centers."

All the while Ashish listened carefully and added thoughtfully, "Mark, in addition, you should also consider the savings accrued when you are operating in the cloud with additional automation, replacing some legacy software with cloud-based SaaS offerings and even the intangibles like ease of attracting skilled talent because your job descriptions will now ask for cloud skills." Mark listened intently and took notes. Over the next hour, the discussion continued with focus on some very specific details. "Well, this has been a very useful discussion. Definitely more than what I was expecting. I really appreciate that," Mark said cheerfully, realizing that the call was coming to an end. "I am glad it was useful, Mark. I will send out a spreadsheet template that will capture the SAP sizing information, and I will include a list of other documents that we would need," Thomas added, always making sure he captured next steps during important sales meetings.

Nolan was rushing through the hall excitedly. His team had just finished creating a 'first-drop' of the prototype application that he had built. He even liked the working name they came up with, 'Project Curie,' after the two-time Nobel-winning scientist. In his excitement, he almost did not notice Mark passing him. Of course, the sharp-eyed Mark did not miss him and called out loudly, "Hey, Nolan, great to see you. Where are you rushing off? Glad I ran into you since I wanted to talk to you anyways. I had a pretty good meeting with the AWS team last week, and we are in the process of getting some pricing and additional savings/benefits information. The business case is shaping up well. I am curious if we received any updated pricing from SAP?" Though Nolan was in a rush, he paused and collected his thoughts before saying, "That's great news, Mark. And I am happy to share that we just received updated pricing numbers from SAP. I will make sure it is sent your way. Also, let's set up a time to review the status of the business case once you have had the chance to incorporate all this new information." Sometimes, these informal encounters were more productive in getting things done rather than formal meetings.

Thomas was intently reviewing the data returned by Mark via email. A few days earlier, Thomas sent him a template spreadsheet to fill out their SAP sizing and server inventory information. Mark had done a good job of collecting all the relevant information and populating the spreadsheet. He had also attached his SAP Early Watch Alert reports and other Utilization reports. Mark had indicated earlier that their internal team would look at the savings and benefits of not renewing the data center lease, so he requested Thomas to exclude that.

Thomas quickly slacked Ashish, "Forwarding you the email received from Mark. Please review, and if you can prepare the draft pricing, we can review it before sharing it back with Mark." Thomas also thought it would be worthwhile to keep Nolan updated. Texting Nolan, he asked if they could connect for a few minutes. Nolan responded almost immediately as if he was expecting the text. Thomas dialed him immediately. "Hey, Nolan, glad to talk to you. I wanted to provide a quick update and discuss a couple of topics with you." "For sure, go ahead, Thomas," the voice came from the other end. "Nolan, we have had a few meetings with Mark to provide some high-level cost toward hosting SAP on AWS. I assume this is going to go as input for the business case. Mark has shared all the data we requested, and we will be presenting him with some pricing in the next few days. I wanted to keep you updated," Thomas shared. "Yeah, Mark did let me know. We ran into each other sometime back. Thanks for keeping me in the loop," Nolan responded nonchalantly. Thomas continued, "That is great. By the way, I also wanted to secure dates for the next session as part of the technical education series. Now we will start getting into operational details, so I think it would be good for Sandeep's team to be well engaged on these topics." "Absolutely, Thomas, I look forward to it, and Sandeep was recently asking about it, so this is good timing. Let me send out some dates and we can go from there," Nolan concluded.

Meanwhile, Elizabeth was in an animated conversation with her executive assistant reviewing and modifying her appointments. She just had ten minutes before the meeting with Mark, Nolan, and Sandeep. Having rattled off half a dozen action items, she shifted her focus to the agenda for the meeting. This was an important meeting given that the SAP modernization program was at an inflection point. Nolan, Mark, and Sandeep trooped in just at the stroke of the hour. After some initial small talk, Mark took charge of the agenda. "I am pretty excited to share that we have made some very good progress on the business case. We had a few primary pillars as we approached this business case. Firstly, we had discussions with the business stakeholders, which yielded key benefits expected from the new S/4 HANA solution and identified important pain points that we would be able to address. Secondly, we received cost estimates from AWS for the cloud hosting as well as some potential benefits of leveraging cloud-based automation and solutions. Thirdly, we received cost estimates from SAP, which, as I understand, have been revised by SAP. The last pillar is around savings from canceling hardware leases and other miscellaneous costs and benefits, which are being addressed by specific teams. Overall, I am pretty confident of the way the business case is turning out." Mark ended on a high note.

Elizabeth who was making a few notes in her big black folder set it aside and chewed on her pen lost in thought. "That looks very comprehensive, Mark. We in fact did receive an updated proposal from SAP, and it looks pretty good. Let's make sure that is incorporated in the business case," Elizabeth shared her thoughts. Sandeep chimed in, "We also have been running sessions with AWS, and our teams are building up a good understanding of AWS fundamentals and designing the SAP on AWS architecture. Very soon we should be doing sessions on day-to-day operations as well as migration strategies." Sandeep glanced toward Nolan while completing his thought. And as if on cue, Nolan spoke up, "Yes, I spoke with Thomas, and the next session is focused on day-to-day SAP operations on AWS. Since your team will be engaged in the execution, it would be critical for them to take the lead on this one." The session ended on a productive note. As everyone exited, Elizabeth called out, "Nolan, can we connect for a quick minute?" Nolan swiveled on his heels and walked up to her desk. "I think the meeting today was productive. Our business case is shaping up well. I see a much clearer path to our SAP modernization goal. Is there a blind spot that we may be missing?" Elizabeth queried. Nolan gave it some thought. "Can't think of any …yet."

Thomas and Ashish were back at the Nimbus office for yet another session, and by now, the Nimbus office was very familiar to the duo. As always, Nolan greeted them at the reception and escorted them to the room. "You should try out this new coffee machine we have installed," Nolan said, pointing in the direction of a contraption that looked like a device out of "Star Trek" than a coffee machine, with its touch screen, various dispensing nozzles, and shiny steel gray body. "It is the same coffee we have started offering on our international flights," Nolan continued. They fiddled with the options and configurations of the machine, and soon the machine dispensed piping hot liquid with the only sound coming from a chime alerting that the brew was ready. A few minutes later the silence was broken by the soft murmur of workshop participants who started streaming in steadily. Thomas and Ashish made their way in, but not before Ashish poured his coffee down the kitchen sink. Surely, coffee served at 30,000 feet did not meet Ashish's high bar at the ground level. Meanwhile, Thomas poured himself another cup to keep company during the session. Most of the faces were very familiar and made their way to greet the AWS team, and a few minutes later Sandeep made his way to the front of the room and shook hands with Ashish and then Thomas.

"Glad to see both of you back again here. Your sessions are very useful, and I look forward to the ones today." Thomas took the lead, "Thanks, Sandeep. We appreciate the partnership, and I am glad the sessions are working well for the team. Also, the session today would be very relevant to you since we are now getting into the operations and execution details from this session onward." Ashish added, "This could be unfamiliar territory for your teams, so I encourage them to reach out to me offline in case there are questions." Sandeep smiled and acknowledged the offer and took a seat close by. After all these sessions, Ashish was quite confident and quickly rolled out the agenda. "So far, we have covered the fundamentals of AWS and basic principles of SAP on AWS. We will now cover some key operational concepts that will help us in running day-to-day operations of SAP on AWS." Setting the stage well, Ashish was all set to start his session.

"Now that we have reviewed the details of the AWS clouds and fundamental components of architecture of SAP on AWS, we will spend today's sessions discussing operational aspects of SAP on AWS including some key topics like high availability, disaster recovery, and operations automation."

High Availability and Disaster Recovery

High availability and **disaster recovery** are not new concepts. Customers running SAP systems have been designing applications to be '*highly available*' coupled with '*disaster recovery*' systems and protocols. Though high availability and disaster recovery are related, they are two different concepts.

Any SAP system has multiple components (Web Dispatcher, application servers, SAP Central Services, database, etc.) and, consequently, multiple points of failure. It is a poor design on the part of the architect if a single failure could render the system unavailable to the end users. The goal with a high-availability architecture is to eliminate these single points of failure and keep the system up and running and available to users for running transactions and queries. Technically speaking, high availability refers to a collection of methods, engineering strategies, and design philosophies aimed at maintaining business continuity and guaranteeing access to data and services for authorized users whenever necessary.

On the other hand, disaster recovery kicks in when the systems actually have gone down despite all fallbacks. SAP disaster recovery refers to the strategies and technologies used to ensure the continuity and recovery of SAP systems and data after a catastrophic event. Together, HA and DR form the "*resiliency*" of SAP systems. In order to understand and design for resiliency, there are some key terms to understand.

Key Concepts for High Availability and Disaster Recovery

In order to understand HA and DR, it is important to familiarize yourself with some key concepts. Given below are the critical ones.

Percentage Uptime

Percentage uptime in SAP, or in any IT system, refers to the proportion of time that the system is available and operational, usually expressed as a percentage of the total time. It is a key metric used to measure the reliability and availability of the system. This concept is especially important in the context of enterprise systems like SAP, which are critical for the daily operations of businesses.

To calculate the percentage uptime, you divide the amount of time the system was operational by the total time period being considered and then multiply by 100 to get a percentage. Here's the formula:

$$Percentage\ Uptime = \left(\frac{Operational\ Time}{Total\ Time} \right) \times 100$$

For example, if an SAP system was operational for 8,760 hours in a year (which is basically the total number of hours in one year), the system's uptime percentage would be 100%. However, if the system was down for 10 hours in that year, the operational time would be 8,750 hours, and the uptime percentage would be calculated as follows:

$$Percentage \ Uptime = \left(\frac{8,750}{8.760}\right) \times 100$$

High uptime percentages (such as 99.9% or higher) are often desired, especially for critical systems like SAP, as they indicate high reliability and minimal downtime. In the context of service-level agreements (SLAs), specific uptime percentages are often guaranteed by service providers, and failing to meet these can lead to penalties or other contractual consequences.

Mean Time to Recovery (MTTR)

Mean Time to Recovery (MTTR) in the context of SAP, or any IT system, refers to the average amount of time it takes to recover a system to its normal operating state after a failure or outage. This metric is crucial for understanding and improving the resilience and reliability of IT services, including complex enterprise systems like SAP. MTTR is an important part of a business's disaster recovery and business continuity planning. It helps organizations to

- **Measure System Reliability**: MTTR offers a quantitative way to assess how quickly a system can be restored after a problem. A lower MTTR indicates a more reliable and resilient system.

- **Plan for Downtime**: Understanding the average recovery time helps businesses plan for potential downtimes and informs strategies for minimizing impact on operations.

- **Improve Response Procedures**: By analyzing MTTR, organizations can identify bottlenecks or weaknesses in their recovery processes and make improvements.

- **Meet SLAs**: Many **service-level agreements** (**SLAs**) include commitments on recovery times, so keeping MTTR low is often a contractual requirement.

In an SAP environment, MTTR might involve restoring databases, restarting services, applying patches, or even switching to a backup server. It's the average time from the start of the incident (when the failure occurs) to the moment the system is back up and running normally.

To calculate MTTR, you sum up the total downtime experienced over a given period and divide it by the number of incidents during that period:

$$MTTR = \frac{Total\ Downtime}{Number\ of\ Incidents}$$

For example, if an SAP system had three incidents in a month, with downtimes of two hours, one hour, and three hours respectively, the MTTR would be

$$MTTR = \frac{2+1+3}{3} = 2\ hours$$

This means, on average, it took two hours to recover from each incident. Reducing MTTR is a key objective in IT operations, as it minimizes the impact of outages on business operations.

Return to Service (RTS)

Return to service (RTS) in SAP refers to the process or time it takes to restore an SAP system or service back to its full operational state after an outage or disruption. Understanding RTS is crucial for organizations that rely heavily on SAP for their day-to-day operations. It involves several key components:

- **Diagnosis and Issue Resolution**: Identifying the cause of the service disruption and implementing a fix. This could involve repairing or replacing hardware, fixing software bugs, or addressing network issues.

- **System Restoration**: Bringing the SAP system back to a fully operational state. This could include restarting services, restoring data from backups, or switching to a redundant system if available.

- **Data Integrity and Validation**: Ensuring that all data within the SAP system is accurate and intact after the service has been restored. This is crucial to maintain the reliability of business processes supported by SAP.

- **Performance Testing**: Confirming that the SAP system is performing as expected and can handle the required workload without issues.

- **Communication**: Keeping relevant stakeholders informed about the status of the outage and the expected time for return to service.

RTS is an important metric for measuring the effectiveness of an organization's response to IT incidents. A lower RTS means the organization can recover more quickly from disruptions, minimizing the impact on business operations. In the context of SAP, which is often mission-critical software for businesses, having a low RTS is essential to maintain continuous business operations and to meet the service-level agreements (SLAs).

Recovery Time Objective (RTO)

Recovery Time Objective (**RTO**) in the context of SAP, or any IT system, refers to the time in which a system must be restored after a disruption in order to maintain business continuity.

In simpler terms, RTO is the maximum allowable amount of time that can pass before the impact of the downtime becomes unacceptable to the business. This time frame includes the duration of the incident itself until normal operations are resumed. It's a critical part of disaster recovery and business continuity planning, helping organizations to set clear expectations and objectives for recovery in the event of an outage.

For SAP systems, which are often integral to the operations of a business, having a well-defined RTO is essential. The RTO will vary from one organization to another, depending on the criticality of the SAP system to their operations. For some businesses, an RTO of a few hours might be acceptable, while for others, particularly those that rely heavily on real-time data processing, an RTO of just minutes may be required.

The RTO helps in several ways:

- **Planning and Prioritization**: Helps businesses prioritize which systems and processes need to be recovered first.

- **Resource Allocation**: Guides the allocation of resources for disaster recovery planning.

- **Setting Expectations**: Establishes clear expectations for recovery timelines both internally within an organization and with external stakeholders.

- **Service-Level Agreements (SLAs)**: RTOs are often part of SLAs with service providers, ensuring that recovery services meet the business's requirements.

Determining the RTO involves understanding the business impact of downtime and balancing this with the cost and technical feasibility of achieving the desired recovery time. It's an essential part of risk management and resilience planning for any business relying on SAP systems.

Recovery Point Objective (RPO)

The **Recovery Point Objective** (**RPO**) in the context of SAP, or any IT system, is a critical metric in disaster recovery and business continuity planning. It refers to the maximum tolerable period in which data might be lost from an IT service due to a major incident.

In simpler terms, the RPO defines how much data loss is acceptable to a business in the event of a disruption, such as a system failure, natural disaster, or cyber-attack. For SAP systems, which often handle critical business processes and store valuable business data, setting an appropriate RPO is crucial. The RPO is typically measured in time: for example, an RPO of one hour means that in the event of a system failure, the business can tolerate losing up to one hour's worth of data. The actual RPO will vary depending on the business's specific needs and the criticality of the data.

Key aspects of RPO in SAP include

- **Data Backup Frequency**: The RPO will influence how frequently data is backed up. A shorter RPO requires more frequent backups.

- **Data Loss Impact**: Understanding the impact of data loss on business operations helps in setting the RPO. For some critical systems, even a small amount of data loss could be significant, necessitating a lower RPO.

- **Disaster Recovery Planning**: The RPO is a key factor in designing disaster recovery strategies. It helps to determine the technologies and processes needed for data backup and recovery.

- **Resource Allocation**: Achieving a lower RPO can require more resources and advanced technology (e.g., real-time data replication), which can influence budgeting and IT resource allocation.

- **Compliance and Regulations**: Certain industries may have regulations that dictate minimum requirements for data protection, impacting the RPO.

For businesses using SAP, an effective RPO strategy will ensure that critical data is not lost beyond an acceptable threshold and that recovery processes are aligned with business needs. Balancing the RPO with the technical capabilities and the cost of data protection solutions is a key consideration in SAP system administration and business continuity planning.

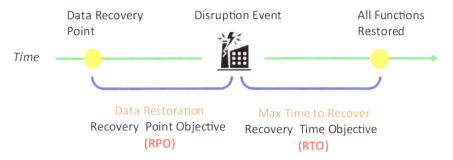

Figure 6-1. *RTO and RPO Explained Visually*

Enterprises typically define different RTO (Recovery Time Objective) and RPO (Recovery Point Objective) targets for various SAP systems based on their criticality to business operations. Core systems like SAP S/4HANA, which handle real-time transactions and financials, often require aggressive RTO and RPO – typically under 15 minutes – to minimize business disruption. In contrast, systems like SAP Solution Manager or SAP Enterprise Portal, which support administrative or internal functions, may have more lenient recovery objectives, allowing for several hours of downtime. This tiered approach ensures cost-effective resilience while prioritizing recovery efforts for the most business-critical workloads.

Failure Scenarios for SAP Systems

When running SAP on AWS, several potential failure scenarios can impact the availability and performance of your SAP systems. Understanding these scenarios helps in planning effective strategies for high availability and disaster recovery. Here are some common failure scenarios:

- **Instance Failures**: Individual EC2 instances running SAP components can fail due to software errors, hardware issues, or other problems. This can lead to the unavailability of specific services or applications until the instance is replaced or recovered.

- **Availability Zone Outages**: Although rare, an entire AWS Availability Zone (AZ) can experience an outage due to power failures, natural disasters, or network issues. Since an AZ represents a distinct data center, its failure can affect all resources deployed within that zone.

- **Network Connectivity Issues**: Network disruptions can occur within AWS or between AWS and the internet or on-premises environments. This can affect the ability to access SAP systems or can impact performance due to increased latency or packet loss.

- **Storage Failures**: Issues with Amazon Elastic Block Store (EBS) or other storage services can lead to data corruption, loss, or accessibility problems. This can affect the operation of SAP databases and applications that rely on persistent storage.

- **Database Failures**: Failures in the database layer, such as SAP HANA or any other supported database, can occur due to software bugs, configuration errors, or hardware issues. This can lead to data inconsistency, loss, or unavailability of database services.

- **Service Disruptions**: AWS services that SAP systems depend on, such as Amazon RDS, AWS S3, or AWS Lambda, can experience disruptions or degraded performance, impacting the overall SAP environment.

- **Security Incidents**: Security breaches, such as unauthorized access, DDoS attacks, or malware infections, can lead to system downtime, data theft, or damage.

- **Human Errors**: Mistakes made in configuration, code deployment, or system maintenance can inadvertently bring down systems or cause data loss.

- **Scaling Limitations**: Inadequate scaling, either vertical or horizontal, can lead to performance degradation or system unavailability during peak load times.

- **Software Bugs and Incompatibilities**: Issues within the SAP software or incompatibilities with the underlying AWS infrastructure can cause system instability or crashes.

To mitigate these risks, AWS recommends implementing a well-architected framework that includes strategies like multi-AZ deployments, data replication, regular backups, auto-scaling, and security best practices. It's also crucial to have a disaster recovery plan and routinely test it to ensure the resilience of your SAP environment on AWS.

Tools and Solutions from AWS

There are multiple solutions available from AWS, which can be used to set up the high-availability architecture as well as perform disaster recovery.

EC2 Auto Recovery

EC2 Auto Recovery is designed to automatically recover an instance in case it becomes impaired due to an underlying hardware failure or a problem that requires AWS involvement to repair. For newer EC2 instances, EC2 Auto Recovery is enabled by default. The other option uses Amazon CloudWatch alarms to trigger the recovery of an instance.

- **How It Works**: You set a CloudWatch alarm to monitor an instance for a specific failure scenario (like system status check failures). When the alarm is triggered, EC2 Auto Recovery is initiated.

- **Recovery Process**: The instance is automatically recovered on a new, healthy host with the same instance ID, private IP addresses, elastic IP addresses, and all instance metadata.

- **Limitations**: Not all instance types support Auto Recovery, and it's only available in certain regions.

AWS Backint Agent for SAP HANA

AWS Backint Agent for SAP HANA is a solution provided by AWS specifically designed to facilitate the backup and recovery of SAP HANA databases to AWS cloud storage services. It acts as a bridge between SAP HANA and Amazon S3, allowing users to leverage the scalability, durability, and cost-effectiveness of AWS cloud storage for their SAP HANA data. Key features are

- **Integration with SAP HANA**: The Backint Agent integrates SAP HANA with AWS using SAP's Backint interface, which is a standard API used for connecting external backup solutions to SAP HANA.

- **Direct Backup to Amazon S3**: It enables direct backup of SAP HANA databases to Amazon S3, eliminating the need for intermediate storage solutions.

- **Support for Database and Log Backups**: The agent supports both full and incremental backups, including data and log backups, providing a comprehensive backup solution.

- **Encryption and Security**: Backups can be encrypted for secure data transfer, and storage integration with AWS Key Management Service (KMS) allows for robust encryption key management.

- **High Durability and Availability**: By utilizing Amazon S3, the backups benefit from the high durability and availability inherent in AWS cloud storage.

- **Cost-Effective Storage Solution**: Amazon S3 provides a scalable and cost-effective storage solution, allowing users to pay only for the storage they consume.

- **Flexible and Configurable**: The agent allows for flexible backup scheduling and configuration, aligning with the specific needs and policies of the organization.

- **Installation**: The AWS Backint Agent is installed on the same server where SAP HANA is running.

- **Configuration**: Users configure the agent to connect to a specific Amazon S3 bucket and set up the desired backup parameters.

- **Backup Process**: During backups, SAP HANA communicates with the Backint Agent, which then handles the transfer of backup data directly to the configured S3 bucket.

- **Recovery Process**: For data recovery, the agent facilitates the retrieval of backup data from S3 and its restoration to the SAP HANA database.

Amazon EBS Snapshots

Amazon EBS Snapshots is a feature provided by AWS that allows users to create backups of their EBS volumes, which are block-level storage volumes used with EC2 instances. These snapshots capture the state of an EBS volume at a specific point in time and can be used for backups, to create new EBS volumes, or for data recovery.

- **Key Features**: Described below are key features of Snapshots:

  - **Incremental Backups**: When a snapshot is taken, only the blocks on the volume that have changed since the last snapshot are saved. This makes the snapshot process efficient in terms of both time and storage.

  - **Data Durability**: Snapshots are stored in Amazon S3, which is known for its high durability. This ensures that the backup data is securely preserved.

  - **Point-in-Time Recovery**: Snapshots provide a point-in-time recovery option. Any EBS volume created from a snapshot reflects the exact state of the original volume at the time the snapshot was taken.

  - **Share and Copy**: Snapshots can be shared with other AWS accounts or copied across AWS regions, facilitating easy data migration and disaster recovery.

- **How Snapshots Work**: Described below are key ways to work with Snapshots:

- **Creating a Snapshot**: When you create a snapshot of an EBS volume, the snapshot captures the volume's state at that particular moment. The initial snapshot might take some time to complete, depending on the size of the volume.

  - **Using Snapshots**: You can create a new EBS volume from a snapshot whenever needed. The new volume is a replica of the original volume as it was at the snapshot time.

  - **Performance Considerations**: While snapshots are taken, you can continue to use the original volume. However, there may be a slight performance impact.

- **Use Cases for Snapshots**: The following are most common use cases for Snapshots:

  - **Data Backup**: Regular snapshots can be scheduled for data backup purposes, ensuring data can be restored to a known state in case of loss or corruption.

  - **Disaster Recovery**: In case of a disaster, you can use snapshots to quickly restore or recreate your volumes in another AWS region.

  - **Data Duplication**: Snapshots allow for easy duplication of data across different environments for testing or analysis.

  - **Volume Migration**: Migrate or upgrade volumes by taking a snapshot and then creating a new volume based on that snapshot, potentially with different configurations.

- **Best Practices**: The following best practices are recommended for using Snapshots:

  - **Regular Scheduling**: Automate the snapshot creation process to ensure regular backups.

  - **Data Integrity**: For consistent snapshots of volumes attached to an instance, it's recommended to stop the instance or unmount the volume before taking a snapshot.

- **Lifecycle Management**: Implement a lifecycle policy to delete old snapshots automatically to manage costs and storage efficiently.

- **Encryption**: If required, use encrypted EBS volumes and snapshots to secure data at rest.

Cluster/Pacemaker Solutions

Certain solutions are available from third-party vendors and are referred to as **high-availability (HA) cluster solutions**. While the AWS infrastructure itself is designed and can be architected for high availability, the clustering solutions are designed to ensure high availability (HA) and manage failover processes for SAP applications and databases. It works by creating a clustered environment where multiple servers (nodes) work together to provide continuous service, even in the event of hardware or software failures. The primary goal is to minimize downtime and ensure business continuity. The clustering software works as follows:

- **Cluster Formation and Management**: The cluster is formed with multiple servers (nodes), each of which can run one or more instances of SAP applications or databases. Cluster management software (like SUSE Linux Enterprise High Availability Extension or Red Hat High Availability Add-On) manages the cluster, overseeing the communication between nodes and controlling resource allocation. The software manages resources like SAP services, applications, databases, file systems, and network resources and also ensures that each service instance is running on an appropriate node within the cluster.

- **Health Monitoring and Failover**: The cluster software continuously monitors the health and status of each node and the SAP services running on them. If a node or service fails (detected through missed heartbeats or health check failures), the cluster software automatically moves the affected services to another node in the cluster. This process is known as failover. A 'heartbeat' is a signal that nodes in the cluster regularly send to each other to monitor the health and status of each node.

- **Load Balancing and Resource Distribution**: The software can distribute workloads across nodes to optimize performance and resource utilization by ensuring that resources are not over-committed on any single node, maintaining balanced operation.

- **Data Replication and Synchronization**: The cluster software works in conjunction with storage solutions to ensure data replication and synchronization across nodes all the while also maintaining data consistency across the cluster, which is especially important for database applications.

- **Quorum and Fencing**: This is an important concept within the clustering software ensuring that a majority of nodes are operational and agree on the cluster's status, preventing 'split-brain' scenarios where two parts of the cluster might operate independently. Fencing isolates a failed node to protect shared resources, while **STONITH** (**Shoot the Other Node in the Head**) is a drastic form of fencing where a failing node is forcibly powered down.

- **Cluster Configuration and Administration**: Admins use graphical or command-line tools to configure and manage the cluster, setting up rules for failover, load balancing, and resource management while also defining policies, such as failover priorities and resource allocation rules.

AWS Elastic Disaster Recovery (DRS)

AWS Elastic Disaster Recovery (AWS DRS) is a fully managed service that enables organizations to **minimize downtime and data loss** by replicating their **on-premises or cloud-based workloads** to AWS. It provides **cost-effective, scalable, and continuous block-level replication**, allowing quick recovery of applications – including SAP systems – without maintaining redundant infrastructure. Some key features of AWS DRS are

- **Continuous Block-Level Replication for SAP Servers**: DRS replicates data from SAP servers (app servers, ASCS, ERS, HANA/AnyDB nodes) at the block level, capturing all disk writes in near real time. This ensures minimal data loss for transactional systems like SAP S/4HANA and efficient replication for non-database servers such as SAP PAS, Web Dispatcher, or Fiori frontend servers.

- **Rapid Recovery of SAP Landscape**: DRS launches EC2 instances for SAP components in a preconfigured order with defined instance types, network settings, and boot parameters. It can also automate restart of SAP services using pre-scripted workflows.

- **Automated Failback to Original Site**: Once the source environment (e.g., on-premises or primary AWS region) is restored, DRS facilitates syncing changes back and switching operations from the AWS recovery site. This enables planned DR testing and cutback to primary with minimal downtime and ensures consistency of critical SAP transactional data during reversion.

- **Non-disruptive Disaster Recovery Testing**: AWS DRS can simulate disaster recovery scenarios in isolated test environments on AWS without impacting production systems or replication.

- **Flexible Recovery Plan Customization**: DRS supports defining recovery blueprints with launch templates, server groupings, boot order, and script execution. Users can customize startup for clustered components (ASCS/ERS with SAP enqueue replication) and automatically trigger HANA database startup and SAPStartSrv processes.

- **Integration**: AWS DRS works with **AWS Systems Manager** or **Step Functions** to orchestrate complex SAP recovery workflows.

- **Cost-Efficient Staging Area for DR Readiness**: AWS DRS uses a low-cost **staging area** with minimal compute (t3.micro/t3.small) and storage for replication data. This avoids high costs of maintaining "warm standby" environments, and the user pays only for minimal replication resources until actual recovery/test launch.

- **Integrated Monitoring and Management**: The centralized AWS DRS Console shows real-time replication status, recovery snapshots, and health alerts. Events and state changes can trigger automation scripts for SAP post-recovery validation. This ensures that systems like SAP BW load chains, IDOCs, or background jobs are correctly resumed post-failover.

- **Support for Multi-AZ and Multi-region DR**: AWS DRS provides flexibility by replicating SAP systems across AWS Availability Zones (HA) or to a separate AWS region (DR). Enables customers to design for regional failures without complex infrastructure replication.

179

Next, let's dive into architecture patterns and compare benefits and limitations of single- and multi-region patterns.

Single- vs. Multi-region Architecture Patterns

SAP systems can be deployed across multiple AZs and even multiple regions balancing the competing requirements of high resiliency and low latency. Let's dive deep into both types of patterns below.

Single-Region Patterns

These patterns are useful when the goal is to reduce network latency since the workloads reside close to each other within the same region. This is also useful in case there are regulatory or sovereignty laws that stipulate the data to be kept within some regional boundaries. The four common single-region patterns are:

- **Single Region and Two AZs for Production**: In this configuration, the SAP HANA instance is set up over two Availability Zones, and SAP HANA System Replication is established on each instance. Both the primary and secondary instances utilize the same type of instance. The secondary instance can operate in either an active/passive or active/active mode. In the active/active mode, the systems connect to a load balancer that distributes workloads across multiple active servers vs. active/ passive clusters where systems connect to the main server, which handles the full workload, whereas the backup server is only activated in the event of a failure. This approach is recommended when using high-availability cluster solutions for automated failover, aiming to achieve virtually zero RPO and RTO.

  However, there is a cost associated with both the cluster software and the idle instance on standby. As usual, the backups can be stored in Amazon S3 buckets using the AWS Backint Agent, and the S3 objects are automatically stored across multiple devices in a minimum of three AZs within a region. Given below is a visual depiction of this architecture.

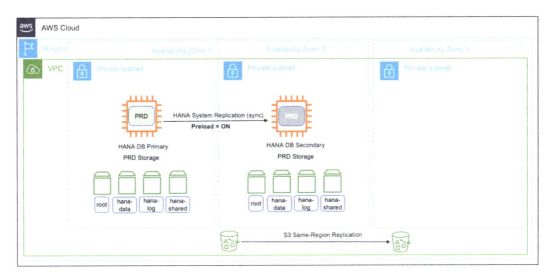

Figure 6-2. *Single-Region (Multi-AZ) Architecture (Variation 1)*

- **Single Region with Two Availability Zones for Production and Production-Sized Non-production in a Third Availability Zone**: This pattern is similar to the above except that a tertiary SAP HANA instance is deployed in a third Availability Zone.

  This architectural design is optimized for cost efficiency. It supports disaster recovery in the rare scenario of losing connectivity to two Availability Zones simultaneously. For disaster recovery purposes, the non-production SAP HANA workload is halted, freeing up resources for the production workload. Nonetheless, activating disaster recovery (involving a third Availability Zone) requires manual intervention. Compared with the approach above, this pattern further enhances availability; there is no restoration required from backups in the case when DR is invoked. The extra expense of the third instance is justified since the idle capacity is employed for non-production workloads. Given below is a visual depiction of this architecture pattern.

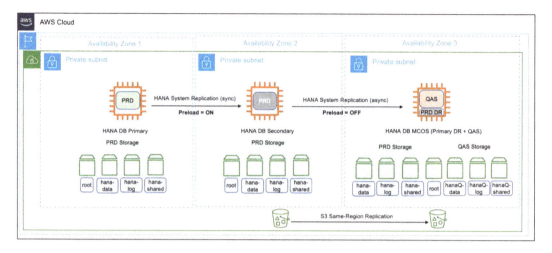

Figure 6-3. *Single-Region (Multi-AZ) Architecture (Variation 2)*

- **Single Region with One Availability Zone for Production and Another Availability Zone for Non-production**: This configuration involves setting up an SAP HANA instance using a two-tier SAP HANA System Replication over two Availability Zones. The secondary instance is an MCOS installation and co-hosts a non-production SAP HANA workload. Both the primary and secondary SAP HANA instances are of the same type, eliminating the need for idle capacity or additional licensing for clustering software.

  However, extra storage is necessary for handling the non-production SAP HANA workloads on the secondary instance. This solution is optimized for cost efficiency and does not include high-availability features. If a failure occurs in the primary instance, the non-production SAP HANA workload is halted, and a takeover is executed in the secondary instance. Given the recovery time involved in restoring services on the secondary instance, this pattern is appropriate for SAP HANA workloads that can tolerate a longer RPO and are used as disaster recovery systems.

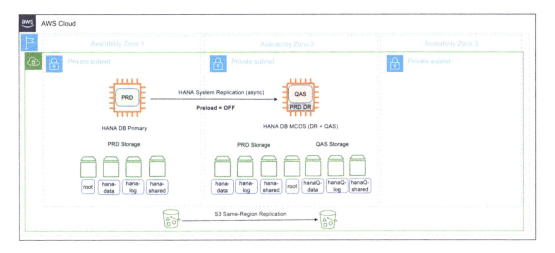

Figure 6-4. *Single-Region (Multi-AZ) Architecture (Variation 3)*

- **Single Region with One Availability Zone for Production**: This
  design involves deploying an SAP HANA instance as a standalone
  setup, without any target systems for data replication. It represents
  the simplest and most cost-effective deployment method.

  However, it's the least robust among all the architectural choices and
  is not advisable for mission-critical SAP HANA workloads. In case of
  a failure, business operations can be restored either through Amazon
  EC2 Auto Recovery for instance failures or by restoring from the most
  recent and valid backups in case of significant issues affecting the AZ.
  The non-production SAP HANA workloads are independent of the
  production SAP HANA instance, allowing them to be deployed in
  any Availability Zone within the region and sized according to their
  specific workload requirements.

  Given below is a visual depiction of this architectural pattern.

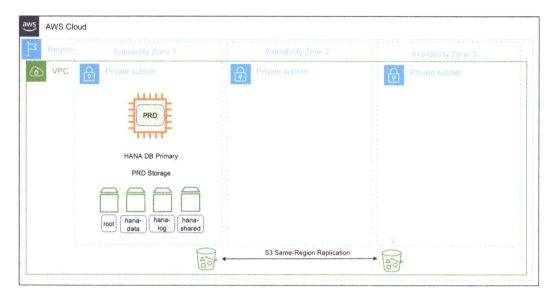

Figure 6-5. *Single-Region (Multi-AZ) Architecture (Variation 4)*

Multi-Region Patterns

Multi-Region patterns are designed to provide **geographic redundancy**, **disaster recovery**, and **low-latency access** for global SAP workloads. These patterns leverage AWS's global infrastructure and inherently have higher latency. This pattern provides geographical separation, which is a requirement for many enterprises. As mentioned, latency has to be considered in this pattern; hence, the distance between chosen regions is an important decision factor. The following are the common multi-region patterns:

- **Primary Region with Two Availability Zones for Production and Secondary Region with a Replica of Backups**: The production instance is deployed across two AZs in a single region providing the high-availability architecture. The backups are stored in S3, Amazon EBS, and AMIs, which are then replicated cross-region.

  In the event a complete region is down (hosting the primary site), the SAP systems can be restored from the backup copies in the secondary region. The RPO is impacted by how often the backup files are stored in S3 and the time taken to replicate the S3 bucket in the secondary region. The RTO is dependent on the time it takes to build the SAP system in the secondary region.

Given below is a depiction of this architectural pattern.

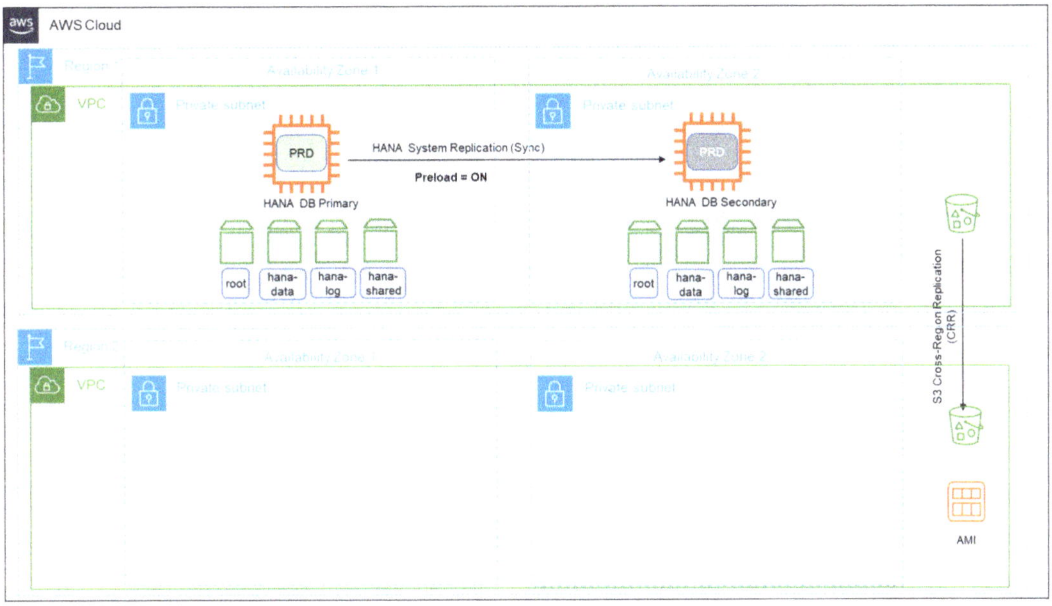

Figure 6-6. *Multi-region Architecture (Variation 1)*

- **Primary Region with Two Availability Zones for Production and Secondary Region with Compute and Storage Capacity deployed in a Single Availability Zone**: In addition to the above pattern, this pattern has compute and storage in an AZ within a secondary region and asynchronous High Availability and System Replication (HSR) set up between the two. If a failure occurs in the primary region, the production workloads are manually switched over to the secondary region. This approach guarantees high availability and disaster tolerance for the SAP systems and offers a faster failover and ensures the continuity of business operations through ongoing data replication.

  However, this method incurs higher costs due to the need to deploy necessary compute and storage resources for the production SAP HANA instance in the secondary region, as well as for the data transfers between regions. This architecture is ideal when there's a need for disaster recovery outside the primary region and when low RPO and RTO are critical. Given below is a visual representation of this architecture.

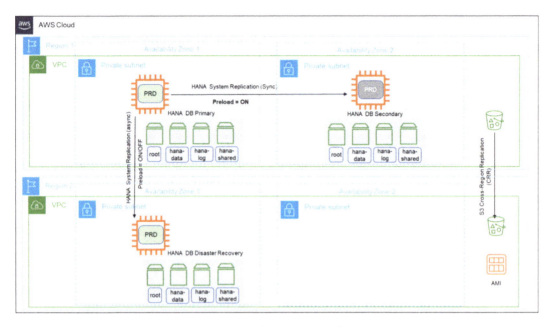

Figure 6-7. *Multi-region Architecture (Variation 2)*

- **Primary Region with Two Availability Zones for Production and Secondary Region with Compute and Storage Capacity Deployed and Data Replication Across Two Availability Zones**: This configuration employs dual two-tier SAP HANA System Replication setups spread across two AWS Regions. Within the same Region, the two-tier SAP HANA System Replication is set up across two Availability Zones, and replication to a secondary Region is achieved through SAP HANA Multi-target System Replication. Additionally, this setup can be enhanced with a high-availability cluster solution to enable automatic failover in the primary region. This design offers safeguards against failures both within Availability Zones and across regions.

  However, transitioning the SAP HANA instance to a different region in case of a failure necessitates manual action. In the event of a secondary region failover, the SAP HANA instance maintains its System Replication in the new region automatically, without the need for manual intervention.

This arrangement is suitable for scenarios demanding the highest possible application availability at all times, along with disaster recovery capabilities outside the primary region, aiming for the lowest RPO and RTO. This pattern is robust enough to handle the extremely rare event of three Availability Zones failing across multiple regions. As expected, the total cost for such an architectural pattern is on the higher side. Given below is a visual representation of this architecture.

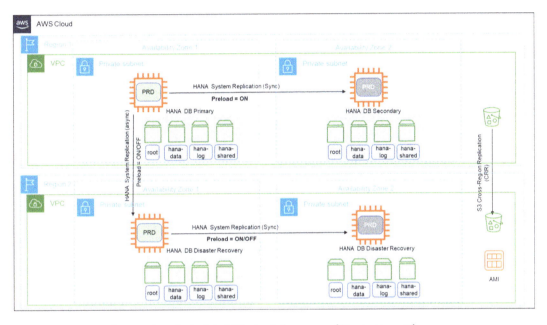

Figure 6-8. *Multi-region (Multi-AZ) Architecture (Variation 3)*

- **Primary Region with One Availability Zone for Production and Secondary Region with a Replica of Backups/AMIs:** The production SAP system is deployed in a primary AZ, while the backups stored in S3, EBS, and AMIs are in a secondary region. In this pattern, the SAP HANA instance is deployed as a standalone installation in the primary region in one Availability Zone with no target SAP HANA systems to replicate data.

  In this scenario, the SAP system lacks high availability. If a complete region failure occurs, the production SAP instance must be reconstructed in the secondary region using an AMI. After launching the instance, the latest backup set can be retrieved from Amazon S3 to restore the SAP HANA instance to a state prior to the disaster. Additionally, the AWS Backint Agent can be used for restoring and recovering the SAP HANA instance, after which client traffic can be rerouted to the newly established instance in the secondary region. For disaster recovery outside the primary region, the RPO is limited by the frequency of SAP HANA backup file storage in the Amazon S3 bucket and the time required to replicate the Amazon S3 bucket to the target Region. The RTO hinges on the duration needed to set up the system in the secondary Region and to resume operations from backup files with this duration varying based on the database size.

This pattern is most appropriate for non-production or non-critical production systems that can withstand the downtime necessary to restore normal functioning. Given below is a visual depiction of this architecture.

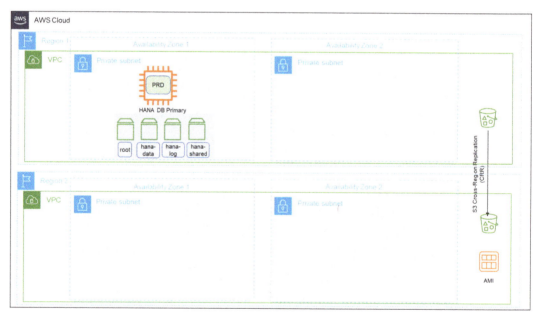

Figure 6-9. *Multi-region Architecture (Variation 4)*

In summary, it is strongly advised to run business-critical SAP instances across two Availability Zones for enhanced reliability. Implementing a third-party cluster solution in conjunction with SAP HANA System Replication is a strategic way to achieve a high-availability configuration. Although incorporating a third-party cluster solution into a high-availability setup may increase licensing expenses, this approach is still recommended. It offers a highly resilient architecture and aims to achieve near-zero RTO and RPO.

Network Considerations for Single- and Multi-Region Architecture Patterns

As seen, the high-availability setups require redirection of network traffic depending on failure scenarios. As reviewed earlier, the starting point for network configuration for SAP on AWS is to create a VPC. Within that, you can configure routing options to direct traffic to specific instances within the VPC or different subnets. All the subnets have a **CIDR** (**classless inter-domain routing**) IP assignment, which resides within the AZ. This CIDR IP assignment cannot be spanned across multiple AZs or reassigned to an instance in a different AZ during failover.

This rerouting issue is addressed via means of **overlay IP routing**. This method allows the AWS network to use a non-overlapping private IP address residing outside the VPC CIDR range of the primary AZ and direct the SAP network traffic to any instance across AZs by changing the routing entry. The SAP systems that are protected by a cluster solution use the overlay IP address assigned to ensure that the HA cluster is still accessible during the failover scenarios.

Routing Options: In order to access the overlay IPs, there are a couple of options for traffic routing:

- **AWS Transit Gateway**: The AWS TGW can be used as a central hub to facilitate the network connection to an overlay IP address from multiple locations as needed. Within the TGW, route table rules allow the overlay IP to access the SAP instance without configuring any additional components.

- **Network Load Balancer**: Another option is to use the NLB for accessing the overlay IP. When a connection request is received by the load balancer, it chooses a destination from the Network Load Balancer target group to forward the network connection request to, which could be an overlay IP address. The NLB is capable of handling millions of requests per second.

Disaster Recovery Options

Following the architecture patterns given above, the disaster recovery for SAP can follow any of the following strategies. Each strategy below is a trade-off between RTO/RPO and cost. Active/passive strategies involve using an operational site, like an AWS Region, to host workloads and handle traffic. A secondary, or passive, site, which could be a different AWS Region, is maintained for recovery purposes. This passive site remains dormant, not serving any traffic, until it's activated during a failover scenario.

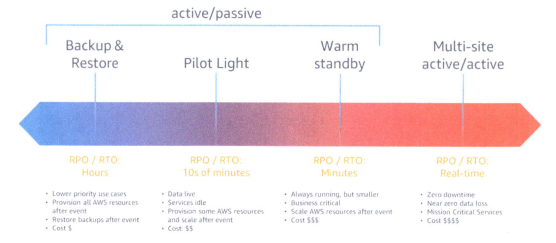

Figure 6-10. *Disaster Recovery Spectrum*

The following are the details of the disaster recovery options:

- **Backup and Restore**: Under this approach a backup of the SAP data is taken using the "AWS Backup" tool. The approach can help mitigate for data loss/corruption or lack of redundancy for workloads deployed in a single AZ. Furthermore, the approach can also help mitigate for a regional disaster by replicating data to another AWS Region. The frequency of the backup will depend on the desired RPO. Also, the backup allows for point-in-recovery restoration. The AWS Backup tool provides a centralized location to schedule, configure, and monitor the backups. In the scenario when a disaster is declared and recovery is invoked, the SAP system is restored via redeployment using 'infrastructure as code' using services like AWS CloudFormation, thereby reducing the RTO. In addition to the data, the code, configurations, as well as AMIs (Amazon Machine Images) that were used to deploy the original EC2 instances should also be backed up.

- **Pilot Light**: In the pilot light method, data is replicated from one AWS Region to another, and a version of the essential workload infrastructure is provisioned. Essential components for data replication and backup, like databases and object storage, are continuously operational. However, other components, such as application servers, are pre-loaded with the necessary application code and settings but remain inactive, being utilized only for testing or activated during disaster recovery scenarios. AWS offers the flexibility to deprovision resources when they're not in use and provision them as needed. A recommended practice for inactive resources is to keep them undeployed, preparing a setup that allows for their rapid deployment ('switching on') when required. This approach differs from the backup and restore method in that the core infrastructure is always ready, providing the ability to swiftly deploy a fully operational production environment by activating and scaling up the application servers. The pilot light strategy reduces the operational cost associated with disaster recovery by limiting the number of resources that are actively in use. Additionally, it streamlines the recovery process during a disaster, as the fundamental infrastructure needs are already established and ready to be activated.

  With this approach, mitigation is also needed against data loss and data corruption. This can be achieved by using a continuous data replication with versioning providing for point-in-time recovery.

- **Warm Standby**: In the warm standby method, a scaled-down yet completely operational version of the production environment is maintained in a different region. This approach builds upon the pilot light concept, enhancing recovery speed since the workload is constantly active in another Region. Additionally, this strategy facilitates easier testing or the implementation of ongoing testing, bolstering confidence in the disaster recovery capabilities. The warm standby and pilot light approaches may seem similar;

191

however, the key distinction is that the pilot light method cannot process transaction requests without additional action being taken beforehand, whereas, in the warm standby approach, the DR site can handle network traffic immediately (at a reduced capacity). The pilot light approach requires additional servers and resources to be 'turned on' and scaled up, while the warm standby only requires scaling up since all the infrastructure and resources are deployed and running. Depending on desired RTO and RPO and cost considerations, either approach can be deployed.

- **Multi-site Active/Active**: In this approach, the SAP workload is run simultaneously in multiple Regions. The users are able to access the system from any of the regions where the system is deployed. This is the most complex and expensive option and offers near-zero RTO (mitigating a data corruption scenario would still rely on backups resulting in non-zero RPO). Since both the sites serve users actively, there is no concept of 'failover.' DR testing checks for workload behavior towards loss of a site, whether the traffic is routed away from the failed site and whether the active site handles all the additional traffic with minimal performance loss.

Security for SAP on AWS

Security for SAP on AWS encompasses a range of practices and technologies designed to protect SAP applications and data when hosted on the AWS cloud platform. This approach is deeply integrated into the AWS Well-Architected Framework, ensuring that SAP workloads benefit from robust, cloud-native security features. AWS offers a robust framework, associated tools, and best practices to maintain the highest level of security standards that help to meet the security and compliance needs of running day-to-day SAP operations. Here's an overview of the key aspects of security for SAP on AWS:

- **Comprehensive Security Model**: AWS employs a shared responsibility model for security. This means while AWS is responsible for securing the underlying infrastructure, customers are responsible for securing their data and applications, including SAP systems.

- **Data Protection**: Protecting data, both in transit and at rest, is a critical aspect. AWS offers various encryption methods and services like AWS Key Management Service (KMS) to enhance data security for SAP workloads.

- **Identity and Access Management**: AWS Identity and Access Management (IAM) allows precise control over who can access your SAP resources on AWS. This includes managing permissions and roles to ensure that only authorized personnel can access sensitive SAP data.

- **Network Security**: AWS provides robust network security features, including security groups, network access control lists (ACLs), and AWS Network Firewalls. These tools help safeguard SAP environments from unauthorized access and network attacks.

- **Monitoring and Compliance**: AWS offers services like Amazon CloudWatch, AWS Config, and AWS CloudTrail for continuous monitoring and logging of SAP system activity. This ensures compliance with security policies and aids in the detection of suspicious activities.

- **Incident Response and Remediation**: AWS provides tools and guidance for responding to security incidents. This includes automated responses to specific threats and comprehensive support for investigating and mitigating issues.

- **Regular Security Assessments**: Conducting regular security assessments and reviews, such as AWS Well-Architected Reviews, helps identify and mitigate potential security risks in SAP environments.

- **Architecture Design Patterns for SAP**: AWS offers specific architecture design patterns for SAP workloads, covering scenarios like internal access, internet egress access, and internet ingress access. These patterns help in securely managing traffic flow to and from SAP systems.

- **Integration with SAP Security Practices**: AWS recommends following SAP Security Notes and News for up-to-date security recommendations specific to SAP workloads, ensuring that the security measures are comprehensive and tailored to SAP applications.

- **Customization and Flexibility**: AWS provides a flexible environment where security controls can be tailored to specific business needs and compliance requirements, ensuring that SAP systems on AWS align with the organization's security posture.

Best Practices and Frameworks for Security of SAP on AWS

AWS has provided certain best practices and frameworks to help with the security of SAP workloads running on AWS. These are included as part of the Well-Architected Review Framework, which provides core principles for the enterprise to establish controls across the entire landscape. The key best practices are as follows:

- **Security Standards as Applicable to SAP**: Standards are documented guidelines outlining policies and best practices for securing systems. They serve as a benchmark for assessing your SAP workload's security. Some standards are obligatory for regulatory compliance, while others, though optional, are beneficial for establishing clear roles and responsibilities. Within this best practice, key components are the following:

  - **Define Security Roles and Responsibilities**: Establishing requirements for the security of your SAP workloads helps in pinpointing risks that need mitigation and ensures that security roles and responsibilities are properly allocated. As part of this, the organization should review:

    - **AWS Shared Responsibility Model**: AWS is responsible for the security of the cloud, and the customer is responsible for the security of their apps and data.

- **Security Foundations Across SAP and AWS**: Review the security standards and compliance certifications supported by SAP and AWS, and identify those pertinent to your industry and country, such as PCI-DSS, GDPR, and HIPAA. Leveraging these controls can enhance compliance and certification efforts, streamlining the process to meet specific security standards.

- **Security Foundations of Service Providers**: When relying on external organizations for managing any aspect of your SAP workload, it's important to evaluate their capacity to adhere to the necessary security controls. This evaluation should encompass both legal and regulatory requirements that your business is subject to.

- **Classify Data with SAP**: The level of data sensitivity influences the necessary controls to reduce risk. AWS recommends consulting standard frameworks relevant to your industry or organization to guide the classification of your SAP workloads and their data. This approach tailors risk mitigation strategies effectively to the specific data types and workloads. As part of this, the organization should review:

  - **Data Classification/Handling Requirements**: Any existing data classification frameworks within your organization. These frameworks assist in sorting data based on its sensitivity, focusing on preserving confidentiality, integrity, and availability. Once the data is categorized, understand the appropriate handling procedures for each classification level. This includes applying specific security controls that align with standards or regulatory requirements like PCI-DSS or GDPR. It also involves addressing common privacy concerns, particularly in managing personally identifiable information (PII). The handling procedures should reflect the sensitivity of the data, ensuring that higher-risk categories receive more stringent protections.

- **SAP Data Types with Specific Handling Rules**: When running SAP systems, there may be unique data handling and storage needs dictated by the business processes. Certain examples are the need for a digital payments add-on to safeguard stored cardholder data; ensuring adherence to PCI compliance standards and HR data residency laws, which may mandate SAP data stay within certain geographic boundaries; etc.

- **Review Need for Specific Security Controls for SAP**: Leverage AWS-provided controls that can help meet any SAP-specific security and compliance needs. As part of this, the organization can review:

  - **Geographical Location Requirements**: Sometimes it may be necessary from a security standpoint to host SAP systems in a specific location. For instance, depending on sensitive data handled, some customers may need to deploy SAP in AWS GovCloud (US), which is designed to host sensitive and regulated data and meet stringent US government security and compliance requirements.

  - **Aligning SAP with Broader AWS Account Strategy**: When managing SAP workloads on AWS, a key factor is your approach to AWS account strategy and the landing zone model, which should align with your organization's security controls. Consideration should be provided to segregate SAP and non-SAP workloads, placing production workloads in a different AWS account from non-production workloads and understanding the organization's existing AWS account management strategy including AWS Organizations and AWS Control Tower for centralized management. All these can enhance security and operational efficiency.

- **Infrastructure and Software Controls to Reduce Security Misconfigurations**: It's advised to implement hardening measures for SAP software solutions and their underlying configurations, including operating system and database patches, parameters, cloud services, and infrastructure. This hardening process is essential for safeguarding all SAP environments, covering both production and non-production setups. The extent of hardening should be in line with the specific security requirements established by your organization. This approach ensures that your SAP systems are robustly protected against potential security threats. Within this best practice, the key components are:

- **Security and Audit Built into SAP Network Design**: Securing network access for your SAP workloads acts as a primary barrier against harmful activities. To determine the necessary ports, protocols, and traffic flows, assess both your business needs and the specific SAP solution in use. Align these with your organization's security standards and leverage available tools and network design patterns for simplification. Regular audits, or audits following any changes, are crucial to maintain robust network protection. As part of this, the organization can review the following:

  - **Network Traffic Flows for SAP**: Network traffic for SAP workloads generally falls into three categories: *inbound*, *outbound*, and *internal*. It is important to discern if the traffic's source and destination are within your trusted network to help define appropriate rule sets. For inbound and outbound traffic, beyond the usual user access and interface connections, it is crucial to consider SAP-specific needs. These include connections to SAP Support through SAP Router and SAP SaaS offerings that may limit access based on source IP addresses. Regarding internal traffic, attention should be given to interactions between different components and systems. This includes both AWS services and shared services within the network. Understanding these traffic patterns is vital for establishing effective and secure network management.

  - **Permit and Restrict Traffic Flows**: Two main strategies for regulating network traffic in and out of AWS VPC are security groups and network ACLs. A security group functions as a virtual firewall at the EC2 instance level, managing both inbound and outbound traffic in a stateful manner. On the other hand, a network ACL provides an optional layer of security for your VPC, acting as a firewall that controls traffic for one or more subnets.

Unlike security groups, network ACLs are stateless. It is also important to account for network components external to the VPC. This includes AWS-provided external network components like CloudWatch endpoints, as well as internet-hosted services such as software repositories for operating system patches. Beyond AWS's standard offerings, SAP offers additional network security options. These include the SAP Router, the SAP Web Dispatcher, and SAP Gateway network-based ACLs. These SAP-specific tools complement AWS services and configurations, helping to either allow or restrict network access to SAP systems effectively. These layered security measures, both from AWS and SAP, work together to create a robust network security environment for your SAP workloads.

- **Protect SAP Data at Rest and Transit**: Given the critical role SAP systems play in business operations and their storage of sensitive data, it is a best practice to encrypt this data both at rest and in transit. This encryption should align with at least one mechanism to satisfy both internal and external security requirements and controls. Beyond what's outlined in the AWS shared responsibility model, AWS offers a variety of encryption solutions. Many AWS services include features that allow for easy activation of encryption, usually with minimal impact on performance. When considering encryption options, it's important to look at both the database level and the SAP application layer. These encryption measures are crucial for safeguarding sensitive enterprise data within SAP systems.

- **Implement a Strategy for Managing Security Events**: Developing a strategic security plan is crucial for addressing both proactive and reactive measures necessary to confront security challenges effectively. This plan should include procedures for logging, detecting, and enhancing protection, which are essential for identifying and resolving security incidents in SAP workloads on AWS.

Key Tools and Services for SAP Security on AWS

AWS provides a comprehensive set of tools that can be used to manage the security for SAP systems on AWS. The key tools and services are:

- **Single Sign-On (SSO)**: Integration between SAP **Business Technology Platform** (**BTP**) and AWS IAM Identity Center allows for secure and streamlined user authentication. This integration supports various **identity providers** (**IdPs**) such as AWS IAM, Okta, and Microsoft Windows Azure Active Directory.

- **AWS Network Firewall**: Offers features such as high availability, stateful inspection of SAP system protocols, web filtering (especially for SAP Fiori), and intrusion prevention. It also includes alert and flow logs integrated with AWS monitoring tools for enhanced traceability and auditability.

- **AWS Shield**: Protects against **Denial of Service** (**DoS**) attacks, ensuring the availability and resilience of SAP applications.

- **AWS WAF (Web Application Firewall)**: Provides protection for web applications, like SAP Fiori, against various web-based threats.

- **AWS Certificate Manager**: Manages public SSL certificates, essential for secure communications.

- **Amazon CloudFront**: Enhances security at the network edge, protecting SAP workloads and complementing AWS Shield and AWS WAF.

- **OS Hardening**: AWS and SAP provide resources and guidance for hardening the operating system of the AWS instances running SAP applications, including specific SAP notes for configuration and security best practices.

- **Data Encryption**: AWS offers encryption for data at rest and in transit, ensuring the confidentiality and integrity of data within the SAP environment. This includes encryption features for Amazon EBS, EFS, and S3.

- **Security Groups and Network ACLs**: These function as virtual firewalls for instances and subnets, respectively, controlling inbound and outbound traffic and adding layers of security.

- **AWS CloudTrail**: Records AWS API calls, providing a history that is vital for security analysis, resource change tracking, and compliance auditing.

- **Amazon Simple Notification Service (SNS)**: Can be used for setting up notifications, such as alerts for SSH logins to AWS instances running SAP.

These tools and services form an integrated approach to securing SAP on AWS, aligning with the AWS shared responsibility model. They ensure that while AWS takes care of the infrastructure security, SAP administrators can focus on securing their data and applications.

Automation for SAP Operations

Businesses seek a reliable and thoroughly tested method for handling their SAP workloads in the cloud. The solution must be secure, swift, and economical, ensuring minimal risk and optimal reliability. Apart from providing infrastructure services for hosting SAP workloads, AWS also offers tools and services for the automation of day-to-day tasks and SAP operations. Automation decreases the need for manual operations, enhances efficiency, and provides organizations with a steady and dependable experience in managing SAP systems. Also, customers are building their own automation solutions using AWS services, and these serve very specific use cases for the enterprise or even business units within the enterprise.

While AWS continues to add more automation capabilities, here are some of the key automation tools.

AWS Systems Manager: A Unified Operations Hub

AWS Systems Manager is a comprehensive management service that helps automate, manage, and monitor AWS and on-premises infrastructure at scale. It offers a **unified user interface** and set of tools to manage EC2 instances, virtual machines, and other AWS resources. It's a key building block in automating operational tasks, improving visibility, and enhancing compliance. Key capabilities include:

- **Automation**: Automate common IT tasks such as patching, backups, configuration changes, and SAP system operations (start/stop) and define workflows as runbooks using AWS-provided or custom automation documents (SSM documents). The trigger is based on events, schedules, or manual execution and can automate daily system restarts, HANA database refresh, or stop/start of SAP landscapes during maintenance windows.

- **Run Command**: Remotely execute shell scripts or commands on managed instances without SSH in order to restart SAP services, check SAP processes (disp+work, HDB), or retrieve system logs remotely.

- **Session Manager**: This can be used to securely log into EC2-based SAP HANA or NetWeaver instances for troubleshooting or configuration without SSH.

- **Patch Manager**: This can be used to automate OS-level patching for managed instances across AWS and on-prem. Users can ensure Linux/Windows OS patches are applied to SAP infrastructure in a controlled, compliant way.

- **Maintenance Windows**: Schedule time slots for running tasks like patching, backups, or SAP restarts.

Monitoring Using AWS CloudWatch Application Insights for SAP

Amazon CloudWatch Application Insights allows for comprehensive monitoring of the entire SAP application stack, including applications, infrastructure, network, and services. It leverages alarms, logs, and event data to automate responses and decrease

201

the **Mean Time to Recovery** (**MTTR**) from system breakdowns. This tool enables the aggregation and easy access of all performance and operational data, including logs and metrics, on a unified platform, eliminating the need to monitor these components in isolation, such as servers, storage, networks, databases, and applications.

CloudWatch Application Insights streamlines the process of setting up observability for the SAP applications, offering clear insights into their health. It automatically identifies and configures essential metrics and logs for various components, including databases, application servers, operating systems, and storage volumes. This service continuously monitors such telemetry data to identify and link any anomalies or errors, alerting the administrator to potential issues in the application.

It generates automated dashboards highlighting these problems for effective troubleshooting, along with further insights to guide towards the possible root cause. This feature enables prompt corrective measures to maintain the health of the SAP applications and prevent impact on end users. It monitors key aspects like Amazon EC2, Amazon EBS, Amazon EFS, SAP security, SAP availability, SAP performance, and the metrics of the high-availability pacemaker cluster. The service provides actionable insights by setting off alarms when predefined thresholds for each monitored metric are reached.

SAP Serverless Refresh

Organizations frequently need to refresh their SAP systems to facilitate testing and production operations. The traditional manual refresh method can be slow, expensive, and cumbersome for SAP administrators. As a more efficient alternative, you can employ an automated solution composed of serverless AWS services, which collectively handle the system refresh tasks. This functionality allows for the updating of an SAP system's test data from another system and is currently compatible with SAP systems using the SAP HANA database management system.

The refresh is executed with a combination of AWS services including Amazon **SNS** (**Simple Notification Service**), Lambda functions, and Systems Manager. The steps to execute are as follows:

A user starts a state machine in AWS Step Functions. In simple terms, it refers to a workflow that coordinates the execution of various tasks that defines the sequence and conditions under which these tasks are executed as part of an application or a process.

- Once the workflow it triggered, a notification goes to the end user via Amazon SNS, and the Lambda function launches an EC2 instance from an AMI (Amazon Machine Image).

- Next, the Lamba function restores the backup by copying the files from Amazon S3 to the EC2 instance hosting the database. Referencing the Parameter Store within Systems Manager, the Lambda function then retrieves values of some key variables like target hostname, target IP address, and target SAP system identifier.

- Once the database restore is complete, the Lambda function performs post-copy tasks. Lastly, a notification is sent back to the end user via Amazon SNS to notify that the refresh is complete. All the while, the Lambda function uses an Amazon DynamoDB table to track the progress of each step.

The advantages of this automation include

- Preserving the configuration of the SAP system

- Boosting productivity, agility, and innovation

- Minimizing downtime to just a few minutes

- Reducing the need for manual labor

- Lowering the likelihood of errors due to human involvement

- Shortening the refresh cycle from weeks to mere days

Automating Startup and Shutdown of SAP Systems

A typical operational SAP system is composed of various Amazon EC2 instances that host essential SAP components, including SAP database servers, application servers, Central Services, and SAP enqueue replication services. Additionally, organizations using SAP frequently integrate the primary SAP systems with other critical solutions for functions like archiving and tax management and also content servers and job management systems. The initiation and termination of such an intricately connected SAP solution requires a particular order of operations.

The administrator can automate the startup and shutdown of SAP systems by using AWS services. This streamlined and regulated method significantly reduces the need for manual input by automating routine and repetitive tasks while adhering to the sequence outlined by SAP administrators. Moreover, this automation allows for the inclusion of scheduling, notifications, and alerts through cloud-specific AWS services. Furthermore, it is equipped to identify and manage dependencies between various SAP and non-SAP applications.

Auto-scaling SAP Applications

The auto-scaling feature for SAP applications can respond dynamically to the demands of SAP application servers. It intelligently scales Amazon EC2 instances up or down based on actual requirements. This functionality is designed to efficiently handle fluctuations in workload, including variations in concurrent user logins, month-end closures, payment processes, and a range of both expected and unexpected workload scenarios. The system is capable of horizontal scaling, which involves starting new compute services to function as application servers when demand increases and stopping these services when the demand decreases.

Auto-scale is achieved by triggering Amazon EventBridge to initiate a Lambda function. This Lambda function collects the local environment variables and parameters including threshold values for system load as defined by the administrators. If the demand is above or below specified thresholds, then the Lambda function directs the AWS Systems Manager to start or stop additional EC2 instances to support the SAP applications.

Automated Operating System Patching

In order to maintain the smooth operations of the SAP landscape, the operating system needs to be patched for updates regularly. This ensures that security improves, systems stay compliant, and unplanned downtime can be reduced to a minimum. AWS Systems Manager can be used to automate the patching of the OS, which reduces the manual effort required to patch and upgrade the OS.

AWS Systems Manager uses its built-in Patch Manager capability, which can automate the process of patching the EC2 instances with security and general OS updates. Depending on the operating system type, the Patch Manager can help patch a whole set of EC2 instances. By creating a "patch configuration," the instances can be patched either on demand or on a predetermined schedule. The Patch Manager also allows for scanning the instances to create a report of missing patches or automatically install the missing patches.

Automated Auditing of SAP Systems and Operating System Configurations

As any organization running SAP would know, there are many configurations to be managed for both the SAP application and the operating systems. These configurations adhere to best practices, meet the audit requirements, as well as meet the requirements for getting the necessary support from third-party vendors. In the traditional approach, these configurations are checked manually and, in most cases, only by sampling and not a complete audit.

'AWS Config,' a fully managed service, provides an inventory of resources, a record of configuration histories, and notifications on configuration changes for security and governance purposes. It enables the user to identify existing AWS resources, document configurations of third-party resources, and export a detailed inventory of all your resources along with their configuration specifics. Additionally, AWS Config allows you to track the configuration of a resource at any given moment. These features are instrumental in compliance auditing, security assessments, monitoring changes in resources, and aiding in troubleshooting efforts. AWS Config can be leveraged to evaluate configuration changes to AWS resources against a defined set of rules. If a change is identified as non-compliant, then it can be alerted to the user. AWS Config comes with predefined managed rules of which many rules apply to SAP workloads. Some of the key rules are **Desired Instance Type**, **Instance Detailed Monitoring**, **EC2 Volume in Use Check, EC2 Volume Encryption Check, S3 Public Read, S3 Server Side Encrypt,** and plenty others.

By leveraging AWS Config, the non-compliant configurations can be notified to the user via Amazon SNS (Simple Notification Service).

Simple Scheduler for SAP Jobs

Scheduling jobs in SAP is a common operational activity for administrators. Typically, SAP users employ the SM37 transaction to execute batch jobs within their SAP systems; however, for more intricate job scheduling that involves dependencies across various SAP systems, users often resort to third-party batch scheduling tools. A major challenge arises when these systems experience downtime or become unavailable for any reason. For SAP customers who rely on external job scheduling tools, the failure of these jobs to execute due to system unavailability can pose significant difficulties. While the impact of such failures might be limited to a single system in some cases, situations where multiple jobs fail to run can lead to costly and time-intensive remedial efforts.

This activity can be automated using '*Simple Scheduler*,' a cloud-native solution built on AWS serverless services including Amazon DynamoDB, S3, Amazon API Gateway, and AWS Step Functions. The user schedules the jobs via a custom frontend (developed by AWS Professional Services), and the key input parameters provided by the user are stored in Amazon DynamoDB.

The job is triggered at the scheduled time by an Amazon CloudWatch Event Rule, which in turn triggers an AWS Step Function. The Step Function then invokes a series of Lambda functions, which reads the job parameters, secures the credentials from AWS Secrets Manager, and triggers the job in the SAP transaction SM37. The flow and sequence of jobs is maintained in the AWS Step Function. On successful completion, the user is notified using Amazon SNS (Simple Notification Service).

Automated HANA Database Patching

HANA DB patching is again an important maintenance activity for SAP administrators to ensure that the system is up to date with security fixes and new features. Customers can leverage AWS Systems Manager to automate this database update/patching activity ensuring consistency and reducing human error, which comes with the manual approach.

As part of this automation, the Systems Manager identifies the target EC2 instance hosting the HANA database based on the tags passed as input. Next, the required update is downloaded from an S3 bucket, and the actual patching activity is executed. Once done, the updated SAP HANA version info is uploaded to the S3 bucket.

AWS Management Console

The **AWS Management Console** is a vital component of AWS's cloud computing platform, providing a web-based user interface for managing AWS services. It is designed to offer a simple, intuitive, and efficient way for users to access and control a wide range of cloud services provided by AWS. Here's a detailed overview:

- **Interface and Accessibility**

  - **Web-Based Interface**: Accessible from a web browser, the console provides a graphical interface to manage AWS services.

  - **User-Friendly Design**: The layout is intuitive, making it easy for both beginners and experienced users to navigate.

  - **Customizable Dashboard**: Users can customize their dashboard to quickly access frequently used resources and services.

- **Service Management**

  - **Wide Range of Services**: The console gives access to a vast array of AWS services including computing (EC2), storage (S3), databases (RDS), and many others.

  - **Service Integration**: Services are well integrated, allowing for seamless management across different AWS offerings.

- **Resource Management and Monitoring**

  - **Resource Deployment and Configuration**: Users can launch and configure resources like EC2 instances, set up VPCs, and create S3 buckets, among other key options.

  - **Monitoring Tools**: The console also incorporates tools like Amazon CloudWatch for real-time monitoring of resources and applications.

- **Security and Identity Management**

  - **IAM (Identity and Access Management)**: The console allows for the creation and management of AWS users, groups, and permissions.

  - **Security Checks**: The console also provides security advisories and best practices to ensure secure deployment of resources.

- **Cost Management and Optimization**

  - **AWS Cost Explorer**: The console comes with AWS Cost Explorer, which is an integrated tool for tracking and analyzing AWS spend.

- **Budgets and Alerts**: Users can also set budgets and receive alerts to manage costs effectively.

- **Automation and Scripting**

  - **AWS CLI and SDK Integration**: The console also supports command-line tools and SDKs for users preferring scripting over the GUI.

  - **Automation Services**: The console has integration with AWS services like CloudFormation for automated provisioning of resources.

- **Support and Documentation**

  - **Access to AWS Support**: The console provides direct access to AWS support within the console for any assistance.

  - **Resource Center**: It also includes documentation, tutorials, and best practices guides.

Mobile Access

AWS Console Mobile Application provides access to the console on mobile devices, allowing for on-the-go management of AWS resources.

In the context of SAP workloads, the console is especially useful for managing and operating SAP systems on the AWS cloud platform. Here's a detailed note on how it is used specifically for SAP environments:

- **EC2 Instance Management**: Launch and manage Amazon EC2 instances where SAP systems can be installed. Configure aspects like computing, storage, and networking according to SAP requirements. Monitor performance and health of instances running SAP.

- **Storage Management**: Utilize Amazon S3 for storing backups of SAP databases and application files. Manage EBS volumes, which can be used for SAP database and application servers.

- **Networking and Security**: Configure Virtual Private Cloud (VPC) for secure network isolation of SAP systems. Set up security groups, network ACLs, and IAM roles for secure and controlled access to SAP resources.

- **Monitoring and Logging**: Use Amazon CloudWatch for monitoring the performance and operational health of SAP environments. Access logs and metrics to ensure optimal performance and troubleshoot issues.

- **Scalability and Elasticity**: Easily scale SAP environments up or down based on demand, leveraging AWS's elastic infrastructure. Utilize auto-scaling to automatically adjust the number of EC2 instances for SAP applications.

- **Backup and Disaster Recovery**: Implement backup strategies using AWS Backup or other AWS services. Configure disaster recovery setups for SAP systems, like pilot light or warm standby.

- **Cost Management**: Monitor and manage AWS costs and usage with AWS Cost Explorer and Budgets. Optimize spending by identifying underused resources or choosing appropriate pricing models.

As was customary, the participants surrounded Ashish asking follow-up questions. "I plan to test out some of the tools you mentioned," "I plan to take up an AWS certification in preparation for our SAP modernization project," and "I can already see some benefits in monitoring our batch jobs" were just some of the comments that Ashish heard.

Sandeep came up and patted Ashish on the back, saying, "That was a great session, Ashish. There were some great ideas for us on how to get started on execution and delivery for SAP modernization especially what this would mean from a day-to-day perspective. I will have some of my team members reach out to you for some more in-depth discussions."

Ashish acknowledged with a smile saying, "Of course. I would be happy to."

Thomas, who always was meticulous with action items, sought out Mark before he left, "Hey, Mark. I sent out the pricing a few days ago. Just wanted to check if you have reviewed and whether you had any questions." "Thanks for checking, Thomas. Yes, I did review the pricing, and I will include your input to our business case. As of now there are no questions, but I am sure our procurement team may have a few at a later stage!"

As the two headed out, Thomas offered, "Hey, Ashish, do you want to grab drinks and dinner? Let's celebrate our mini-success." "For sure, amigo."

CHAPTER 7

Innovation Beyond Infrastructure with SAP on AWS

After having covered the infrastructure details in previous chapters, this chapter will focus on innovations and use cases for SAP beyond infrastructure, using AWS technology. This will include three core pillars, data and analytics, applications and APIs, and artificial intelligence and machine learning.

It was the start of the busy travel season, and it naturally meant that things quickly got busy at Nimbus. The technology team saw direct impact of this enhanced activity, with additional support for ticketing operations, customer support, and, most importantly, customer experience. During the travel season, "we at Nimbus work even harder so that our customers can take time off peacefully" was an oft-repeated mantra at Nimbus. But even during these busy times, Elizabeth did not lose sight of her long-term priorities. She pulled in the core team on the SAP modernization initiative. The meeting was held a bit early in the day at 7:30 AM, so as not to disrupt work for the travel season. No one complained.

Elizabeth got to the point quickly, "I think we are at an inflection point with our SAP modernization program. My goal for our discussion today is to tie up loose ends and plan any remaining next steps with precision. I would like to get a firm date by which we can present our final plan to Micah and then eventually to the board. Can we go around the room to review each aspect?"

Mark started, "My focus is the business case and the buy-in from business stakeholders. As far as the business case, I have the inputs regarding benefits and SAP license costs and just recently received the pricing information from AWS. I have included all of it, and the

© Tushar Srivastava 2025
T. Srivastava, *Modernizing SAP with AWS*, https://doi.org/10.1007/979-8-8688-1579-9_7

business case seems very promising. Regarding the buy-in from the business stakeholders, you are already aware of the strong partnership we have forged there, and we have full support from them in managing the change. I don't see that as a risk."

Elizabeth nodded in acknowledgment and moved over to Sandeep. "My team's focus is the delivery of the solution and ongoing operations. I have already been working with our regular 'system integrator' partners on supporting us with delivery and passed the costs to Mark. Also, since the delivery and operations will involve the new component of the cloud, I have had discussions with AWS on understanding the operating model in the cloud. Those meetings have been very useful. Again, I don't see much risk there."

Sandeep looked around the room to see if there were questions. As Elizabeth was ready to move on, he remembered something and continued, "After speaking with AWS and doing my research, I think the cloud can also benefit this program, beyond just infrastructure. I will engage with AWS on this topic." Sandeep finally concluded. Elizabeth cocked her head a bit and said, "Interesting. Yes, let's dig into that."

Nolan finally had a chance to speak and chimed in, "I have been working the partnership with both SAP and AWS. SAP did send out an updated quote, and AWS has overall been impressive. They have been doing a great job of educating us and focusing on the success of this program. They have smart people on the team." Elizabeth nodded in acknowledgment. She seemed to be thinking over something before saying, "Nolan, I would like to have a meeting with the other cloud providers to see what they have to offer. I would like just you and me at that meeting."

There was stunned silence in the room, before Nolan broke it and confirmed, "Yes, for sure. I can arrange that."

Back in the Amazon office, Thomas's screen flashed with a notification. He had his scheduled one-on-one meeting with Amy coming up in 15 minutes. Both of them were in the office and planned to do the meeting in person. He figured he still had a few minutes to wrap up some routine emails. Amy walked into the room just with a coffee cup even as Thomas was settling in with his laptop and related paraphernalia. The conversation covered regular day-to-day issues before Amy said, "Also, let's discuss our position with Nimbus. What is the latest on that?"

Thomas was prepared and started, "We have done detailed sessions with them to cover technical topics and have also provided them with high-level pricing. They have also received pricing from SAP, and they would be taking the business case to the CFO and the board within the next four to six weeks. We still have a few topics to cover with them, which we will do over the next couple of weeks." Amy listened thoughtfully. She got up and paced around the room before commenting, "Are we looking around corners? Everything seems to be moving just too smoothly. While you continue with the sessions, also ask for a meeting with Elizabeth and Nolan, just for you and me. Let's try to stay ahead of the curve." Thomas's mind was already racing even before the meeting came to an end.

Sandeep was waiting in the conference room while he read the latest article in 'Harvard Business Review' that spoke about the role of artificial intelligence at the workplace. He kept highlighting text from the article on his Kindle device, intending to share it with his team. Nolan walked in and greeted Sandeep, "Our very own scientist, always reading up something." Sandeep smiled as he put away the device and got up to shake hands with Nolan. After the initial chatter, Sandeep got to the point, "Nolan, I wanted to talk to you about the SAP modernization project and specifically around AWS." Nolan leaned in and said, "Yes, you mentioned in the email and I am all ears." Sandeep continued, "Remember the other day in the meeting with Elizabeth I mentioned innovating with SAP on AWS beyond infrastructure. I have read about use cases where we can leverage AWS beyond just infrastructure for SAP. I would like to include that as part of our plan sooner rather than later." Nolan nodded and simply said, "Very good. How should we proceed?"

Having anticipated this question, Sandeep said, "I think we need to meet with the AWS team and not a large audience, but just you and me. I want to do some in-depth discussions before baking it into our plans. Let me know what you think?" Nolan sat there and thought for a while. "Sandeep, I am not opposed to the idea, and I am sure there are some benefits that you have researched. However, Elizabeth is now asking us to also look at alternatives to AWS. I am not sure how much deeper we should get here before we fully know what Elizabeth has in mind." The two men sat silently in a thoughtful mood. Sandeep stared at his watch and said, "Well, I am not sure what Elizabeth is thinking, but let me move ahead with this conversation with AWS. I am sure it won't be wasted. Anything we learn would be of value, and if we do pivot to a different provider, at least we have some additional inputs to compare against." "Very well, let's move ahead then," Nolan responded.

As Nolan wound up for the day, an email popped up that caught his attention. It was from Thomas. Thomas was asking to meet with him and Elizabeth to discuss the next steps on the engagement – specifically, to discuss key dates and the path forward. Nolan re-read the email. Here he was planning to engage other cloud providers and now Thomas's probing email. He thought he might have to stall, but then he needed to keep AWS engaged on the key topics for Sandeep. He felt like this situation was right out of a rom-com, where one partner was asking the other about their future. Well, this is no relationship; this is business, *Nolan thought to himself trying to reconcile his conflicting emotions. Nolan spent the next day securing the contacts and sending out emails to the other cloud providers. Not a difficult task, since most technology vendors were already knocking on Nimbus's door constantly. Before the day ended, Nolan had received eager responses from each of the cloud providers. He asked Elizabeth's executive assistant to help schedule this series of meetings. Before long, the meetings were scheduled, and Nolan was invited to each of them. Elizabeth's executive assistant was really good, knowing exactly the priorities of his boss. Nolan however had still not requested for one meeting yet, the one that Thomas had asked for.*

"Hello, is this Thomas?" "Yes, this is Thomas." "Hi, Thomas, this is Sandeep Krishnan from Nimbus. Hope you are doing well today. I thought a call would be easier than email."

"Hey, Sandeep, thank you. I am doing well. How can I help?"

Pleasantries were exchanged for a short while before Sandeep got to the point, "As you know, I am responsible for the delivery of the overall SAP modernization engagement, and I read about some of the innovation that AWS can provide that is beyond just infrastructure. I wanted to dig deeper into that with a limited audience." Thomas heard Sandeep intently and responded, "Yes, you are right. We do have offerings beyond just infrastructure, and I would be happy to walk you through those. I can send you some high-level overview via email and also coordinate on dates with you. Ashish will also participate in the discussion. Hope that works?" Sandeep was very happy with Thomas's thoughtful response and eagerly agreed to the plan. Thomas immediately sent a message out to Ashish.

The next day Thomas got Amy and Ashish together for a virtual meeting. "Sandeep called me yesterday. He wants to set up a focused session around how AWS can support SAP modernization beyond just infrastructure. He wants this session to be with a smaller audience. Also, to add, I texted with Nolan, and he did confirm that this is definitely a key part of the engagement." "We should easily be able to cover that topic. I can do as deep or as light as Sandeep wants," Ashish added. Amy was lost in a thoughtful mood. Her cat made an appearance much to Thomas and Ashish's amusement, but she did not notice. Finally, Amy spoke up after fiddling with her controls, "Sorry, I was speaking on mute. It is interesting that they want to get into the beyond infrastructure conversation. It shows that they are beyond the foundational considerations and are serious about taking SAP to the cloud as part of this modernization effort." "I guess so," Thomas responded in a bit subdued tone. Ashish responded a bit more enthusiastically, "I will put together the content. And, Thomas, let me know what dates we plan to deliver. I can plan my travel accordingly."

A few more sundry items were discussed and the meeting concluded. Just then Amy asked, "Hey, Thomas, did Nolan respond to your request for the meeting?"

"Not yet. I will follow up again," Thomas replied, with an air of wistfulness.

Dates were soon finalized, and Ashish and Thomas showed up at the Nimbus office. It seemed like a second home to both. It had been only a few minutes, before Nolan and Sandeep both came to the lobby. After the usual formalities, both got access to the building.

"Thanks for making the time today," Sandeep said graciously.

"Of course, it is our pleasure," Thomas was quick to respond. Nolan and Ashish in the meanwhile were engaged in an animated discussion on the features of the latest phone that Ashish had acquired.

As everyone was settling in, Ashish said, "I will use slides; however, since it is a small group, I will use the whiteboard more, and let's keep it interactive." Sandeep opened up his journal and also his laptop to take as much notes as he could. Ashish fired up his presentation and walked up to the whiteboard. He tested out a few markers before settling on one. He wrote the word "INNOVATION" in big block letters and started the presentation.

Innovation for SAP with AWS

When running SAP in the cloud, customers usually start with an infrastructure foundation in the form of compute, storage, and network services. As customers mature in the operations of SAP on the cloud, there are other ways to innovate with AWS beyond just infrastructure that are relevant in the context of SAP. This innovation has the following pillars:

- **Data and Analytics**: The ability to leverage AWS services to get better insights from SAP data.

- **Applications and APIs**: Connect SAP with various AWS microservices to build newer business processes and extend existing capabilities.

- **Artificial Intelligence and Machine Learning**: Leverage AI (artificial intelligence), generative AI and ML for SAP.

All these together form the key pillars of innovation beyond infrastructure for SAP on AWS.

Data and Analytics

One of the core pillars of innovation, data and analytics is where most customers start their innovation journey with SAP. SAP stores a lot of transactional data for the enterprise, and running analytics on that provides some good insights for both leadership and frontline users.

Why Is SAP Data Important?

For SAP users, embracing data analytics is not just about handling vast amounts of data efficiently; it's about transforming that data into strategic insights that can drive business value and success. Data analytics plays a critical role for SAP users for several reasons:

- **Informed Decision-Making**: SAP systems often contain a wealth of data across various business functions. Data analytics allows users to extract meaningful insights from this data, enabling more informed and evidence-based decision-making. It helps identify trends, patterns, and anomalies that might not be apparent from simply reviewing raw data.

- **Enhanced Business Processes**: By analyzing data from SAP systems, organizations can identify areas for process improvement. This might include streamlining operations, reducing costs, or improving efficiency. For instance, analytics might reveal bottlenecks in supply chain processes or opportunities for cost savings in procurement.

- **Predictive Analysis**: Advanced data analytics, including machine learning algorithms, can be used to forecast future trends based on historical data. This predictive capability is invaluable for areas like inventory management, demand forecasting, and financial planning.

- **Customer Insights**: SAP systems often contain detailed customer data. Analytics can help in understanding customer behaviors, preferences, and needs, leading to more effective marketing strategies, product development, and customer service.

- **Risk Management**: Data analytics aids in identifying and mitigating risks. By analyzing patterns and trends, companies can foresee potential issues in areas like compliance, finance, and operations and take proactive measures to address them.

216

- **Performance Measurement**: Analytics helps in measuring and tracking key performance indicators (KPIs) across different business functions. This enables organizations to assess their performance over time and against industry benchmarks or specific goals.

- **Integration of Data Sources**: SAP users often deal with data from multiple sources. Analytics helps in integrating and making sense of these disparate datasets, providing a more comprehensive view of the business.

- **Real-Time Analysis**: Modern data analytics tools, when integrated with SAP, can provide real-time insights. This immediacy is crucial for operational decision-making and responding quickly to market changes.

- **Customization and Personalization**: By understanding patterns and trends in customer data, businesses can tailor their offerings and communications to better meet individual customer needs and preferences, enhancing customer satisfaction and loyalty.

- **Competitive Advantage**: Effective use of data analytics provides a competitive edge. It enables organizations to be more agile, responsive, and customer-focused than those that don't leverage such insights.

How Does AWS Help?

Data and analytics for SAP on AWS encompasses a comprehensive set of strategies, tools, and services designed to optimize the extraction of insights from data stored in SAP systems using the powerful capabilities of AWS cloud services. This integration brings together the robust **enterprise resource planning** (**ERP**) functionalities of SAP with the scalable, flexible, and advanced analytical capabilities of AWS. The end-to-end solution can be viewed in the following stages:

- **Data Extraction**: In this context, the data is extracted from SAP, which serves as the source, to a designated target within the AWS ecosystem. This operation creates a duplicate of the data, a step undertaken to facilitate ease of access and to enhance performance. By replicating data in this manner, we ensure that it is readily available in an environment optimized for efficient utilization and swift processing, thereby aligning with the operational needs and objectives. While there are multiple SAP tools as well as third-party tools for extracting SAP data, the focus below is on the AWS-specific tools and services:

- **Database-Level Extraction**: In some use cases, there is a need to pull the data at the database level. This approach is distinct in its ability to access the raw, unprocessed data, offering a comprehensive and granular view of the information stored within the SAP database. Direct database extraction can be faster than application-level extraction, as it bypasses the business logic layer. This method allows access to all data, including historical, log, and audit data, which might not be accessible through standard SAP interfaces. For customized reporting requirements, direct database queries can provide the necessary flexibility. This extraction is done using either *AWS Glue* or *AWS Lambda* using JDBC drivers or Node.js/Python packages. This method involves writing additional custom code while providing no specific support for 'Change Data Capture.' The whole setup involves minimal steps and is serverless. The data once extracted is typically moved to S3 for storage. In some cases, frequent database-level extraction may cause performance issues, and there could be licensing implications also.

- **Application-Level Extraction**: This is a more preferred way of extracting data from SAP since it retains the business logic and validation rules defined in SAP. This ensures data integrity and consistency with SAP transactions and processes. Also ensured is that table relationships, customizations, and package configurations are retained. Lastly, there could be licensing restrictions from SAP in pulling the data directly from the database level. Other benefits include less transformation work outside SAP as well as support for 'Change Data Capture.' The data is extracted either in the IDOCs/RFC or ODATA protocols. The data can be extracted using AWS Lambda, AWS Glue, or SAP OData Connector and moved to Amazon S3.

- **Data Storage**: When conducting data analytics for SAP on AWS, the data storage architecture is key to ensuring efficient analysis, scalability, security, and optimal performance. AWS offers a range of storage and database services suitable for different types of data and analytics needs. Amazon S3 is often used to create data lakes. It's ideal for storing large volumes of structured, semi-structured, and unstructured data from SAP systems. Data lakes on S3 can integrate data from various SAP modules, along with data from other sources, providing a centralized repository for comprehensive analytics.

- **Data Analysis**: Once the data is extracted and stored within S3, various tools can be used for analyzing the data depending on specific use cases.

  - **Amazon Athena** is an interactive query service provided by AWS that makes it easy to analyze data directly in Amazon Simple Storage Service (Amazon S3) using standard SQL. When it comes to SAP data analytics, Athena allows users to run SQL queries against the SAP data stored in S3 without the need to set up or manage any servers or data warehouses. This serverless approach can significantly simplify the infrastructure required for data analysis. Athena is designed to handle large-scale datasets, making it well suited for the vast amounts of data typically generated by SAP systems. It automatically scales to accommodate the size of the data being queried, ensuring fast performance even with large datasets.

  - **Amazon Redshift** is a fully managed, petabyte-scale data warehouse service in the cloud provided by AWS. It plays a significant role in enhancing the capabilities of SAP data analytics by offering a powerful platform for large-scale data storage, aggregation, and complex querying. Redshift is optimized for handling large volumes of data, a common scenario with SAP systems. Its columnar storage and massively parallel processing (MPP) architecture enable fast query performance, crucial for analytics on large SAP datasets. Redshift can integrate with SAP BW and other SAP applications either directly or through intermediary data integration tools like AWS Glue or third-party ETL tools. This allows for seamless extraction, transformation, and loading (ETL) of SAP data into Redshift. Being a fully managed service, Redshift handles tasks like provisioning, configuring, monitoring, backing up the warehouse, and applying patches and upgrades, reducing the management overhead for businesses.

- **Amazon OpenSearch Service** is a fully managed service that makes it easy to deploy, operate, and scale Elasticsearch, an open source, real-time distributed search and analytics engine. The service provides real-time search and analytics capabilities, which can be particularly beneficial for analyzing large volumes of SAP data. It enables quick and efficient searching, filtering, and aggregation of data, facilitating faster insights. Amazon Elasticsearch is well suited for analyzing log and event data generated by SAP systems. This can include system logs, transaction logs, and audit logs, which are critical for monitoring, troubleshooting, and security analysis.

- **Data Consumption**: All the analysis tools Redshift, Athena, and OpenSearch can integrate seamlessly with *Amazon QuickSight*, a scalable, serverless, embeddable, machine learning–powered business intelligence (BI) service designed to provide fast and reliable insights and advanced analytics capabilities to users of all skill levels.

Users can create interactive dashboards and visualizations with a simple, user-friendly interface. This functionality is crucial for transforming complex SAP data into understandable and actionable insights. These visualizations can include charts, graphs, pivot tables, and other visual elements that make it easier to understand trends, outliers, and patterns in SAP data. Dashboards and reports can be easily shared with stakeholders within and outside the organization.

QuickSight also allows for the embedding of interactive dashboards in applications or websites, enhancing the reach and utility of SAP data analytics. QuickSight also offers mobile applications for iOS and Android, allowing access to dashboards and analytics on the go, which is valuable for decision-makers and field workers needing real-time access to SAP data insights.

The latest feature Amazon Q incorporates machine learning capabilities, such as anomaly detection, forecasting, and natural language queries, which can be applied to SAP data to uncover hidden insights and automate predictive analytics. Amazon Q brings a significant advancement in data interaction by allowing users to ask business questions in natural language and receive answers in the form of visualizations or numeric results. It allows for *natural language querying*, allowing users to type in questions about their data in plain English, just like having a conversation with the system.

For instance, a user could ask, "What were the total sales last quarter?" or "Which product category had the highest growth in 2022?" With machine learning–powered insights, Amazon Q uses machine learning algorithms to interpret the questions, determine the intent, and then query the relevant datasets to provide answers. It continuously learns from the patterns of questions asked, becoming more accurate and efficient over time. The feature of instant visualization allows auto-generation of charts or graphs, based on the question. This feature makes data analysis more accessible and intuitive, especially for users who might not be skilled in data analytics.

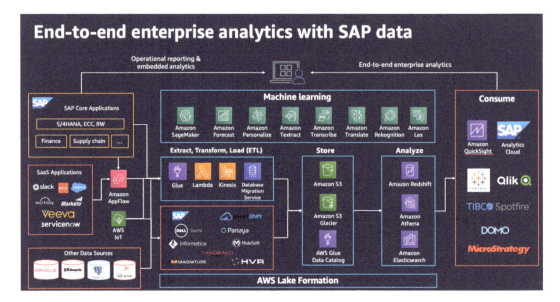

Figure 7-1. *End-to-End Enterprise Analytics with SAP Data*

Applications and APIs

The traditional approach to innovation with SAP has been one of custom development. However, recently, customers have started taking the approach of a 'clean core' and doing the innovation outside of the core. Developers are looking to use AWS services in conjunction with the SAP application and connecting via API calls. An API (Application Programming Interface) is a set of rules and protocols that allows different software programs to communicate and exchange data.

Concept of Clean Core

The concept of a *clean core* refers to a strategic approach in managing and customizing SAP S/4HANA environments. This concept emphasizes maintaining the core system – the standard SAP S/4HANA – as 'clean' or free from custom modifications as much as possible.

Benefits of a clean core include the following:

- **Simplified Upgrades and Maintenance**: By keeping the core clean, businesses can reduce complexities associated with system upgrades and maintenance. Standard SAP updates and patches can be applied more smoothly without the need to reconcile custom code.

- **Reduced Total Cost of Ownership (TCO)**: A clean core approach minimizes the need for extensive custom development and testing, leading to lower costs over the system's lifecycle.

- **Increased System Stability**: Standard SAP code, without extensive modifications, tends to be more stable and reliable, reducing the risk of system issues and downtime.

- **Future-Proofing**: Keeping the core clean ensures that the system remains adaptable and ready for future innovations and capabilities that SAP may introduce.

SAP encourages users to adopt standard processes and best practices embedded in S/4HANA. Where customization is necessary, SAP advises using the provided extensibility frameworks. The clean core concept in SAP S/4HANA is about striking a balance between customization and standardization. It aims to leverage the robust, innovative capabilities of S/4HANA while maintaining a stable, efficient, and easily upgradable core system. This approach is fundamental in enabling businesses to stay agile and responsive in a rapidly evolving digital landscape.

Operational Approach to Maintain a Clean Core

Given below are certain approaches to maintaining a clean core as part of day-to-day operations:

- **Core System Integrity**: In the clean core approach, the core SAP S/4HANA system is kept free from custom code modifications. Instead of altering the standard code of the core system, customizations and enhancements are encouraged to be built using extension frameworks provided by SAP.

- **Use of Extension Frameworks**: SAP provides various tools and frameworks for extending the functionality of S/4HANA without directly modifying its core. These include SAP Fiori apps, SAP BTP (Business Technology Platform), and in-app and side-by-side extensibility options. In-app extensibility allows users to add fields, create custom business logic, and develop new UIs within the S/4HANA environment. Side-by-side extensibility involves creating custom applications that run on the SAP BTP and interact with S/4HANA via APIs.

- **Role of APIs in Extension Frameworks**: APIs (Application Programming Interfaces) play a crucial role in the clean core concept. They are essential in enabling integration, automation, customization, and extending the capabilities of SAP systems. APIs are a fundamental component in the SAP landscape, providing the necessary infrastructure for integration, customization, automation, and extending the capabilities of SAP systems. They are instrumental in ensuring that SAP solutions remain flexible, efficient, and capable of adapting to the evolving technological and business environments. Here's how APIs help enable this:

  - **Integration with Other Systems**: APIs are the key to integrating SAP systems with other internal or external software applications. This includes CRM (customer relationship management) systems, ERP (enterprise resource planning) systems, third-party applications, and various other business tools. They allow seamless data exchange between SAP and non-SAP systems, ensuring that business processes run efficiently across the entire organization.

  - **Enabling Real-Time Data Access and Transactions**: APIs provide real-time access to data in SAP systems. They allow other applications to retrieve and update data in SAP systems as business events occur, supporting real-time decision-making and operational efficiency. This real-time capability is crucial for applications like ecommerce, where immediate access to inventory, pricing, and customer data is essential.

  - **Extending SAP Functionality**: APIs enable the development of custom solutions that extend the functionality of standard SAP software. Businesses can build bespoke applications or extensions that cater to their unique processes and requirements. This extensibility is especially important in areas where specialized functionality is needed that SAP may not natively provide.

- **Facilitating Cloud Services and SaaS Integration**: As businesses increasingly move toward cloud-based services, APIs are essential for integrating SAP systems with cloud platforms and software as a service (SaaS) applications. APIs enable SAP systems to interact with cloud services for various purposes, including data storage, analytics, machine learning, and more.

- **Supporting Mobile Applications and Remote Access**: APIs are crucial for connecting SAP systems with mobile applications, allowing remote access to SAP data and functionality. This supports a mobile workforce and enhances business flexibility.

- **Automation of Business Processes**: By using APIs, businesses can automate workflows and processes, reducing manual effort and increasing efficiency. APIs allow various systems to communicate and transfer data automatically, streamlining business operations.

- **Enhancing Customer Experience**: APIs enable the integration of SAP systems with customer-facing applications, providing customers with up-to-date information, personalized experiences, and efficient service.

- **Complying with Standards and Regulations**: APIs help ensure compliance with data standards and regulations by controlling how data is accessed and shared between systems, which is critical for maintaining data security and privacy.

How Does AWS Help Support a Clean Core

AWS provides solutions for integration of the SAP core (SAP S/4HANA system) via APIs and other solutions, and specifically the core integrates with AWS services to build and extend business processes. As a first step, we review integration patterns and approaches. While there are many SAP-provided and third-party solutions, here the focus is on AWS solutions.

- **AWS Glue SAP OData Connector**: The AWS Glue SAP OData Connector represents a significant advancement in data integration capabilities between SAP systems and AWS cloud services. This native connector enables organizations to seamlessly extract, transform, and load data from their SAP environments into AWS data lakes and analytics platforms without the need for third-party tools or complex custom development. The AWS Glue SAP OData Connector for SAP uses the SAP ODP framework and OData protocol for data extraction. This framework acts in a provider–subscriber model to enable data transfers between SAP systems and non-SAP data targets. The connector leverages the standardized OData protocol, which is built on web technologies such as HTTP, to provide secure and reliable access to SAP data across various external applications and platforms. The connector offers several notable features and benefits:

- **Support for OData Protocol (v2/v4)**: The connector natively integrates with SAP OData services, enabling streamlined access to structured SAP data without custom APIs or ABAP development.

- **Serverless Architecture Integration**: Built on AWS Glue's serverless framework, it allows users to build and execute data pipelines without provisioning or managing infrastructure.

- **Incremental Data Extraction**: The connector supports incremental data loads using delta tokens or timestamp-based filtering, enabling efficient synchronization and near-real-time data integration.

- **Secure and Configurable Connectivity**: Secure access to SAP systems is achieved using HTTPS, with support for authentication methods such as Basic Auth and OAuth 2.0. Glue connections simplify the management of endpoint and credential configuration.

- **Automatic Schema Inference and Catalog Integration**: AWS Glue automatically infers the schema of SAP OData entities and integrates them into the AWS Glue Data Catalog, enabling consistent metadata management across AWS analytics services.

- **Simplified SAP Data Integration**: By abstracting the complexities of SAP's data structures and protocols, the connector empowers data engineers to access SAP data using familiar tools and workflows within AWS Glue.

- **Real-Time Analytics Enablement**: With support for delta-based extraction, the connector facilitates near-real-time data ingestion, which is essential for up-to-date reporting, dashboards, and machine learning use cases.

- **Reduced Development Overhead**: The connector eliminates the need for custom SAP-specific coding, significantly reducing the time and resources required to build and maintain SAP data pipelines.

- **Broad Compatibility with AWS Services**: Data extracted using the SAP OData Connector can be stored in Amazon S3, transformed with AWS Glue, queried via Amazon Athena or Amazon Redshift, and leveraged for AI/ML applications using services such as Amazon SageMaker.

- **AWS Step Functions**: Amazon Step Functions is a cloud service provided by Amazon Web Services (AWS) that enables developers to coordinate multiple AWS services into serverless workflows. It is designed to facilitate the building and execution of complex, multi-step applications by orchestrating various AWS services and functions. When it comes to API integration, Amazon Step Functions offers several important features and capabilities:

  - **Workflow Orchestration for API Integration**: Step Functions allows you to orchestrate various AWS services, including API Gateway, Lambda, and others, into a seamless workflow. This capability is crucial for integrating different APIs in a coordinated manner, especially in complex applications involving multiple steps or stages.

- **State Management**: One of the key strengths of Step Functions is its state management capability. It keeps track of the state of each step in your workflow, which is essential for managing complex integrations where different services and APIs interact with each other.

- **Visual Workflow Management**: Step Functions provides a visual interface for designing and monitoring your workflows. This makes it easier to understand, modify, and manage your API integration processes, especially for complex workflows involving multiple AWS services and external APIs.

- **Error Handling and Retry Logic**: Step Functions offers built-in error handling and retry mechanisms. This feature is particularly important for API integrations, where network issues or intermittent failures of external services can disrupt the workflow.

- **Scalability and Performance**: As a managed service, Step Functions scales automatically based on the demands of your workflows. This ensures that your API integrations can handle high volumes of requests and data without manual intervention.

- **Integration with AWS Lambda and API Gateway**: Step Functions integrates seamlessly with AWS Lambda and API Gateway, enabling you to create comprehensive API-driven applications. You can trigger Lambda functions in response to API calls, process the data, and then move to the next step in your workflow.

- **Synchronous and Asynchronous Execution**: Step Functions supports both synchronous and asynchronous execution of steps in your workflow. This flexibility is crucial for API integrations, where some processes might require immediate response, while others can be processed asynchronously.

- **Cost-Effective and Efficient**: With its pay-per-use pricing model, Step Functions can be a cost-effective solution for orchestrating API integrations, particularly for workflows that are not continuously running.

- **Amazon API Gateway**: Amazon API Gateway is a fully managed service provided by AWS that makes it easy for developers to create, publish, maintain, monitor, and secure APIs at any scale. It acts as a 'front door' for applications to access data, business logic, or functionality from backend services. Here are some key features and aspects of Amazon API Gateway:

  - **API Creation and Deployment**: API Gateway allows developers to quickly define APIs that act as the interface to their backend services, whether those services are running on AWS (like Lambda functions or EC2 instances) or elsewhere (like on-premises servers).

  - **Serverless Integration**: It integrates seamlessly with AWS Lambda, enabling the creation of a completely serverless architecture. This means you can run your backend code without provisioning or managing servers.

  - **Support for RESTful and WebSocket APIs**: API Gateway supports both RESTful APIs and WebSocket APIs. RESTful APIs are used for standard request–response interactions, while WebSocket APIs allow for real-time, two-way communication.

  - **Traffic Management**: It provides features for handling traffic management, such as throttling and version management, to ensure that backend operations can handle incoming requests at scale without degradation in performance.

  - **Security**: Security is a key aspect of API Gateway. It offers multiple mechanisms for controlling and managing access to your APIs, including AWS Identity and Access Management (IAM) roles and policies, Amazon Cognito User Pools for authentication, and API keys.

  - **Monitoring and Logging**: Integration with AWS CloudWatch and AWS X-Ray allows you to monitor the performance of your APIs, log requests & responses, and trace and debug issues in your APIs.

- **Transformation and Validation**: API Gateway can transform incoming requests and outgoing responses, which is useful for converting between different data formats or validating requests before they reach your backend.

- **Cost-Effective and Scalable**: Like many AWS services, API Gateway follows a pay-as-you-go pricing model. It can automatically scale your APIs to handle varying loads, making it cost-effective for both low- and high-traffic scenarios.

- **API Lifecycle Management**: It supports different stages of the API lifecycle, such as development, testing, and production, allowing you to manage different versions and deployments of your APIs.

Given below is the architecture for using Amazon API Gateway in the context of SAP applications.

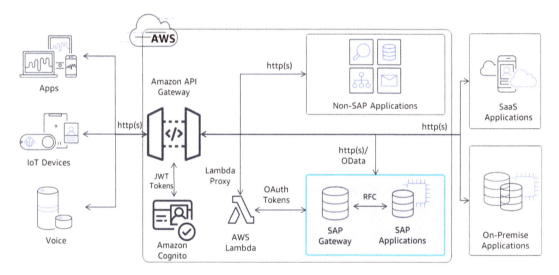

Figure 7-2. *Amazon API Gateway and AWS Lambda Connecting with SAP and Non-SAP Applications*

- **Amazon EventBridge**: Amazon EventBridge, particularly in the context of API integration, offers a highly efficient and scalable way to handle event-driven data flow between various services and applications. In this context, an "event" is a significant change or occurrence within a system, often triggered by user interactions, system states, or external factors. It stands out as a powerful service for integrating APIs from different sources, including custom applications, AWS services, and third-party SaaS applications. Here are some key points to consider when using Amazon EventBridge for API integration:

- **Event-Driven API Integration**: EventBridge enables an event-driven architecture where APIs can be invoked in response to events. This approach is highly efficient for scenarios where actions need to be triggered automatically based on certain conditions or changes in data.

- **Seamless Connection with AWS and External APIs**: It can route events from AWS services, SaaS applications, and custom applications. This makes it an ideal tool for integrating APIs from diverse sources, enabling them to communicate and interact seamlessly.

- **Custom Event Buses for Organizing APIs**: You can create custom event buses in EventBridge to manage events from specific sources or for applications. This organization enhances the management and routing of API calls and responses within your architecture.

- **Flexible Event Routing and Filtering**: EventBridge allows for detailed routing rules and event filtering. This means you can specify which events should trigger which API calls, allowing for a granular and precise control over your API integrations.

- **Scalability for High-Volume API Calls**: As a managed service, EventBridge can handle a high volume of events and API calls without the need for manual scaling. This scalability is crucial for applications that experience variable loads or have high-throughput requirements.

- **Reduced Latency in API Communication**: By utilizing an event-driven model, EventBridge can reduce the latency typically associated with polling mechanisms in API integrations. Events can trigger API calls in real time as they occur.

- **Enhanced Reliability and Error Handling**: EventBridge provides robust reliability for event delivery. It ensures that events triggering API calls are delivered reliably, and it can be configured to handle errors or retries in API interactions.

- **Integration with AWS Lambda and Other Services**: Often used in conjunction with AWS Lambda, EventBridge can trigger Lambda functions that then interact with APIs, creating a powerful, serverless integration pattern that is both efficient and cost-effective.

- **Simplifies Complex Workflows**: For complex integrations involving multiple APIs, EventBridge can orchestrate and manage the workflow, ensuring that API calls are made in the correct sequence and with the appropriate conditional logic.

- **Monitoring and Logging**: Integration with AWS CloudWatch for monitoring and logging allows you to track the performance and health of your API integrations, providing valuable insights and aiding in troubleshooting.

- **AWS SDK for SAP ABAP**: The AWS SDK for SAP ABAP is designed to facilitate an interface in the ABAP programming language for accessing the range of services provided by AWS. This **Software Development Kit** (**SDK**) enables the creation and implementation of various ABAP components, including Business Add-Ins (BADIs), reports, transactions, and OData services, utilizing AWS services such as Amazon Simple Storage Service (S3), Amazon DynamoDB, and Amazon Translate. Additionally, this SDK supports development for ABAP-based systems, with compatibility extending to SAP NetWeaver version 7.4 and onward.

The AWS SDK for SAP ABAP deploys a client library of modules that are consistent and familiar to ABAP developers. Through a set of simple ABAP classes, it addresses the task around security, data formatting, and API connectivity so ABAP developers can focus on developing the use case with AWS services using only a few lines of code. The AWS SDK for SAP ABAP supports SAP NetWeaver ABAP version 7.4 and above.

Use Cases for Applications and APIs

There are many use cases for building applications for SAP using AWS services via APIs. Most such use cases are for serving three primary stakeholders – customers, partners, and employees. Most of these stakeholders are served by various SAP business processes through multiple channels like voice-enabled applications, web applications, mobile applications, etc., and their expectation is to consume SAP services just like any other consumer service they may be used to in their homes and personal life. To meet this requirement, SAP services and data need to be available via API rather than being tied to a specific user interface. Most of the use cases fall under the following broad categories:

- **Mobile**: In the modern business landscape, mobile applications play a pivotal role, and their integration with SAP systems has become increasingly significant. This transition not only improves operational efficiency but also enhances user experience, providing a competitive edge in today's digitally driven market.

- **Web Channel**: Web channel applications in SAP are pivotal in enabling businesses to leverage digital channels effectively by creating feature-rich, integrated web applications that enhance user experience and streamline ecommerce and self-service functionalities.

- **AR/VR**: In the dynamic field of enterprise technology, the integration of Augmented Reality (AR) and Virtual Reality (VR) with SAP systems represents a significant advancement. This integration facilitates innovative and immersive experiences, enhancing various business processes and operations. AR and VR applications can transform how data is visualized and interacted with in SAP systems. Complex datasets can be represented in three-dimensional spaces, providing intuitive and interactive ways for users to analyze and understand data. AR and VR technologies on SAP on the AWS platform are particularly beneficial for training and simulation purposes. They provide realistic and immersive environments for training employees, especially in scenarios where real-life training is risky, expensive, or impractical. AR/VR use cases are also particularly useful in remote assistance and collaboration, product design, and customer experience (virtual showrooms) among others.

- **Voice**: Voice applications like Amazon Alexa are increasingly becoming a pivotal element in enhancing the capabilities of SAP systems. Integrating voice technology with SAP's robust enterprise resource planning (ERP) software offers innovative ways to interact with complex business processes, making them more accessible and efficient. Voice applications introduce a more intuitive and user-friendly way to interact with SAP systems. This shift is particularly beneficial for users who may find traditional ERP interfaces daunting or cumbersome. Voice applications facilitate real-time interaction with SAP systems. Users can quickly query system data or initiate transactions through voice commands, leading to faster decision-making and increased productivity. When combined with AI and machine learning, voice applications in SAP can provide more personalized and context-aware interactions, further enhancing user experience and operational effectiveness while providing local language support.

- **Chatbots**: In the evolving landscape of digital business solutions, chatbots have emerged as a key technology in enhancing the functionality and user experience of SAP systems. Chatbots in SAP systems offer a conversational interface, making it easier for users to interact with complex ERP functionalities. This approach simplifies tasks such as data retrieval, input, and system navigation. Chatbots can handle routine and repetitive tasks, such as answering common queries, scheduling tasks, or updating records. This automation frees up human resources for more complex and value-added activities, while in customer-facing roles, SAP-integrated chatbots can significantly improve service quality and response times as they can handle a wide range of customer inquiries, from order status to product information, enhancing overall customer experience. Chatbots in SAP can be integrated across various modules like sales, finance, procurement, and HR, providing a unified conversational interface across different business functions.

- **Industrial IoT Integration**: The **Internet of Things** (**IoT**) has become a transformative force in the modern business landscape, and its integration with SAP systems is particularly impactful. This combination of SAP and AWS for IoT harnesses the vast capabilities of IoT, SAP's powerful ERP solutions, and AWS's robust cloud infrastructure, leading to innovative and efficient business. IoT devices generate vast amounts of real-time data. Integrating this data into SAP systems allows businesses to gain immediate insights into various operations, from supply chain management to customer interactions. IoT-enabled SAP systems can monitor and optimize business processes in real time. This includes automating routine tasks, reducing downtime through predictive maintenance, optimizing resource utilization, and combining with analytics, which can lead to improved decision-making. IoT devices can be used for continuous monitoring and management of physical assets, and in sectors like manufacturing and utilities, IoT integration with SAP helps in monitoring environmental conditions and ensuring compliance with health and safety regulations.

Examples of SAP Applications Built with AWS Services

There are many actual examples where applications have been built by leveraging SAP processes, data, and AWS services. Discussed below are two examples.

Detecting Manufacturing Defects

For any manufacturing organization, detecting defects on the assembly line has a direct impact on the bottom line. For years, the standard method of defect prevention is sampling and visual inspection. This method relies heavily on human skill/judgment, sample size, and manpower available.

Inherently, this method is not scalable, and as a result metrics like *First Pass Yield* (number of defect free output units divided by total number of input units) remain low. In recent years, organizations have started using camera vision as a detection method, but usually it is not integrated with the MRP or SAP systems. Users have to manually enter the defects in SAP. A novel solution to this problem comes in the form of using AWS solutions integrated with the Quality Management module of SAP. The following AWS services are used for this solution:

Amazon Lookout for Vision is a machine learning (ML) service offered by AWS that helps detect anomalies and defects in physical objects using computer vision. The service can be integrated with many types of computer vision cameras to take the input feed. Some key aspects of Lookout for Vision are as follows:

- **Anomaly Detection Using Machine Learning**: Lookout for Vision uses machine learning to identify anomalies in images of objects. It can detect issues such as cracks, dents, or irregularities in production lines, often with more accuracy and consistency than human inspection.

- **Easy to Train and Deploy**: The service does not require deep machine learning expertise. Users can train the model by providing images of both normal and defective products. The service then automatically creates a model that can identify defects.

- **Real-Time Inspection**: Once the model is trained, it can be used for real-time inspection of products on production lines. This allows for immediate identification and rectification of issues, improving product quality and reducing waste.

- **Integration with AWS Services**: Being part of the AWS ecosystem, Lookout for Vision can easily integrate with other AWS services for enhanced functionality, such as data storage, analytics, or IoT services.

- **Scalability and Security**: As an AWS service, Lookout for Vision offers high scalability to handle varying volumes of inspection data and robust security features to protect sensitive information.

- **Continuous Learning and Improvement**: The service can continuously learn from new data, improving its accuracy and effectiveness over time.

- **Use Cases Across Industries**: The service is applicable across various industries like manufacturing, automotive, electronics, and consumer goods, where quality control is crucial.

SAP QM (Quality Management) is a component specifically designed to support quality management processes within an organization. It is an integral part of the logistics function within SAP and interacts with other modules like **Material Management (MM)**, **Production Planning (PP)**, and **Sales and Distribution (SD)**. Here's an overview of its key features and functionalities:

- **Quality Planning**: SAP QM enables the creation and management of quality plans, inspection plans, and testing equipment. Quality planning involves defining how the quality control processes should be implemented, including the specification of inspection characteristics, procedures, and the necessary resources.

- **Quality Inspection**: The module facilitates the inspection of materials based on quality requirements defined in the quality plans. This includes the recording of inspection results, tracking the quantity of materials inspected, and determining whether materials should be accepted or rejected.

- **Quality Certificates**: SAP QM can generate quality certificates that provide proof of compliance with specified quality standards for both incoming and outgoing goods.

- **Quality Control**: This aspect involves ongoing quality checks and monitoring. It allows for the identification and tracking of defects and supports the implementation of corrective actions to mitigate quality issues.

- **Integration with Manufacturing**: SAP QM is tightly integrated with production processes, enabling quality checks during various stages of manufacturing. It ensures that the quality of the product meets the required standards before, during, and after production.

- **Quality Notifications**: The module allows for the creation and management of quality notifications, which document problems or defects identified in goods. These notifications can trigger specific workflows for addressing and resolving quality issues.

- **Audit Management**: SAP QM supports quality audits by managing audit plans, conducting audits, and tracking audit results. This helps in ensuring compliance with internal and external quality standards and regulations.

- **Reporting and Analysis**: The system offers comprehensive reporting and analysis tools, providing insights into quality metrics, process efficiency, and the effectiveness of quality control measures.

- **Vendor Evaluation**: It integrates with procurement processes, enabling evaluation of vendors based on their quality performance, thus ensuring that the quality of purchased materials meets the required standards.

SAP QM is essential for organizations looking to maintain high-quality standards in their products and processes. By integrating quality management directly into the workflow of other business processes, it helps reduce waste, improve product reliability, and ensure customer satisfaction.

The solution consists of integration of Lookout for Vision with SAP QM as per the steps below:

- **Physical Equipment (Camera) Setup**: The manufacturing facilities usually have existing camera setups for assembly lines. Certain sophisticated camera systems can directly (or via a client application) feed the images to Amazon S3, or the images can be fed manually.

- **Image Store**: The images obtained from the assembly line are stored in Amazon S3.

- **Setup of Defect Detection Model**: The Lookout for Vision service is set up and fed a dataset of 'good' product images as well as defective images. Based on this, the machine learning model understands how to run inference on the actual assembly line images.

- **Orchestration and API Integration**: We could have used EventBridge or Step Functions to orchestrate the process. However, in this case, since we are using only one service, we can simply use a Lambda function. The Lambda function in this case will get notified of any new image coming into Amazon S3. Next, it would invoke the Lookout for Vision service and test the new image against the ML model. If the image is defective, the Lambda function connects to SAP via the OData protocol and API and passes the result into SAP. The defect is then logged into SAP QM, and based on configuration within SAP, the next action is taken. This could be in the form of a notification, defect log, or any other action.

The overall solution is elegant and can be scaled to track defects in all output products coming out of an assembly line. This not only reduces defect rate but creates a rich dataset to further do a causal analysis as to why certain defects show up. Given below is the visual representation of the solution.

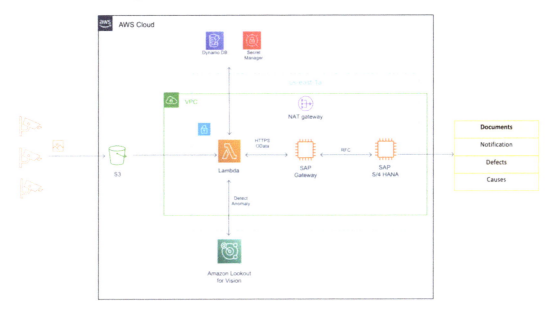

Figure 7-3. *Detecting Manufacturing Defects with SAP QM and AWS Services*

Intelligent Document Processing

As part of regular operations, any organization processes multiple documents every day. These are documents like invoices, contracts, tax reports, and sales orders, among others, typically coming in via various channels like emails, payment systems, and order management systems. Manually processing such documents has a heavy downstream impact since it can cause process delays, drain on labor, and direct revenue loss in case of manual errors. As a result, organizations are constantly looking for ways to digitize the documents and process them electronically.

This also helps to store the document contents digitally. One way to solve the problem is via using services like Amazon Textract, Amazon Comprehend, and Amazon Translate.

Amazon Textract is a service provided by AWS that uses machine learning to automatically extract text, handwriting, and data from scanned documents. It goes beyond simple optical character recognition (OCR) to also identify the contents of fields in forms and information stored in tables. Here are some key features and functionalities of Amazon Textract:

- **Text and Data Extraction**: Textract can extract printed and handwritten text from documents, forms, and tables. It's capable of handling various document formats like PDFs, images, and scans.

- **Form and Table Recognition**: Unlike basic OCR tools, Textract can understand the layout and structure of documents. It can recognize and extract data from forms (like the data in specific fields) and from tables, understanding the relationships between different cells.

- **Machine Learning Technology**: Textract uses machine learning models that have been trained on a vast array of documents. This allows for accurate extraction of information even from complex or low-quality documents.

- **No Manual Configuration Needed**: Textract requires no manual setup or templates. It automatically detects and extracts the relevant information from documents without the need for specific rules or custom code.

- **Integration with Other AWS Services**: Extracted data can be easily integrated with other AWS services for further processing, storage, or analysis. For example, it can be stored in Amazon S3, processed in Amazon SageMaker, or used to trigger workflows in AWS Lambda.

- **Use Cases Across Industries**: Textract is useful in various industries for processes like automated form processing, maintaining compliance records, digitizing archives, processing invoices, and extracting data for analytics.

- **Security and Compliance**: As with other AWS services, Textract is designed with security in mind. It complies with various certifications and standards, ensuring that data is handled securely.

- **Scalability**: Textract is scalable, able to handle large volumes of document processing without significant delays, making it suitable for businesses of all sizes.

Amazon Textract provides a powerful solution for businesses and organizations looking to automate the extraction of text and data from documents, thereby reducing manual efforts, improving accuracy, and streamlining document processing workflows.

The workflow can be set up as below:

- **Document Storage**: Let's say that we want to process invoices. The invoice documents are first uploaded to an Amazon S3 bucket using a custom SAP ABAP program.

- **Text Extraction**: The customer ABAP program will then use **AWS SDK for SAP ABAP** to invoke the Amazon Textract API and extract the data elements from the document.

- **Optional Step (Translation)**: As an additional step if the documents are in multiple languages, the extracted data is sent to Amazon Comprehend to detect language and then Amazon Translate to translate the input language into the preferred output language.

- **Processing the Document**: Based on the final extracted information, the custom ABAP application then performs invoice processing and validation as per rules set up in SAP.

- **Error or Additional Step Handling**: If there are errors in the invoice, then the application would trigger email notification by invoking **Amazon SNS (Simple Notification Service)**. Further, if any additional approvals are required, then an approval workflow or additional orchestration can be triggered using Amazon Step Functions.

Overall, the AWS SDK for SAP ABAP comes in handy when creating business processes from within the SAP environment and there is a need to invoke one or multiple AWS services. Intelligent document processing is a good example of such a use case. Given below is the visual representation of this use case.

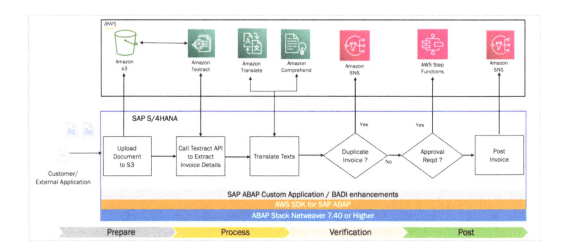

Figure 7-4. *Intelligent Document Processing with SAP and AWS Services*

Artificial Intelligence and Machine Learning

Artificial intelligence (AI) and machine learning (ML) are closely related fields that have become integral to many aspects of technology and everyday life, driving innovation and efficiency across various industries.

AI refers to the simulation of human intelligence in machines that are programmed to think and learn like humans. The term can also be applied to any machine that exhibits traits associated with a human mind, such as learning and problem-solving. The primary goal of AI is to enable the creation of systems that can function intelligently and independently.

AI can be classified into two main types:

- **Narrow AI (or Weak AI):** These systems are designed and trained for a specific task. Virtual personal assistants, such as Apple's Siri, are a form of narrow AI. They operate within a limited predefined range of functions.

- **General AI (or Strong AI):** This is a type of AI that fully replicates human intelligence, meaning it can understand, learn, and apply knowledge in different domains. This form of AI is still a theoretical concept and not yet realized.

AI incorporates multiple disciplines, including computer science, psychology, linguistics, philosophy, and neuroscience, and utilizes various approaches and tools, such as logic, rule-based systems, and decision trees.

Machine Learning is a subset of AI that involves the creation of algorithms that enable computers to learn and improve from experience. ML focuses on the development of computer programs that can access data and use it to learn for themselves. The process of learning begins with observations or data, such as examples, direct experience, or instruction, to look for patterns in data and make better decisions in the future based on the examples that we provide.

Key concepts in ML include

- **Supervised Learning**: The model is trained on a labeled dataset, meaning that each training example is paired with an output label. The model learns to predict the output from the input data.

- **Unsupervised Learning**: The model is trained using a dataset without labels, and the system tries to learn the patterns and structure from the input data.

- **Reinforcement Learning**: The model learns to make decisions by performing certain actions and receiving rewards or penalties in return. It's about taking suitable action to maximize reward in a particular situation.

- **Deep Learning**: A subset of ML that uses neural networks with three or more layers. These neural networks attempt to simulate the behavior of the human brain – albeit far from matching its ability – allowing it to 'learn' from large amounts of data.

While AI and ML can be incredibly powerful and versatile, it's important to remember that they are tools designed and used by humans and reflect the intentions, strengths, and biases of their creators. As these technologies continue to evolve and become more integrated into our daily lives, understanding their mechanisms, capabilities, and implications is essential for leveraging their benefits and mitigating potential risks.

Evolution of AI and ML

The history of artificial intelligence (AI) and machine learning (ML) is a fascinating journey through time, marked by visionary ideas, theoretical advancements, and technological breakthroughs. This field has evolved over decades, reflecting the dynamic interplay between human curiosity, technological progress, and practical applications. The seeds of AI were planted in the 1940s with the development of the first electronic computers like the ENIAC, which showed that machines could perform complex calculations at unprecedented speeds, and in 1950, Alan Turing published his seminal paper, 'Computing Machinery and Intelligence,' proposing the *Turing Test* as a criterion of intelligence, a fundamental concept in the philosophy of AI. Early AI research focused on problem-solving and symbolic methods. Successes in these domains led to optimism and predictions that general artificial intelligence was just around the corner; however, due to the limitation of 'rule-based learning,' the field suffered from reduced funding and ebbing of interest. Advances in computational technology led to a shift toward 'machine learning,' where computers develop the ability to learn from and make predictions on data. Early ML pioneers began developing the backpropagation algorithm that allowed neural networks to adjust hidden layers, laying the groundwork for deep learning. The explosion of the internet and the digitalization of society resulted in the generation of vast amounts of data. This big data became the fuel for machine learning, as algorithms require large datasets to learn effectively. The advent of deep learning, powered by big data and advances in computational power (GPUs), led to breakthroughs in AI. Neural networks, particularly convolutional neural networks (CNNs) and recurrent neural networks (RNNs), began outperforming other methods in tasks like image and speech recognition. AI and ML have become integral to various applications, from autonomous vehicles and healthcare diagnostics to personalized recommendations and natural language processing (NLP).

Role of Cloud Technology in the Growth of AI and ML

The integration of cloud technology with AI and ML is transforming the business landscape, offering scalable, flexible, and efficient solutions. The convergence of these technologies is not just enhancing existing business models but also enabling the creation of new paradigms in service delivery, operational efficiency, and innovation. Broadly, the cloud helps amplify these technologies in the following ways:

- **Scalability and Flexibility**: Cloud technology provides a scalable infrastructure for AI and ML, allowing businesses to adjust resources based on demand. This flexibility supports the processing of large datasets and the computational needs of complex AI models, facilitating growth without the need for substantial up-front capital investment in physical infrastructure.

- **Accessibility and Collaboration**: Cloud-based AI services democratize access to advanced technologies, enabling businesses of all sizes to leverage AI and ML without the need for specialized hardware or expertise. This levels the playing field, allowing smaller players to compete with larger corporations. Moreover, cloud platforms facilitate collaboration, enabling teams to work together on AI/ML projects from different locations in real time.

- **Cost Efficiency**: By utilizing cloud services, businesses can significantly reduce costs associated with data storage, management, and computation. The pay-as-you-go model of cloud services ensures that businesses only pay for what they use, optimizing operational expenses and reducing the need for large initial investments.

- **Enhanced Data Management and Analytics**: Cloud platforms provide sophisticated tools for data storage, processing, and analysis, which are fundamental for AI and ML applications. These tools, combined with cloud-based AI services, enable businesses to gain insights from their data, driving informed decision-making and strategy development.

- **Innovation and Speed to Market**: The cloud accelerates the development and deployment of AI and ML applications. With the infrastructure and platform services provided by cloud providers, businesses can focus on innovation and product development without worrying about underlying hardware or scalability issues. This leads to faster prototyping, testing, and deployment of AI-driven solutions, reducing the time to market.

- **Security and Compliance**: While cloud technology introduces concerns about data security and privacy, reputable cloud service providers invest heavily in securing their infrastructure and ensuring compliance with regulatory standards. Businesses can leverage these investments and the advanced security features of cloud platforms to protect their data and AI models, ensuring they meet industry regulations and standards.

- **Sustainable Development**: Cloud providers are increasingly focusing on sustainable practices, offering businesses a greener alternative to traditional IT infrastructure. By leveraging cloud services, businesses can reduce their carbon footprint, contributing to their corporate social responsibility goals and aligning with global sustainability efforts.

The fusion of cloud technology with AI and ML is a powerful catalyst for business transformation. It offers scalability, cost efficiency, and access to advanced analytical tools, driving innovation and competitive advantage.

However, businesses must also be cognizant of the security, ethical, and regulatory challenges associated with these technologies. By strategically embracing cloud-based AI and ML solutions and addressing these challenges, businesses can unlock new opportunities and thrive in the digital era.

Implications of AI and ML for Businesses

The growth of AI and ML technologies represents a paradigm shift in the business landscape, heralding a new era of operational efficiency, innovation, and competition. AI and ML technologies have experienced exponential growth in recent years, primarily due to advancements in computational power, availability of large datasets, and improvements in algorithms. Businesses across various sectors are leveraging these technologies to transform their operations, products, and services. Some key implications for businesses are:

- **Enhanced Decision-Making**: AI-driven data analytics enable businesses to make informed decisions by providing insights that were previously inaccessible. Predictive analytics and trend analysis powered by ML can forecast market trends, consumer behavior, and potential risks, leading to more strategic decision-making.

- **Operational Efficiency**: Automation of routine tasks through AI significantly reduces human error and increases productivity. ML algorithms can optimize supply chains, manage inventory, and streamline processes, leading to cost reduction and improved efficiency.

- **Personalization and Customer Service**: AI enhances customer experience through personalized services. Chatbots and virtual assistants, powered by natural language processing, provide 24/7 customer service, while recommendation systems personalize user experiences in ecommerce, streaming services, and more.

- **Innovation and Product Development**: Businesses are harnessing AI to drive innovation. From drug discovery in pharmaceuticals to design in automotive industries, AI and ML are speeding up research and development, leading to faster innovation cycles.

- **Market Competition and Disruption**: AI and ML are leveling the playing field, allowing startups to compete with established players by offering innovative, technology-driven products and services. Conversely, businesses that fail to adapt risk becoming obsolete.

- **Ethical and Regulatory Challenges**: The growth of AI and ML brings forth ethical considerations related to privacy, bias, and accountability. Businesses must navigate regulatory landscapes and societal expectations, ensuring that their use of AI is transparent, ethical, and compliant.

- **Workforce Transformation**: While AI automates certain tasks, it also creates opportunities for new job roles focused on AI and ML management, oversight, and ethical considerations. Businesses must invest in reskilling and upskilling employees to stay competitive in the AI-driven market.

The rapid growth of AI and ML technologies is reshaping the business world, offering unprecedented opportunities for innovation, efficiency, and customer engagement. However, it also presents challenges that require careful navigation. Businesses that strategically embrace AI and ML, while addressing the ethical and regulatory implications, will be well positioned to thrive in this new era.

Significance of AI and ML Technology for SAP Customers

Like all aspects of technology, SAP customers can also draw a lot of value from leveraging AI and ML technology. AI and ML significantly enhance the value of SAP by automating processes, providing actionable insights, and enabling more informed decision-making. These technologies infuse traditional SAP with intelligence, transforming them into dynamic tools that can predict, adapt, and react in real time. Here is a high-level overview of how AI and ML are enhancing the value of SAP:

- **Process Automation**: AI and ML automate routine and repetitive tasks within SAP, such as data entry, invoice processing, and report generation. This not only reduces the risk of human error but also allows staff to focus on more strategic, value-added tasks.

- **Predictive Analytics**: ML algorithms can analyze historical data and identify patterns to forecast future trends. This can be particularly valuable in areas like demand planning, inventory management, and maintenance scheduling. Businesses can use these insights to optimize their operations, reduce costs, and improve customer satisfaction.

- **Enhanced Decision-Making**: AI enhances decision-making by providing managers and executives with deep insights and actionable recommendations. Instead of relying solely on historical data, AI-powered ERP systems can analyze a wide range of variables in real time, providing a more holistic view of the business and its environment.

- **Improved Customer Service**: AI can analyze customer data and interactions to provide a personalized experience. For instance, it can recommend products based on previous purchases or predict when a customer might need support. This not only improves customer satisfaction but also opens new opportunities for sales and marketing.

- **Supply Chain Optimization**: AI and ML can significantly improve supply chain management by predicting disruptions, optimizing inventory levels, and automating procurement processes. This leads to more efficient operations, reduced costs, and improved ability to respond to market changes.

- **Enhanced Compliance and Risk Management**: AI-powered SAP can monitor transactions and operations in real time to ensure compliance with regulations and internal policies. They can also predict potential risks based on patterns and trends, allowing businesses to take proactive measures to mitigate them.

- **Employee Productivity and Engagement**: AI can streamline HR processes within SAP, such as recruitment, onboarding, and performance management. It can analyze employee data to identify patterns related to productivity, satisfaction, and retention, helping organizations to create better work environments and foster employee engagement.

- **Cost Reduction and ROI Improvement**: By optimizing operations, reducing errors, and improving decision-making, AI and ML can significantly reduce costs. The automation of routine tasks also leads to higher productivity, while predictive maintenance can prevent costly downtimes. These factors contribute to an improved ROI for SAP systems.

AI and ML are not just add-ons but fundamental elements that transform SAP into a more intelligent, responsive, and efficient enterprise solution. They enable businesses to move from reactive to proactive and predictive management, enhancing every aspect of operations from the supply chain and customer relationship management to human resources and financial management. As AI and ML technologies continue to evolve, their integration into SAP will become increasingly sophisticated, further enhancing the value and capabilities of these systems.

Generative AI for SAP: Beyond the Hype

Generative AI, a subset of AI focusing on generating new content, data, or solutions based on learned patterns and information, significantly enhances the value of SAP systems. It does so by introducing innovative capabilities that transform how businesses interact with data, make decisions, and automate processes. The technology is in its early stages; however, certain use cases are already emerging:

- **Advanced Data Generation and Simulation**: Generative AI can create realistic and coherent data based on existing patterns, useful for scenario planning and simulations. Businesses can use these capabilities to model various scenarios (e.g., market changes, supply chain disruptions) and devise strategies, enhancing decision-making and preparedness.

- **Content Creation and Documentation**: Generative AI can automate the creation of business documents, reports, and communications. It can generate summaries from large datasets, write coherent reports, and even draft email responses, saving time and ensuring consistency in business communications.

- **Personalized Customer and Employee Experiences**: By understanding patterns and preferences, generative AI can create personalized content for customers and employees. For customers, this could mean personalized product recommendations or tailored marketing messages. For employees, this could involve personalized learning and development content or automated, context-relevant support in their work processes.

- **Predictive Maintenance and Manufacturing**: In manufacturing settings, generative AI can predict when machines or components are likely to fail or require maintenance. Beyond prediction, it can also generate solutions or recommendations for maintenance schedules, optimizing operations and preventing downtime.

- **Automated Data Entry and Integrity**: Generative AI can automate data entry by extracting information from unstructured data sources (e.g., emails, documents) and entering it into SAP. It can also enhance data integrity by generating missing data or correcting inconsistencies, ensuring that decision-makers have accurate and complete information.

- **Customization and Configuration**: Generative AI can assist in the customization and configuration of SAP itself. By understanding the specific needs and workflows of a business, it can suggest or even implement custom configurations, enhancing SAP's effectiveness and user experience.

- **Risk Assessment and Mitigation**: Generative AI can analyze various risk factors and generate potential mitigation strategies. It can simulate the impact of different strategies, helping businesses to choose the most effective approach to managing risks.

Generative AI significantly enhances the value of ERP systems by bringing in capabilities that automate complex tasks, generate new insights, and offer innovative solutions to business problems. It transforms SAP from being mere repositories and processors of information to proactive, intelligent platforms that can predict, adapt, and generate value in dynamic business environments.

Leveraging AWS for AI and ML for SAP

AWS offers a comprehensive suite of AI and ML services designed to empower developers, data scientists, and businesses to build intelligent solutions. These services cover a wide range of applications, from data analysis and predictive modeling to natural language processing and image recognition. The AI and ML services in AWS can broadly be categorized into three main layers: AI services for ready-made intelligence, ML services for custom machine learning model development, and ML frameworks and infrastructure for expert ML practitioners. Utilizing these, users can build specific use cases that are also relevant in the context of SAP data and business processes.

- **ML Frameworks and Infrastructure**: AWS provides a rich set of machine learning (ML) frameworks and infrastructure options designed to cater to the needs of ML practitioners and researchers. These frameworks and infrastructure offer the tools and environments necessary for building, training, and deploying machine learning models at scale. Key components include

  - **Amazon EC2 Instances for ML**: The EC2 P3 and P4 instances are GPU-powered instances ideal for machine learning and high-performance computing. They are equipped with NVIDIA Tensor Core GPUs and, as a result, offer high throughput and performance.

  - **AWS Deep Learning AMIs**: The Deep Learning AMIs (Amazon Machine Images) are preconfigured with popular deep learning frameworks to enable rapid deployment of deep learning environments. Some of the key supported ML frameworks include TensorFlow, PyTorch, Apache MXNet, and others. These AMIs and frameworks are easy to customize and offer greater flexibility in designing the ML models.

- **Elastic Inference**: Elastic Inference allows attaching GPU-powered inference acceleration to any Amazon EC2 or Amazon SageMaker instance, ideal for scenarios where the compute capacity of a full GPU instance is not required, making it a cost-effective solution for running inference on large models.

- **Purpose-Built Processors**: Amazon also offers high-end processors Inferentia and Trainium for the purposes of machine learning. While Amazon Inferentia focuses on optimizing the inference phase of machine learning workflows, Amazon Trainium is specifically engineered for the training phase, which involves teaching a model to make predictions or perform tasks based on a given dataset.

- **ML Model Building Tools (SageMaker)**: Once the user has access to the infrastructure, next, they would like to build specific ML models. Amazon SageMaker is a fully managed service that enables developers and data scientists to quickly and easily build, train, and deploy machine learning (ML) models at scale. It removes the heavy lifting from each step of the machine learning process, making it easier for users to develop high-quality models. SageMaker offers a range of capabilities and tools designed to simplify and expedite the ML development lifecycle. Key features of SageMaker are:

  - **Ground Truth**: This feature helps in building highly accurate training datasets for machine learning quickly. SageMaker Ground Truth offers easy access to human labelers and provides built-in workflows and interfaces for common labeling tasks.

  - **Notebooks**: SageMaker provides Jupyter notebooks that are fully integrated with the platform, making it easy to explore and visualize data as well as to write, run, and debug code.

- **Studio**: Amazon SageMaker Studio is the first fully integrated development environment (IDE) for machine learning. It provides a single, web-based visual interface where a user can perform all ML development steps.

- **Canvas**: Amazon SageMaker Canvas is a visual, no-code tool designed to allow business analysts and other non-developer users to create ML models without writing code.

- **Autopilot**: SageMaker Autopilot automatically builds, trains, and tunes the best machine learning models based on your data while allowing you to maintain full control and visibility.

- **Training**: This feature allows the user to train and tune the model. It supports a broad array of built-in algorithms, frameworks, and interfaces for custom algorithms, ensuring flexibility and ease of use.

- **Inference**: SageMaker enables developers to deploy ML models for inference and provides an HTTPS endpoint where ML models can be invoked.

- **Experiments**: This feature allows users to organize, track, compare, and evaluate machine learning experiments and model versions.

- **Debugger**: SageMaker Debugger provides real-time monitoring of model training, detecting and alerting on issues and anomalies to improve model accuracy.

- **Model Monitor**: This feature continuously monitors the quality of the machine learning models in production. It detects and alerts on deviations in model quality, such as data drift.

- **Data Wrangler**: SageMaker Data Wrangler reduces the time it takes to aggregate and prepare data for machine learning from weeks to minutes.

- **Feature Store**: Amazon SageMaker Feature Store is a fully managed, purpose-built repository to store, retrieve, and share machine learning features.

- **Clarify**: This feature provides bias detection and model explainability to improve the transparency and explainability of the ML models.

- **AI Services**: On top of SageMaker, the user can leverage a host of purpose-built AI services that are designed for specific use cases. Based on the primary purpose and functionality, the AI services are classified as below:

  - **Language Services**

    - **Amazon Transcribe**: Automatic speech recognition (ASR) service to convert speech into text

    - **Amazon Polly**: Text-to-speech (TTS) service to convert text into lifelike speech

    - **Amazon Lex**: Service for building conversational interfaces into applications using voice and text

  - **Text Services**

    - **Amazon Comprehend**: Natural language processing (NLP) service to extract insights and relationships from text

    - **Amazon Translate**: Neural machine translation service for translating text to and from multiple languages

    - **Amazon Textract**: Service to extract text and data from scanned documents

  - **Computer Vision Services**

    - **Amazon Rekognition**: Image and video analysis service for identifying objects, people, text, scenes, and activities. It also offers facial recognition capabilities.

    - **Personalization and Recommendation Services**

    - **Amazon Personalize**: Machine learning service to create individualized recommendations for customers using their applications

    - **Amazon Forecast**: Time-series forecasting service based on machine learning and built for business metrics analysis

- **Search Services**

  - **Amazon Kendra**: Enterprise search service powered by machine learning to find information across various content repositories

- **Fraud Detection and Security Services**

  - **Amazon Fraud Detector**: Fully managed service to identify potentially fraudulent activities and online scams

  - **Amazon Lookout for Metrics**: Service to detect anomalies in business and operational data

- **Industrial Applications**

  - **Amazon Lookout for Equipment**: Service that uses machine learning to identify abnormal equipment behavior and provide alerts

  - **Amazon Monitron**: End-to-end system that uses machine learning to detect abnormal behavior in industrial machinery

  - **Amazon Lookout for Vision**: Service that uses machine learning to identify defects and anomalies in physical products

  - **Amazon Panorama**: A machine learning appliance and SDK that allows organizations to bring computer vision to on-premises cameras

- **Amazon Bedrock**: Amazon Bedrock is a fully managed service that provides access to a selection of high-performance foundational models (FMs) and Large Language Models (LLMs) through a unified API. This service features models from top AI organizations, including AI21 Labs, Anthropic, Cohere, Meta, Stability AI, and Amazon. It comes equipped with many features essential for the development of generative AI applications, ensuring adherence to security, privacy, and responsible AI practices. The key features and benefits of Bedrock for building generative AI applications are as follows:

- **Selection of Premier Foundational Models (FMs)**:
  Amazon Bedrock simplifies the integration and utilization
  of a diverse array of top-performing FMs. This platform
  offers a streamlined developer experience, enabling swift
  experimentation within its playground environment and
  seamless model inference through a singular API. This design
  allows for the flexible incorporation of FMs from multiple
  providers and ensures easy adaptation to the most current
  model versions with minimal adjustments to the existing
  codebase.

- **Model Personalization**: Bedrock empowers users to tailor
  FMs to their specific requirements using their own datasets,
  all through an intuitive visual interface that eliminates the
  need for coding. Users can simply choose their training and
  validation datasets hosted on Amazon S3 and, if necessary,
  fine-tune hyperparameters to optimize model performance.

- **Dynamic and Fully Managed Agents**: Bedrock enables
  the construction of agents capable of executing intricate
  business operations, ranging from arranging travel and
  handling insurance claims to crafting advertising campaigns,
  preparing tax filings, and overseeing inventory. These agents
  dynamically interact with your company's systems and APIs,
  leveraging the cognitive prowess of FMs to dissect tasks,
  devise an orchestration strategy, and implement it effectively.

- **Enhanced FM Capabilities with Native RAG (Retrieval-
  Augmented Generation) Support**: Through Knowledge
  Bases for Amazon Bedrock, users can securely link FMs to
  their proprietary data repositories for retrieval augmentation,
  all within the confines of the managed service. This
  connection significantly augments the inherent capabilities
  of the FMs, rendering them more adept and informed about
  your specific domain and organizational context.

- **Data Security and Compliance**: Bedrock is committed to upholding stringent security and privacy protocols. It aligns with common compliance standards including SOC, ISO, HIPAA eligibility, and GDPR, offering a secure and compliant environment for your AI endeavors. Bedrock has attained CSA STAR Level 2 certification, affirming its adherence to industry best practices and robust security measures. Within Bedrock, your content remains exclusive to your use, never contributing to the enhancement of base models nor being shared with model providers. Bedrock ensures that your data is always encrypted, both in transit and at rest, and provides the option for encryption with your own keys. Moreover, AWS PrivateLink facilitates a secure, private connection between your FMs and your Amazon Virtual Private Cloud (Amazon VPC), ensuring data remains shielded from internet exposure.

SAP users can leverage this wide variety of services, frameworks, and purpose-built infrastructure to build new use cases within SAP that leverage AI and ML services.

Example Use Case

For customers who want to extend the capabilities of SAP with the help of AI and ML technology, there are many use cases including automating order entry (Amazon Transcribe/Textract), predictive maintenance (Lookout for Equipment), automating health and safety inspection (Amazon Rekognition), and others. Here, we will review a specific example of processing exceptions in SAP using Amazon Nova Agentic AI.

Using Amazon Nova Agentic AI for Exception Processing in SAP

Overview: Exception processing in SAP encompasses the detection, diagnosis, and resolution of anomalies that disrupt standard business processes - such as blocked invoices, failed IDocs, delivery discrepancies, or master data errors. Traditionally, these exceptions demand manual intervention, which can be time-intensive, error-prone, and operationally costly.

Amazon Nova Agentic AI introduces a transformative approach to exception handling by enabling intelligent agents capable of autonomous, multi-step reasoning and task execution. These agents are purpose-built using generative AI models and tightly integrated with enterprise systems like SAP. Nova agents can proactively identify exceptions, understand their root causes, and either resolve them autonomously or escalate them to human users with detailed context and recommended actions.

Key Features: Amazon Nova Agentic AI provides several capabilities tailored to streamline SAP exception workflows:

- **Autonomous Agents with Specialized Skills**: Nova provides purpose-built agents trained to handle specific SAP exception types (e.g., order blocks, invoice errors) with domain expertise.

- **Tight Integration with SAP Data Sources**: Through services like **AWS Glue** and **OData connectors**, Nova can ingest structured SAP data for real-time processing.

- **Multi-step Reasoning and Workflow Orchestration**: Agents use chain-of-thought prompting and reasoning to perform stepwise analysis, cross-checking of SAP tables, and orchestration of resolution steps using APIs.

- **Contextual Awareness and Memory**: Nova agents retain session memory and context, allowing them to learn from historical exceptions and improve accuracy in repeated cases.

- **Natural Language Interface**: Users can interact with Nova agents using natural language within platforms like SAP Fiori, Microsoft Teams, or Amazon Q, simplifying collaboration.

- **Human-in-the-Loop (HITL) Collaboration**: When needed, agents escalate unresolved cases with full audit trails and recommended actions for human review.

Benefits: The application of Amazon Nova Agentic AI in SAP exception processing delivers significant operational advantages:

- **Increased Efficiency**: Automates up to 70–80% of repetitive exception handling tasks, reducing the workload on SAP support teams.

- **Faster Resolution Time**: Exceptions are detected and acted upon in near real time, minimizing business process delays.

- **Improved Accuracy**: Reduces manual errors in exception analysis and remediation by relying on structured logic and data.

- **Scalability**: Handles a high volume of exceptions simultaneously across multiple SAP modules (SD, MM, FI, etc.) without requiring proportional increases in manpower.

- **Business Continuity**: Ensures smoother end-to-end SAP workflows by proactively addressing disruptions before they escalate.

- **Actionable Insights**: Provides root cause summaries, trend analysis, and recommendations, helping SAP administrators refine underlying configurations or master data.

Working Principles: The operational flow of Amazon Nova Agentic AI in an SAP environment can be summarized in the following stages:

- **Triggering an Exception Detection Workflow**: A Nova agent can be scheduled or event-triggered (e.g., on IDoc failure, status change, or BAPI error response) via CloudWatch Events, SAP PI/PO, or Amazon EventBridge.

- **Data Collection**: Agents extract relevant data from SAP via OData services or historical logs indexed through AWS Glue and Lake Formation.

- **Root Cause Analysis**: Using LLM-based reasoning, the agent validates document chains (e.g., PO → GR → Invoice), checks master data inconsistencies (e.g., missing partner functions), and queries SAP logs (e.g., SM21, ST22) or error tables.

- **Decision Execution**: Depending on rules and confidence score, the agent automatically updates SAP (e.g., unblock invoice, correct quantity), sends notification to stakeholders (via Amazon SNS or email), or escalates with rationale if confidence is low.

- **Feedback and Learning**: The agent logs the outcome, gathers feedback from the human user if involved, and uses the result to refine future actions using a reinforcement feedback loop (enabled via Amazon Bedrock with retrieval-augmented generation or fine-tuning workflows).

Use Cases in SAP:

- **Blocked Sales Orders (SD)**: Identify block reason, check credit limits, and release if thresholds are met.

- **Invoice Exceptions (FI/MM)**: Resolve quantity mismatches by checking GR and PO alignment.

- **Delivery Delays (MM)**: Suggest alternate vendors or expedite existing orders.

- **Master Data Inconsistencies**: Detect missing fields and auto-correct based on predefined templates or lookups.

Amazon Nova Agentic AI revolutionizes exception processing in SAP by bringing intelligent automation, contextual decision-making, and seamless integration to critical business workflows. This reduces manual effort, improves responsiveness, and enables enterprises to manage exceptions at scale while focusing human effort on strategic exceptions that truly need attention.

As the discussion came to an end, Sandeep got up and shook hands with Ashish. "That was a great discussion, Ashish. Not only the insights, but your skill of breaking down complex topics into simple terms has been just amazing." Ashish smiled and while wiping away the whiteboard said, "Thanks, Sandeep, for the kind words. I am glad that you found the session useful." Nolan also patted Ashish on the back and with a smile said, "Great job, Ashish. I am glad we have you on team Nimbus."

As everyone trooped out of the conference room, Thomas walked alongside Nolan and asked casually, "Nolan, I am curious, how is your overall plan coming along?"

"It is coming along well. We are almost ready with the business case and are ready to take it to the CFO and the board. Should happen soon," Nolan responded making positive eye contact with Thomas.

"That is some great news. AWS is definitely looking to be a part of this journey with Nimbus, as we have been so far. I think it is important that we meet with Elizabeth to finalize the next steps. I have not received a reply to my meeting request yet," responded Thomas knowing he was in a position of trust. Nolan almost froze in his stride, even as Sandeep and Ashish were already walking away.

"For sure, Thomas, all in good time," responded Nolan laconically.

Elizabeth had just walked into the house and was hanging her car keys when Sophia came running in, almost bumping into her. Of course, she was very excited, with her birthday celebrations coming up in less than a week. The whole Nelson household had been planning for this for months. "Sorry, Mom, but can you help me pick out the outfit? I have two laid out and I could use some help," she pleaded. Elizabeth smiled and put down her backpack.

"Sure, sweetie, I will come upstairs," Elizabeth said with a smile on her face. Though tired, Elizabeth never gave up any opportunity to spend time with the kids, especially Sophia. She was looking forward to Sophia's birthday party.

The rest of the week was progressing fast, and it was already Thursday. Elizabeth was headed to her office from the parking lot, mentally making a note of everything she needed to do, which included ordering the cake for the birthday party. She also was preparing herself for an important meeting with Nolan.

Elizabeth had just gone through her morning emails when Nolan knocked on the door. "Ready for our ten o' clock?" he queried with a smile. Elizabeth looked up from her desk, still absorbed in some thoughts, and gestured Nolan to sit down. In a few minutes, she wrapped up her email and set aside the laptop.

"Sorry. Something running in my mind. But I am all ears now," Elizabeth said with an apologetic shrug.

"I have a few updates for you, but I did want to understand where you stand on some points," Nolan responded, immediately getting Elizabeth's full attention. Nolan continued, "Firstly, Sandeep's session with AWS went well. There is a lot Sandeep's team can accomplish innovation-wise with SAP on AWS. There are many use cases that would work well in our environment.

Second, Mark has emailed the final copy of the business case to both of us. I have reviewed it, and it looks very compelling and very well written."

"Yes, the business case has turned out well. I just glanced through, and he has made the changes I requested. Let me give some time to it tomorrow. Also, I am very glad that Sandeep is building confidence in his delivery capability and viewing the cloud as an enabler for innovation. This way the cloud is not just viewed as infrastructure but more than that," Elizabeth was quite emphatic in her response.

Nolan smiled and continued, "Very cool, that brings me to my question. Over the past month, we have also spent time reviewing offerings from other cloud providers. What is our direction?"

Elizabeth pushed back on her chair, removed her glasses, and said, "I hate to respond to a question with a question, but I am curious, what do you think of the other cloud providers?"

Nolan thought for a while, wanting to give a measured response, before saying, "The other cloud providers have some good features and offers; however, I think AWS has a more comprehensive offering and its solutions are more mature, and AWS has been in the business longer than others." Elizabeth rocked forward on her chair, almost slamming her desk, "That is a good assessment, Nolan. How else would we have known?" Nolan looked sideways, bemused. "Oh, I notice you have a pending cake order," Nolan remarked as his eye caught a glance of the receipt on the desk.

"I assume it is for Sophia's birthday," he concluded with a smile. Elizabeth's eyes twinkled. "Sharp eye, Perez. By the way, let's plan to secure time with the CFO's office to review the business plan and numbers with him before we go up to the board. But before that, this weekend, I am going to be busy with Sophia's birthday celebrations." Nolan left the room, knowing well what he needed to do. Elizabeth's words kept ringing in his head, "How else would we have known ..."

The next day passed without much buzz. Elizabeth, in a decidedly cheerful mood, left a bit early heading to the bakery to pick up her cake order. The cake looked wonderful, just perfect for the occasion. Elizabeth had just stepped out when her phone rang. With her bag and cake in hand, she was in no position to take the call. After placing the cake gingerly on the passenger seat, she glanced at her phone. The call came from the office. Before she could think any further, the phone rang again. Without wasting time on courtesies, the quivering voice on the other end said, "Elizabeth, madam, this is Doris from ticket support operations. Can you please come back to the office? We are noticing some weird activity ..." And the voice trailed off.

This better be good, *Elizabeth said to herself and headed back to the office. As soon as Elizabeth got to her floor, there were already twenty people teeming about. Nolan and Mark were already there with anxious looks on their faces. The experienced Mark spoke first, "The ticketing operations started seeing some complaints earlier in the week, but they thought it was the usual holiday rush. However, the complaints have become worse since today afternoon. We notice that certain customers are unable to book travel."*

"I am assuming we have checked the system performance and other parameters? Is it just additional load that the system is choking under?" Elizabeth offered, trying to find answers. A young engineer spoke up, "If I may, I don't think it is the system load. It is just that users are unable to even access the system, while peak user load during this period was at about 35%. It is as if the system is deliberately not letting users in. The symptoms seem consistent with a cyber-attack."

Elizabeth's brows furrowed with concern. "Let's head to the operations center," Elizabeth said. As everyone started to move, she added, "I will join in a few minutes. I need to get something from my car and put it in the fridge."

The operations center felt like a war room. System parameters were checked every few minutes. Most people had left for the day, and the key experts were being called back in. Elizabeth was listening attentively to the security engineer. "We are under a DDoS (Distributed Denial of Service) attack. Some malicious agent is creating bots that are attacking our ticketing system."

"Our ticketing system has a lot of sensitive customer and payment data," Elizabeth added. The engineer continued, "They could be after our customer data like passport information and credit card details, which sell for a premium on the dark web." "Or even our customers' loyalty miles," Elizabeth said thoughtfully. Elizabeth turned around to address the room, and the leader in her instinctively kicked in. "All right, everyone, as we all now know, we are under attack. We don't know what our enemy wants, but we will do all it takes to protect our house. We have the best of Nimbus in the room, and others are rushing in. Please make one last call and let your loved ones know that we will be back once we have defeated the enemy. This could be two hours or two weeks. And remember, they may be your loved ones, but we still are not sharing details with anyone, not just yet. And I am not going anywhere." The room roared with thundering applause. As teams settled in, Elizabeth stepped out and called Ben. "Hey, honey, something big has come up at work. I may be stuck here for a while, and unfortunately, I can't share much. Don't worry about me. Just make sure you throw Sophia the best birthday party ever. Love you." "Love you, honey, and don't worry. You take care of whatever problem is out there."

It was only a few minutes when Elizabeth's phone buzzed. It was an angry text from Sophia. Elizabeth ignored it. As the room got to work, Elizabeth pulled in a few key people and shared, "We have two key priorities: one is to get our customers to be able to transact on the system and, second, not allow the attack to scale. Limit the impact of the attack."

"We can track the IP address of where the attack is originating and try limiting it with an access control list," the head of cyber-security chimed in. "I am also in touch with a few partners who may have some counter measure solutions," he added.

"Can we also set up a monitoring station to see how the attack is progressing?" Elizabeth asked. "Lastly, let me make the call. I think our C-suite leaders should know."

Her phone buzzed a few more times during the short meeting. More angry texts from Sophia. Elizabeth chose not to respond. She put her phone on silent mode and turned off all notifications. Elizabeth made the tough call to call the CEO first. Of course, he needed all the answers to how and when would the problem be fixed. Elizabeth owned up and said she did not know. Over the next few hours, Elizabeth informed each of the C-execs personally. It was close to midnight, and the team was playing a cat-and-mouse game with the attackers, adding more capacity and restricting access for the attackers, who eventually found alternate routes. Elizabeth asked the teams to go on rotation, had food ordered for everyone, and arranged for sleeping bags. The team took turns to sleep.

The next morning the room was abuzz with activity. Some members of key partners had come in person. Elizabeth was still not ready to have virtual participants. Most of the C-suite had come down to check on the team and the progress. The attackers were gaining more control of the systems; however, the Nimbus team was pulling back. Real customers did see the systems slow down, but not completely shut down. Ticketing operations continued, though at a slower pace. Elizabeth pulled her cyber-security expert into a standing meeting with the CEO.

"We continue to see a slowdown of operations, but we are still afloat. The attackers are targeting certain vulnerabilities in our system, which we are patching and fixing right now. I assure you we are not moving from here till we have everything back in control. The good thing is they do not have access to our data. That is our most valued asset," Elizabeth rounded it off for the CEO.

Meanwhile, Ben was doing his best to keep Sophia in high spirits. He continued to put up the decorations and make small talk when appropriate. Ethan and Pepper tried their best to help. Sophia continued to be in a foul mood and was not happy that her mom was not around for such an important event. What got her even more upset was that she did not even know what kept her away, other than it was a work emergency. Sophia's anger stemmed from her feeling that her mom always prioritized her work before her family. She looked at her phone, but still no reply from Mom. Pepper was cuddling by her feet, and she rubbed her hand on his head. She finally got up from the couch and lent a helping hand to Ben. Ben just looked at her with a smile.

It was late afternoon, and the team was semi-exhausted. The situation was turning into a scrappy stalemate. The engineers were still working on a permanent fix to eliminate the attackers from the system. Just then one of the engineers monitoring the attack shrieked, "I think the attackers have a different plan. They just got hold of some data and encrypted it."

Elizabeth rushed to the monitor. So did a dozen others.

"Wow, this is more than a simple attack. This is a ransomware attack," said a voice. "When did this happen?" "Did they make demands?" "How should we respond?" The room was drowning in a din of chaos as everyone was voicing questions and raising

concerns. Elizabeth raised her voice, "Hold on, everyone." She looked at the engineer and asked, "What data did they encrypt?" "Not a whole lot, about 2 GB, and it was test data we use for new product development, so not actual data, yet." "Take down all systems. Go offline now."

There was dead silence in the room. "Are you sure? Our business operations will have to fall back on manual processes. Flights will be canceled, pilots and crew won't be assigned, and there will be chaos at the airports." Some concerns were raised from different corners.

"Whatever happens, we are not going to pay bitcoin ransom to these attackers," Elizabeth responded calmly. She then turned around to her smartest security engineer, "How much time would we need to set up additional firewall and tight security so that we can bring the data back up?" "I guess three to four hours," he replied nervously. "Not good enough. I am staking my career on this decision, but we can't be completely down for four hours. You have two hours."

Elizabeth looked to the CEO. "This is my decision, and you can fire me right now or fire me tomorrow, but I trust my approach. I want to go completely offline now."

The CEO looked her straight in the eye. "I trust you, but you better come out clean on the other end." The CEO turned to his operations head and said, "Relay messages to all airports that we are going offline, and don't create panic."

"Thank you, sir," Elizabeth smiled.

All systems were made offline simultaneously. Access to both public and private network connectivity was shut down. The security engineer hand-picked two additional colleagues and got to work. Elizabeth huddled with Nolan and the head of cyber-security. "We cannot screw this up. Not just me, but everyone's job is on the line. And most important, it is Nimbus's reputation on the line. How should we plan the next steps? Our vendors are close to a breakthrough. I think we should be close to repelling the attackers with the new security protocols and measures. We are also scanning continuously for malicious activity."

Nolan was lost in thought, not paying attention. Suddenly he spoke, "Elizabeth, once we have the additional firewall and security, let's not bring the systems back up right away. Let us bring them back up one at a time and then again take a few offline and then bring them back up. If we create a timed sequence, we can track how the attackers are moving and which data are they going after. We can then trace their path along the data. Maybe we could then shut them out completely." "Brilliant, why did I not think of that?" the head of cyber-security exclaimed.

The operations at the airport did not melt down in chaos. Everyone pitched in whether it was paper-based boarding passes, over-the-phone crew assignments, or calm but assertive customer service. Back in the operations center, the engineers continued to work feverishly. At about 90 minutes one of them shouted across the room, "We are ready to test!" A non-critical system and its data were brought back up with the new protection. Everyone was watching with bated breath.

Within three minutes the attackers tried to access the system. Two minutes passed, then three, and then ten. The attackers were not able to penetrate. Everyone in the room broke into applause and hugged each other.

"We are not done yet," Elizabeth popped the party bubble. "Let's bring the system back online and then offline again in the specific sequence we designed in the last hour. We still don't know the size or shape of our enemy. We don't yet know what we are dealing with."

The team continued to run the sequence. The attackers kept following. This continued for a while. It was getting late in the evening. The systems were responding well, and operations were reaching back to normal levels, slowly but surely. Some of the executives left, but the team continued to stay back. Elizabeth was still firmly in the room.

The morning of the next day, Ben woke up with the sun getting into his eyes from behind the window. He checked his phone. It was 7 AM and still no news from Elizabeth. "Wake up, sleepy heads. It is Sunday morning and we have a party to host!" Ben urged the kids. It was Sophia's idea to have a brunch birthday party, so she knew there was not much time left. Everyone was quick to get ready. At around 11 AM, the guests started trickling in – Sophia's friends, neighbors, family friends. Everyone was having a good time, but invariably someone would ask about Elizabeth. Ben had arranged a few party games, which kept everyone busy. As the party drew to a close, friends said their goodbyes, and Ben packed generous portions of the leftovers for the guests. "I will never forgive Mom for this. It was so embarrassing. The one time she needs to be here, she is dealing with work, and we have not even heard from her," vented Sophia with her face turning red.

Even as Sophia was having her outburst, Ben slouched on the couch, tired from all the work over the weekend. Ethan cuddled up to him. Ben flicked on the TV remote and was surfing channels. The news channel caught his attention. The popular news anchor Oliver Brinkman spoke in a grave tone, "This is breaking news! Now taking you live to the headquarters of Nimbus Airlines, where early reports are coming in of a cyber-attack. Teri, what do we know?"

Teri White was standing in front of half-a-dozen news vans parked right outside the Nimbus office and said, "Thanks, Oliver. As you said, these are very early reports, but we understand that on Friday afternoon Nimbus came under a cyber-attack. The incident started small but then snowballed. There are Nimbus employees who have been working nonstop for the past 48 hours, and the good news is that the attack was unsuccessful. This is still a developing story. Back to you, Oliver." Sophia came running down and gaped open-mouthed at the TV. Finally, Ben and she looked at each other.

For 90 minutes the Nelson family did not move an inch from the couch. They kept watching the news over and over trying to piece together what exactly was happening at Nimbus. Ben's knees were hurting, and he went out for a short walk to stretch. Within minutes, Sophia yelled, "Dad, come back here. They just mentioned Mom's name." Ben came running back almost tripping over. On the TV screen they saw Teri again, who seemed to be speaking directly to them.

"Finally, we have some Nimbus executives with us, CEO Eric Taylor and CIO Elizabeth Nelson. Thanks for joining us. Eric, can you tell us more about this cyber-attack?" Eric started in a somber tone, "About 48 hours ago, we came under attack, which started innocuously, but soon started impacting our ticketing systems. The systems are back up now to about 95% capacity, and I wish to thank our customers, partners, and especially employees who stood by us all this time. I would like to specially call out the exemplary leadership of our CIO Elizabeth Nelson who has commanded the operations center all through this crisis." The camera now focused on Elizabeth, and Teri smiled at Elizabeth before saying, "That is some great praise from your boss." Elizabeth broke into a smile. "Walk us through what happened."

Having barely slept over the past two days, Elizabeth looked frazzled, but was in complete control as she spoke, "As noted, about 48 hours ago, we noticed some slowing down of our ticketing system with customers complaining that they were unable to complete transactions. Some of the support operations leads noticed unusual activity and network traffic. Our team soon got together on a Friday evening, and we realized we were under a DDoS attack, which basically means that bots were slowing down our systems. Our team got together and also engaged some partners to look for a permanent fix and increase network capacity in the meantime. For a while, it was a cat-and-mouse game. Late yesterday we realized that the attackers were actually looking to do a ransomware attack. Their goal was to capture our data and encrypt it and demand ransom in cryptocurrency. Fortunately, we decided to go completely offline and prevented the ransomware attack on our data. Our superb engineers and partners came up with security fixes late yesterday. Since yesterday we have been cautiously bringing systems back online and testing thoroughly. We are almost 95% back up and should be fully functional in the next hour. I could not be prouder of this team." Teri was listening intently and responded, "That is job well done, Elizabeth. Do you know who was behind the attack?" Without hesitation, Elizabeth responded, "A group called DarkMaze. The authorities have been in touch with us, and it looks like they have been behind some high-profile attacks. They could not beat us though!"

It was almost nine in the evening. The Nelsons already had dinner. Ben was now getting ready to tuck Ethan in. Just then the garage door opened, and Pepper ran towards it. A tired but triumphant Elizabeth walked in. She was smiling and stretched out her arms, and everyone was wrapped in a collective hug for what seemed like eternity. Ethan was the most excited. "Mom, we have been seeing you on TV for the past three hours!" Ethan said, even as he helped haul away Elizabeth's bag and purse. Ben offered, "You must be tired. Let me fix you your favorite snack." After a few minutes, it was just Sophia and Elizabeth together.

"By the way, I did not forget." Elizabeth smiled, placing a brown paper bag on the kitchen counter and pulling out the beautiful birthday cake. Sophia burst out crying and hugged her mom tightly. "I am so sorry for all the mean things I texted." Still hugging, stroking Sophia's hair, Elizabeth responded jokingly, "Well, I stopped reading them after the first couple. Happy birthday, sweetie." And tears rolled down her own cheek.

CHAPTER 8

Migration Execution and Ramping Up to Cloud

This chapter will go into details on planning your SAP to AWS migration and how to ramp up the SAP systems to the AWS cloud.

It was a month since the cyber-attack was thwarted by Nimbus Airlines. The media was still abuzz and full of praise for the Nimbus leadership, especially Elizabeth who was recognized for her leadership in that crucial moment. Multiple federal agencies were doing more frequent meetings with the Nimbus leadership while Elizabeth herself had been declining more media interviews than ever before. There were other priorities that she was focusing on. It was 11 AM on a Tuesday, and Elizabeth had called on Mark, Sandeep, and Nolan to 'revisit' the SAP modernization program.

"Because of the events of the past month, we lost some momentum on this strategic SAP modernization program; however, I think we need to get things back on track," Elizabeth made some opening remarks.

Mark made additional observations, "We have the business leaders all primed for this transformation, so we need to leverage that energy." "We also have a fair understanding of the effort it would take for execution since we had productive meetings with SAP and AWS. We are also close to finalizing a services partner," Sandeep chimed in. "Well, we definitely got to review the business case with the CFO's office and present it to the board," added Nolan. "All very good observations," commented Elizabeth, straining her brow in some thought. "I do want to spend time with AWS on a few 'execution'-related topics," added Sandeep as an afterthought. "I think it's time we paid them a visit," Elizabeth remarked.

Thomas almost jumped out of his seat after reading the email. After weeks of silence, Nimbus wanted to meet at the AWS office. Also included in the agenda was a key topic around migration execution. He called Nolan immediately.

© Tushar Srivastava 2025
T. Srivastava, *Modernizing SAP with AWS*, https://doi.org/10.1007/979-8-8688-1579-9_8

As soon as the call was done, Thomas wasted no time in securing 30 minutes on the calendar with Amy and Ashish. Thomas opened up the meeting excitedly, "I got an email today from Nolan and had a quick phone call with him. Understandably, the Nimbus team was busy in the aftermath of the cyber-attack; however, they want to get the SAP modernization program back on track. They also want to include some topics on migration execution. And they want to do all this in person at the AWS office." Thomas could see Amy breaking out in a smile on the video screen. "Looks like they are getting really serious now," Amy quipped. "I can get the technical content together, and since we will have only leadership, I can keep it at a high level," Ashish added his inputs. "I will get the dates secured, as well as the conference room, lunch, and other logistics. Got to make myself useful," Thomas chuckled.

A few days had passed, and Elizabeth was getting ready for her meeting with Micah. The no-nonsense CFO had a knack for cutting through the fluff and getting to the heart of the matter quickly. Elizabeth was engrossed in some last-minute discussions with Mark and Nolan to go over some final details of the business case.

"We have a solid foundation here. And we are being reasonable with our ask. I am sure Micah would like what we have put together," Elizabeth remarked as she reviewed some of the final numbers. Elizabeth continued, "However, I know what Micah is going to ask us. The numbers are one part of the story, but he would want to see the groundwork, preparation, and the alignment with strategic partners. If he is convinced, he will set us up for success for the meeting with the board."

Mark and Nolan nodded along in agreement. It was almost time, and Elizabeth packed the sheaf of papers in her bag. She proceeded to Micah's office with Mark trying to catch up. Nolan stayed back. "Elizabeth, Mark, so nice to see both of you," Micah said cheerfully, getting up from his desk to welcome them both in the room. "I am glad we are doing this early in the day. I have a meeting with the investor relations team in the afternoon, and my brain is usually fried after that." The CFO was in a good mood. There were smiles all around in the room. Elizabeth handed out a printed copy of the business case for Micah to read. Mark hooked up his laptop and flashed the presentation on the screen. Elizabeth took charge of the whiteboard and uncapped the marker, almost as if unsheathing a sword for battle. Micah in the meanwhile was already circling numbers and highlighting text on the paper copy.

It was about 90 minutes, and Nolan was now getting a bit fidgety. The meeting with Micah already overshot 30 minutes, and there was no sign of anyone coming out. He thought about checking with Micah's executive assistant, but wise counsel prevailed.

Another 15 minutes passed, and Nolan could finally hear footsteps. He waited in anticipation as three individuals came out from the CFO's office. There were smiles all around before Micah finally shook hands and patted Mark and Elizabeth on the back before heading back to his office.

"Hey, Nolan," Elizabeth called out as soon as she saw him in the distance. "How did it go?", shot back Nolan. "What do you think?" Mark replied with a smile. "Let's debrief for a bit in my office. Nolan, can you text Sandeep and see if he is available too?" Elizabeth addressed Nolan. In about 15 minutes all four of them were in Elizabeth's office.

Elizabeth wasted no time in getting to the crux, "Micah loved how thorough the plan was. He did have a few comments on the specific numbers, but we can address those. He appreciated the attention to detail with the preparation work and alignment with partners. He especially liked our research around cloud options since that is something new for us as an organization." Mark added, "He also commended us on getting the business stakeholders on board for this large transformation." "So what next from here?" queried Nolan. "And what timelines should we work with?" Sandeep added. "All good questions," Elizabeth replied with a smile. She continued, "Nolan, let's get a meeting with AWS at their office. Mark, please work with me directly to refine the business case based on Micah's feedback and prepare for the board presentation. Lastly, Sandeep, can you get with SAP as well as the implementation partner to put together a project plan. We can then plan the start date accordingly." The meeting was dismissed soon with clear instructions for everyone.

The appointed day came soon. Thomas had gone over the preparations a few dozen times, and he arrived early at the AWS office. As he made his way up to the conference room, he noticed that Ashish was already there, coffee in one hand and working on the whiteboard with the other. Lost in thought, Ashish barely acknowledged Thomas's presence. About an hour later, Amy made her way to the room. "Look at you guys. Everything under control," Amy said with a laugh looking at Ashish and Thomas dropping her bag on her selected seat. Just then Thomas got a call from the front office informing him of visitors. Thomas rushed to the elevators and made his way down to the reception area. Thomas quickly ushered the Nimbus team to get pictures taken and get them their temporarily issued badges. The well-organized Thomas had already submitted a ticket to the front desk resulting in a quick turnaround.

The entire team made its way up the elevator. As the elevator opened on the tenth floor, Thomas directed the Nimbus team to the conference room. Mark and Nolan made their way in followed by Sandeep and then Elizabeth. Lastly, Thomas made his entry and then closed the conference room door behind him. Greetings and handshakes were exchanged all around. Amy made special efforts to introduce herself to everyone.

Everyone settled in, and Elizabeth quickly made opening comments, "This is a wonderful office. I love the attention to detail. Also, I would like to thank the entire AWS team for the support over the past few months with all the education and clarifications around SAP on AWS. The SAP modernization program is extremely important to Nimbus, and AWS has made a significant contribution in us being able to come thus far on this journey."

Nolan added, "Agree with everything Elizabeth said. Ashish is by far the most complete technical expert I have met, and Thomas has great attention to detail and takes time to understand our needs and viewpoint. It has been a wonderful relationship." "Thank you so much for the kind words, and in Ashish and Thomas, you have the best of the best at your service," Amy responded with a smile. Thomas took the opportunity and spoke, "Thanks again, Nimbus team, for the trust placed in us. It has been a wonderful journey so far with all of you, and we continue to move forward. Before we proceed, I would love for the Nimbus team to share the progress so far and expectations from AWS going forward."

Nolan responded on behalf of the Nimbus team, "We are definitely looking to modernize our SAP system and upgrade to the latest S/4HANA release. We also look to minimize custom code and overall improve the experience of our internal customers."

There was some silence. "Let me add some more context," Elizabeth added, as she opened up her little black journal.

"Nimbus has always prided itself on being a pioneer and forefront of technology. Right from in-flight entertainment, in-air phone service, and many such innovations, we have always broken new ground. At the same time, we do not invest in technology for technology's sake. Over the past few years, we have received a lot of feedback from our business stakeholders that they need more modern processes, analytics, and reporting out of our SAP systems. Our evaluations show that rather than simply doing 'Band-Aid' fixes, we have to modernize our SAP systems. Also, early in the evaluation process, we realized that the cloud will play an important role in our SAP modernization journey. Over the past few months, AWS has also demonstrated the value it can bring to our SAP systems backed by impressive credentials and an equally impressive client list. We also did our due diligence and spoke to your competitors, and that strengthened our belief that AWS is the right choice. While we do have some technical topics to cover today, the meeting today is essentially to understand how well AWS is aligned to our goals and how would we partner in this epic journey we are about to undertake. I expect nothing less than 100% commitment to our success."

Elizabeth ended her fine speech, and the room fell eerily silent. No one was speaking. A few minutes later Thomas cleared his throat to break the silence and spoke up, "Those were some great insights, Elizabeth. AWS is fully committed to your success, and we will continue to work backward from your end goal. Not just the team in the room, but our leadership would be invested in your success." As Thomas ended, Amy looked directly at Elizabeth and addressed the Nimbus team, "Our end goal is not just to help modernize SAP for you, but to build a long-term relationship. We want to see success beyond just this one transaction and build a solid foundation for Nimbus to reimagine its overall business and deliver value to your internal stakeholders and your end customers. We are in this for the long run."

"How do I follow up after such stirring speeches?" Ashish spoke up to break the silence. The room greeted him with a round of laughter. Ashish continued, "I connected with Sandeep offline to understand the ask for today's meeting. Per our discussion, Sandeep is interested in reviewing the migration execution options. I suggested that we also review the ramp-up scenarios and use cases, which can then become the foundational elements upon which we could build further. Without much delay, let me dive into it right away."

Migration Execution

The overall execution of the migration of SAP systems to AWS consists of the following steps.

Migration Planning

Once an organization has made a decision to modernize SAP and move it to AWS, there are a few options to consider when executing the migration. Careful consideration of these options will ensure a successful migration with the lowest impact on business operations. When migrating to AWS, the customer has the option of changing the operating system or database on which SAP is running. Usually, the target database is SAP HANA, and the target OS is a version of Linux. However, in certain scenarios customers may choose not to change the OS and database during a migration.

- **Homogeneous Migration**: Homogeneous migration refers to moving SAP systems from one environment to another while keeping the operating system and database platforms consistent. This approach is typically simpler as it involves fewer changes to the SAP landscape. This type of migration is generically known as 'rehosting.'

- **Heterogeneous Migration**: Heterogeneous migration involves changing the OS or DB platform as part of the migration process. This type is more complex due to the transformations required but can offer benefits such as performance improvements, cost savings, or alignment with strategic IT goals. This type of migration is also generically known as 're-platforming'.

SAP HANA Sizing

Once the migration strategy is defined in line with business requirements, the next step is to size the SAP landscape in the target (AWS) infrastructure. Sizing involves the following key components:

- **Memory Sizing**: The standard way to size the memory requirement for SAP on AWS is to look at peak memory utilization of the existing SAP system, which can be obtained from the SAP Early Watch Alert reports, a free automated service available from SAP. Also, standard SAP sizing reports can be utilized for this purpose.

- **Instance Sizing**: As stated earlier, AWS provides instances certified for SAP, designed to satisfy the unique performance demands of SAP HANA. Once the sizing requirements are established for the SAP HANA system, these needs can be aligned with the appropriate sizes of the EC2 instance families. Essentially, the peak memory needs of the SAP HANA instances are matched with the maximum memory capacity offered by the chosen EC2 instance type. Additionally, selecting the right types and sizes of storage volumes is crucial for achieving the best performance from the SAP HANA database.

- **Storage Sizing**: Storage sizing for SAP on AWS involves estimating the required storage capacity and performance based on the specific needs of SAP systems such as S/4HANA, BW/4HANA, or ECC. Key factors include the database size, expected growth rate, backup retention policies, and I/O throughput requirements. AWS offers a range of storage options like Amazon EBS for high-performance block storage, Amazon S3 for backups and archives, and Amazon FSx for shared file systems. Proper sizing ensures optimal performance, cost efficiency, and scalability while aligning with SAP's best practices and the AWS Well-Architected Framework.

- **Network Sizing**: Another factor to consider is the amount of data to be transferred to AWS as part of the migration. The data transfer rate depends on the network bandwidth (faster rate with higher bandwidth) and is a factor impacting the total downtime. For non-production systems where the downtime is not critical, a smaller network pipe can help to reduce costs. Once the acceptable downtime and associated network cost are agreed upon, then the right connectivity option can be considered (Direct Connect or VPN).

Migration Tools

There are various AWS-provided, SAP-provided, and third-party tools available that can be used for executing the migration, and each tool is suited to a specific migration strategy.

- **AWS Migration Hub Orchestrator**: AWS Migration Hub Orchestrator is a service designed to help plan, orchestrate, and automate the migration of applications to AWS. It provides a central hub to manage migration workflows, enabling users to define, execute, and monitor migration tasks across multiple AWS services and partner tools. The key focus of AWS Migration Hub Orchestrator is to simplify the process of application migration by offering a structured and repeatable migration workflow, thereby reducing the complexity, risk, and time associated with migrations.

    Key Features of AWS Migration Hub Orchestrator:

    - **Workflow Automation**: Allows for the creation of custom migration workflows to automate and orchestrate the steps involved in migrating applications to AWS

    - **Centralized Management**: Offers a unified dashboard to track and manage the progress of multiple migration projects

    - **Integration**: Supports integration with AWS services and third-party migration tools, facilitating a broad range of migration scenarios

- **AWS Launch Wizard**: AWS Launch Wizard for SAP is a service aimed specifically at simplifying the process of sizing, configuring, and deploying SAP systems on AWS. It provides a guided user interface that automates the provisioning of AWS resources based on best practices and SAP-certified guidelines. AWS Launch Wizard helps users to quickly deploy SAP applications by automating tasks such as infrastructure provisioning, including compute, storage, and networking components.

  Key Features of AWS Launch Wizard:

  - **Simplified Deployment**: Offers a guided UI to simplify the process of deploying SAP environments on AWS, making it accessible even to users with limited AWS expertise.

  - **Customizable Templates**: Provides preconfigured templates based on AWS and SAP best practices, which can be customized to meet specific requirements.

  - **Reuse of Templates**: AWS Launch Wizard enables reuse of deployment templates, streamlining future SAP environment setups with consistent configurations. This reduces manual effort, speeds up deployments, and ensures standardized best practices.

  - **Cost Estimation**: Includes up-front cost estimates and allows users to adjust configurations to optimize costs before deployment.

- **HSR**: SAP HANA **High Availability and System Replication** (**HSR**) provides a mechanism for replicating data from a primary SAP HANA system to one or more secondary systems in real time (this is used in the setup of HA or DR environments). After the target environment for SAP has been set up on AWS using AWS Launch Wizard, this instance can be set as the target system of HSR from the source environment. Once the data is fully synchronized, the system can switch over to the AWS environment with minimal impact on business operations.

- **SUM DMO**: SAP Database Migration Option (DMO) is a feature of the SAP Software Update Manager (SUM) that simplifies the migration process of SAP systems to a different database, upgrade of the SAP system version, or both simultaneously. DMO with System Move helps to migrate SAP systems from an on-premises environment to AWS by using a DMO tool and a special export and import process, leveraging AWS services such as Amazon S3, Amazon EFS (over AWS Direct Connect), and Storage Gateway file interface. AWS Launch Wizard for SAP can then be used to rapidly provision SAP HANA instances and build the SAP application servers on AWS, whenever ready to trigger the import process of the DMO tool. The SUM DMO tool is capable of transforming data from any database to SAP HANA or SAP ASE, simultaneously handling OS migrations, release/enhancement pack updates, and Unicode transformations. The output is generated as flat files, which are then conveyed to the designated SAP HANA system on AWS. In the second phase of DMO with System Move, these flat files are imported to reassemble the migrated SAP application, incorporating the data, code, and settings.

"That was a wonderful session. Ashish, as usual, did a fantastic job. It gives me some good insights into our options and will help us plan better with our professional services partners," Sandeep said, effusive in his praise for Ashish. "Glad to be of help," responded a smiling Ashish.

After a productive session, the Nimbus team bid farewell to their hosts and headed back. As the team left, Thomas looked at Amy and Ashish and said, "Let's grab some dinner, shall we?" Both Amy and Ashish nodded in agreement almost together. The trio picked a 'hole-in-the-wall' Persian restaurant, and the place did not disappoint. Aromas of fresh herbs wafted through the sparsely decorated place. The walls had some large rugs pinned up, and there was a big poster of a Persian village scene. It all added to the ambiance. The gentle waiter took their order and placed some complimentary 'naan' bread on the table.

Ashish asked casually, "So what does everyone think of the meeting today?"

Thomas put down his half-eaten bread and replied, "I have a very good feeling from this meeting. They have reviewed the business case with the CFO. Today they reviewed migration strategies with us. These are all indications that they are moving forward with the SAP modernization soon. Also, they have spent so much time with us, exploring AWS capabilities, and today they made a point to come to our office, which again indicates their preference for AWS."

Both Ashish and Amy listened intently. Amy took her time before speaking up, "I think a key factor for them, Elizabeth specially, would be the cultural fit and how we engage as a partner, beyond just technical capability. Everyone else in the room evaluated us on a specific capability, but eventually looks like it will be Elizabeth's decision. I hope we have done enough." Amy high-fived the two and took the check that the waiter had just placed. She glanced at it quickly and placed her corporate expense card carefully inside.

It had been a week since Elizabeth had presented the business case for SAP modernization to the Nimbus board. The feedback was pretty positive, but they were still waiting for the formal approval. It was due any day. It was a Friday afternoon, and Nolan's screen suddenly flashed with a group message. Elizabeth just messaged Mark, Sandeep, and Nolan with just one word "Approved" and plenty of exclamation marks.

Nolan wasted no time in getting up from his desk and making his way to Elizabeth's office. Mark and Sandeep followed a few minutes later.

"Congrats, everyone. It was an intense few months, but we learned a lot and now have the budget to modernize our SAP systems on the cloud," Elizabeth said. There was palpable excitement in the room. "I haven't felt so excited since we moved from punch cards to mainframes, and yeah I am indeed that old," joked Mark and the room broke out into laughter. Fist bumps and congratulations were exchanged all around the room. "We have a lot to work on now," Sandeep said as the excitement settled a bit in the room. Soon the team dispersed, soaking in the good news while welcoming the weekend. "Nolan, can you wait a bit?" Elizabeth asked. "Sure." "Nolan, I wanted to thank you for all the support during the past few months. I could not have done this without you," Elizabeth said in a tone of genuine gratitude. "Of course, not a problem. It was all teamwork," responded Nolan. "You must be really proud of yourself now, Elizabeth. First, the positive coverage after the cyber-attack and, now, this approval for the SAP modernization program," Nolan enquired gently. Elizabeth looked Nolan in the eye and smiled. "You know, Nolan, at every stage in life, priorities change. I am indeed very happy about the board's approval, but you know what actually made my day today? I was waiting for the board decision, so that I can take a short vacation. I just booked tickets for Sophia and myself for a road trip in Europe. I am fulfilling an old promise and fixing some mistakes of the past."

A few days had passed since the board decision. It was a bright sunny afternoon, and Thomas was wrapping up a document that he was working on. Based on some well-meaning advice from a colleague, Thomas shut off his email application while doing focus *work. Now, as he was ready to take a break, he thought of quickly popping in to check his messages. As he was clearing some of the routine emails, Thomas noticed one from the head of procurement at Nimbus, from about an hour ago. He quickly clicked open the email.*

It read:

Dear Thomas, after careful evaluations and engagement with your team over the past few months, Nimbus Airlines has decided to move forward with AWS as the cloud service provider for our SAP modernization program. We see a strong value proposition from AWS in terms of technical capabilities to support our complex SAP landscape and the deep level of engagement displayed by your team during the past few months. Another key aspect, which is very important to Nimbus, is the cultural fit between Nimbus and AWS and the commitment to our shared success and not just your self-interest alone. The AWS team has won our trust on this critical aspect, also echoed in direct feedback from the office of the CIO, Elizabeth Nelson. Congratulations and we will be in touch for next steps.

Thomas jumped from his seat and re-read the email again. His heart was pounding faster than ever. He fumbled with his phone for a bit and quickly called Ashish. Soon Ashish, Amy, and Thomas were on a call. There were smiles all around and virtual high fives. "Congrats, guys. This is great news!" Amy said with excitement. "It's all teamwork," Thomas said smiling into the camera. The usually unflappable Ashish was also sporting a broad smile. They chatted briefly for a few minutes, and then looking at Thomas through the computer screen, Amy said, "I will send your email out to the leadership. This is some huge news." As the call concluded, Ashish added, "You know what this means. The real work begins now, and it will be a long and exciting journey."

It was a bright Thursday afternoon as Thomas waited patiently at the Sky High Café not too far away from the Nimbus headquarters. Nolan walked in and immediately spotted Thomas. The two exchanged warm greetings as Nolan sat down. "Pretty good view with all the airplanes taking off and landing," Thomas said peering out of the window beside their table. "Oh yeah, I heard that this place has been around ever since the airport came up and, in those days, people flocked to see the planes in action," Nolan remarked. The waiter took their drinks order and pointed to the window promising to bring the drinks out before the next flight took off. Nolan spoke up, "Congrats on the announcement that AWS will be our cloud service provider for the SAP modernization program. I am excited to have AWS as part of this journey, and your team has earned every bit of it." "Thanks for the trust. It was a team effort, and we are as excited to be a part of this,"

Thomas added. The drinks came as promised and the food arrived a few minutes later. Both of them were deeply engrossed in sharing ideas, and time flew by. Nolan glanced at his watch and exclaimed, "Oh wow, I did not know it was this late. Guess we don't realize it when having a good time." Thomas responded with a smile. As the check came in, Nolan insisted on picking the tab. As they were ready to leave, Nolan looked straight at Thomas and said, "Thomas, a big thank you for all the work you did with the Nimbus team all these months. We may not have been the easiest to work with, but you rallied your team well and truly worked in Nimbus's interest. We could not have asked for a better account rep to support us." For a few seconds Thomas was at a loss for words before responding, "I am glad that we have been able to make a positive contribution so far and look forward to supporting team Nimbus on the road ahead. And thank you, Nolan, for all your support and advice during this time."

The two bumped their fists and clasped a strong handshake, almost together glancing outside the window where a Nimbus Airlines flight was taking off and was just about to reach the clouds.

CHAPTER 9

Customer Case Studies

This chapter consists of actual customer case studies, giving a glimpse of the journey they took toward SAP modernization with AWS solutions and technology. These stories can be a reference point for other customers who are looking to undertake a similar journey themselves.

CHS Inc.: Connecting the Physical to the Digital

In conversation with Mukesh Kakani, Product Delivery Manager, SAP Platform Team, and Nathan Souer, Senior Cloud Infrastructure and DevOps Engineer

What comes to your mind when you think CHS? While the average consumer may not be able to recognize the brand right away, for thousands of farmers, ranchers, and cooperatives, CHS immediately evokes a strong connection with the land. With a strong focus on the agronomy, grains, food processing, and energy, CHS is committed to empowering its stakeholders to grow their business.

In 2016 when Mukesh Kakani joined the team at CHS as part of the technology organization, he clearly understood that the key to success for him and his team was to be able to connect the physical with the digital. How could digital technology, which you cannot "touch or feel," add value at CHS where the physical connection to land and landowners played a vital role in the success of the organization? In 2019, three years after Mukesh started at CHS, an opportunity presented itself.

In 2013, CHS embarked on a journey to move away from legacy ERP systems for various business units to SAP as the standard ERP across the enterprise. The agriculture business unit was the first to go live on SAP on ECC 6.0 with a special focus on finance and agriculture commodities management. The company also made investments in on-premises hardware to host the SAP systems. In early 2019, CHS was looking to

© Tushar Srivastava 2025
T. Srivastava, *Modernizing SAP with AWS*, https://doi.org/10.1007/979-8-8688-1579-9_9

upgrade SAP from ECC 6.0 to S/4HANA in order to meet newer business requirements. While doing preparations for the move, the team also looked at hardware considerations and realized that the current hardware was ageing and would need to be replaced in 2020. Further evaluations showed that they would run into a similar situation in another five years. It was at this juncture that CHS made the decision to move SAP to the cloud while doing this upgrade to S/4HANA.

Mukesh and his team are responsible for the SAP platform within CHS, and as part of this modernization program, worked with the Cloud DevOps and Platform team to build a roadmap for SAP in the cloud. Nathan Souer, a nine-year veteran at CHS and part of the Cloud DevOps team, worked closely with Mukesh and his team and the broader set of stakeholders to help convert this modernization vision to reality. In early 2019, the CHS team set up a proof of concept on various cloud service providers to test performance of each. As part of the effort, SAP S/4HANA 1809 was installed on each, and each cloud service provider was to provide a set of automation and high-availability cluster setups, since the HA setup was a critical requirement for CHS. As part of the proof of concept, CHS evaluated the cloud providers on multiple parameters including alliance with SAP, relationship with CHS, innovation strategy & vision, automation (infrastructure as code and automation for SAP implementations), and platform cost. After a detailed evaluation, CHS picked AWS as the cloud service provider, and the SAP modernization project was kicked off around September 2019. And it was in early 2020 when the COVID pandemic hit and brought the entire project to a standstill.

The pandemic changed lives in many ways for people around the globe, and the CHS project team was no different. They could not proceed with the project for a good six months, and the modernization program was put on hold. However, one silver lining was that since all the infrastructure was provisioned in the cloud on AWS, they could simply turn off the systems and incur no costs. "We could only do this on the cloud and not if we were working with on-premises hardware," says Nathan emphatically. Six months later as everyone started getting used to the new normal, the SAP modernization project at CHS came back to life out of hibernation. Working with partners and AWS Professional Services for SAP, the team took a 'brownfield' approach to the S/4HANA modernization (transferring existing data, workflows, and certain customizations) and deployed automation scripts for provisioning the environment. The initial system setup took six months where they took time to deploy automation scripts for environment provisioning and made sure everything was set up right, including load balancer, application, database components, high-availability cluster and automated as much as possible.

They also ensured that the cluster setup for high availability and disaster recovery was architected per CHS's requirements. The team followed the proper methodology for S/4HANA migration, testing and making sure everything worked right the first time. After the setup for the first system, all subsequent systems were provisioned much quicker, reusing templates and automation. Finally in December 2021, CHS went live with the new S/4HANA system in production without any issues.

Looking back, Mukesh said this critical project was not just an amazing learning experience, but it resulted in a mindset shift internally. Before the project, the SAP ECC system was managed by a third-party service provider, and operations were run in a traditional manner. There was a server team, SAP Basis team, infrastructure team, and a lot of operational overhead resulting in longer cycle times for innovation and continuous improvement projects. Now, Mukesh's team is known as the SAP Platform team, and they are able to 'self-service' most of their infrastructure needs rather than depend on Nathan's team or other teams within the organization. They are able to spin up new HANA environments to troubleshoot/innovate, which is very convenient and cost-effective on the cloud compared to the on-premises setup. This has led to quicker turnaround on projects. Nathan added that one of the most critical outcomes of this project is a robust high availability and disaster recovery setup compared with the on-premises environment where the DR site was simply set up across the other side of the town. On AWS they have a very robust pacemaker architecture with primary in Availability Zone 1, secondary in Availability Zone 2, and disaster recovery in a different region. This setup is more robust and helps achieve the NZDT (near-zero downtime) requirement during all maintenance activities such as system upgrades, operating system patching, SAP kernel upgrades, HANA DB upgrades, and other related activities. The team uses AWS SSM (Systems Manager) for the upgrade and patching activities including system start and stop. The user is able to go to the AWS console and execute the automation for a set of systems instead of patching individual systems as in the on-premises world. For example, the operating system patching on-premises needed 11 hours downtime, and on AWS is only four hours. With further automation, it is being brought to near zero. Another benefit that the team sees is around SAP system monitoring. Using AWS tools like CloudWatch and CloudTrail, the team now has a lot of system information and is able to proactively act on it rather than being reactive. The project has been extremely successful, and the template and learnings from deployment for the agriculture business are being used for subsequent business units including energy.

When asked to comment on lessons learned and advice, Nathan immediately says, "You can automate more than what you think you can." "Also, the sooner you can automate, the better since it has a compounding effect. The work–life balance has been definitely better with all the automation," Nathan adds. Further, another learning that Nathan shares is that the cloud is more secure given all the tools and solutions like security groups, VPCs, and account segregation that AWS offers. Mukesh adds that the operating model does not map one to one between on-premises and cloud. Certain tasks go away, certain tasks are new, and there are new opportunities. Moving to the cloud is not simply a change in technical infrastructure, but also impacts how teams are organized, new skills, and overall shift in mindset when making the transition to the cloud. "The teams work in a more agile fashion, and we are breaking down silos, though silos (farm storage towers) are an important part of CHS's agriculture business," signs off Mukesh with a smile.

Ergon Inc.: Committed to "Doing Right"

In conversation with Jana Branham, Executive Vice President and Chief Information Officer, and Paul Shook, Vice President of Digital Business Solutions

'Doing Right' as an organization, for its products, planet, and people, is a core value that Ergon lives by. Taking a peek at Ergon's 'Doing Right' report for 2023 boldly proclaims that Ergon's legacy is built around doing the right thing. This core value has its roots in the vision laid down by founder Leslie Lampton. After serving in the Navy in World War II and the Korean conflict, Mr. Lampton returned to his hometown Jackson, Mississippi, with plans to enter the oil business. While many businesses were moving to Texas to capitalize on the oil boom, Leslie Lampton made a commitment to stay in his home state of Mississippi, starting the business in 1954 with a used delivery truck and two employees. Ergon today is a well-diversified organization, engaged in a number of industries related to the refining and marketing of specialty oils, asphalt, thermoplastic resins, petrochemicals, propane, and the necessary infrastructure to support those businesses.

Jana said that Ergon was an early adopter of SAP as the ERP for running the business. Having deployed SAP in 2003, Ergon was running ECC 6.0 with core areas of financials, material management, and business warehouse. However, since implementing SAP in

2003, no major enhancements or modernization efforts were done with SAP apart from the support packs to keep security current. The talented team worked hard, but over the years standard practices were not followed leading to customizations. The company was growing via acquisitions, and it needed a modern ERP that would be an aid to this future growth. After deep consultations with the business stakeholders, Jana, Paul, and their team evaluated all options and after careful consideration chose to modernize SAP by adopting the SAP RISE offering to deploy SAP S/4HANA on AWS. The model was to deploy greenfield SAP S/4HANA, one business unit at a time with the plan to expand functionality and improve business processes in order to make systems more scalable and provide greater benefit to the business. Paul added that the SAP S/4HANA implemented with a focus on standard processes would allow them to take advantage of a clean core resulting in easier upgrades and quicker integrations of acquired companies. Also, additional functionality for the back-office processes was going to be a huge benefit as they sought to automate current manual processes in the new S/4HANA world. Eliminating complexities in the processes and coding would also provide huge benefits and allow for the scalability as they grew. The cloud also would allow them to engage in the AI tools offered by SAP and their cloud service provider, AWS. The journey started in November 2023 and was planned as an 18-month journey with one business unit. As stated, it was a greenfield deployment with addition of a new module Supply Chain for Secondary Distribution (S4SCSD). Paul and Jana agreed that going from on-premises to the cloud would be a big step for not just Ergon IT but the business as well. They would be living in two systems until they got all businesses and back-office functionality to the SAP S4 RISE environment.

SAP's direction on RISE and offering new functionality to RISE customers first was important to Ergon, since it meant fewer options if they remained on-premises. Having talked to other customers who underwent a similar journey, Ergon saw the full maturity of RISE and specifically the benefits of SAP RISE on AWS, including reliability, platform maturity, and innovation offered via AWS-native services. "AWS also brought in a pool of skilled SAP resources, which was a great comfort knowing we could lean on them during implementation," added Jana. Paul further added, "As we researched on-premises vs. RISE, AWS was invaluable in helping us understand the differences and provided great insight to our process and our decision-making. We also liked the ability to spin up and spin down for short periods with AWS. We were able to get a 30-day trial license from SAP and spin up an environment to perform a proof of concept. This was very helpful before we decided to add to our SAP order form on the existing term." Overall, the Ergon team felt comfortable with AWS as the cloud service provider than other cloud options based on all the reasons above.

Reflecting on the benefits that the organization is realizing from this major change, Jana and Paul shared that the new system will provide greater functionality to their corporate services groups and business function using the system and the Fiori apps will be a great improvement for the business users providing simplicity in their daily work. They are also excited about Signavio as a new process tool and that will allow them to improve and see where costly deviations are occurring. The audit team is especially excited about the potential benefits that this new tool will offer them in their auditing practices. As stated previously, they are also creating a system that is more scalable as Ergon continues to grow through acquisitions, which is a huge plus for the organization. When asked to share their learnings with other customers, they said, "Choose wisely your systems implementer. Get many references from AWS, SAP, and the implementer you are evaluating. Only buy what you need right now since you can always add more modules later to the order form."

Jana imbibes the "Doing Right" philosophy in her own information technology team at Ergon. Back in 2017, when Ergon's CEO asked for ideas for giving back to communities on an enterprise-wide level, Jana suggested Toys for Tots, and employees in the corporate office were quick to join in. Led by Jana's information technology team, it is now an annual fundraising event for Ergon, and Jana said that they love this charity because it meets the needs of the community where they live and serve and all the donations go directly to children in need.

In fact, their process for embarking on the SAP modernization journey reflects the philosophy of 'Doing Right.'

Epilogue

Dear reader, I hope you have enjoyed this flight with Nimbus Airlines on their "SAP to AWS" cloud journey. In fact, it is not a coincidence that this fictional company is called Nimbus (a type of cloud)! I enjoyed the process of writing the book, especially trying to decide what topics were relevant and what could be left out. Another challenge that I relished was creating a fictional narrative and taking that to a logical conclusion, taking care not to dilute the technical content. That balancing act was a very valuable learning experience.

Over the course of this book, every chapter builds upon the concepts of the previous. As a result, we started from the basics of cloud fundamentals, evolution of cloud computing, and AWS overview. Next, we reviewed the SAP and AWS technical partnership and the benefits of running SAP on AWS. The next few chapters of the book covered design aspects, covering design of the AWS cloud, design of the AWS infrastructure for SAP, and finally design of the operating model. Once we were comfortable with the fundamentals and then the design aspects, we moved onto innovation, migration, and ramping to the cloud and ended with actual customer case studies. I am confident that this flow would help you, the reader, appreciate all the aspects of modernizing SAP with AWS and would help you in your own SAP on AWS cloud journey.

Like any transformation journey, modernizing SAP with AWS cloud requires a shift in mindset of not simply treating AWS like another data center for SAP, but rather exploring the full capabilities that the cloud offers and helping your stakeholders adopt those changes and realize benefits. In fact, this journey does not have a destination, but rather this is an ongoing process and continuous evolution.

I would love to hear from you if you have any feedback or comments or if you would like to connect to discuss your own modernization journey.

Happy "modernizing"!

© Tushar Srivastava 2025

T. Srivastava, *Modernizing SAP with AWS*, https://doi.org/10.1007/979-8-8688-1579-9

Index

A

Access control lists (ACLs), 193
ACLs, *see* Access control lists (ACLs)
Agriculture business, 281, 283, 284
AI, *see* Artificial intelligence (AI)
Air-Connect project, 73
ALB, *see* Application load balancer (ALB)
Amazon EBS snapshots, 175–177
Amazon Elastic Compute Cloud (EC2), 13
Amazon FSx, 53
Amazon Lookout for Vision, 236
Amazon Machine Images (AMIs), 142, 191
Amazon Nova Agentic AI, 257–260
Amazon Q, 221
Amazon Simple Storage Service (S3), 13,
      17, 151, 152
Amazon Web Services (AWS), 8
    access controls and traffic
      management, 22, 23
    availability zone, 99, 100
    compute (Amazon EC2), 19, 20
    connectivity, 21, 22
    data centers, 97–99
    defined, 12
    edge locations, 27
    factors, 27
    geographic proximity, 25
    high-speed communication, 27
    infrastructure (*see* AWS infrastructure)
    infrastructure services, 13
    local zones, 26, 102, 103
    narrative, SAP deployments, 91–97
    network architecture, 108
    network backbone, 105
    outposts, 103, 104
    pay-as-you-go model, 14
    physical networking equipment, 106
    PoPs, 104
    pricing, 20, 21
    public debut, 13
    region, 26, 100–102
    SAP resources, 285
    SAP specialist, 1
    scalability challenge, 12
    security and compliance, 28–30
    security group, 22
    services, 23–25
    shared vision, standardized
      infrastructure, 12
    storage (Amazon S3), 17–19
    techno-functional consultant, 14
    upgrade and patching activities, 283
    VPC, 21, 106–113
AMIs, *see* Amazon Machine
    Images (AMIs)
API economy, 11
API Gateway, 228
Application-level extraction, 218
Application load balancer (ALB), 134
AR, *see* Augmented reality (AR)
Artificial intelligence (AI), 213
    Amazon Nova Agentic AI, 257–260
    classification, 242
    cloud technology, 244–246

B

GPSR Compliance
The European Union's (EU) General Product Safety Regulation (GPSR) is a set
of rules that requires consumer products to be safe and our obligations to
ensure this.

If you have any concerns about our products, you can contact us on

ProductSafety@springernature.com

In case Publisher is established outside the EU, the EU authorized
representative is:

Springer Nature Customer Service Center GmbH
Europaplatz 3
69115 Heidelberg, Germany